White Party, White Government

White Party, White Government examines the centuries-old impact of systemic racism on the U.S. political system. The text assesses the development by elite and other whites of a racialized capitalistic system, grounded early in slavery and land theft, and its intertwining with a distinctive political system whose fundamentals were laid down in the founding decades. From these years through the Civil War and Reconstruction, to the 1920s, the 1930s Roosevelt era, the 1960s Johnson era, through to the Ronald Reagan, George H. W. Bush, Bill Clinton, George W. Bush, and Barack Obama presidencies, Feagin explores the effects of racial and class realities and the ongoing demographic changes on the present and future of the U.S. political system.

Joe R. Feagin is Ella C. McFadden Professor at Texas A&M University. He has done research on racism and sexism issues for 46 years and has served as the Scholar-in-Residence at the U.S. Commission on Civil Rights. He has written 58 scholarly books and nearly 200 scholarly articles in his research areas, and one of his books (*Ghetto Revolts*) was nominated for a Pulitzer Prize. His recent books include *Systemic Racism* (Routledge 2006), *The White Racial Frame* (Routledge 2010), and *Racist America* (2nd edition, Routledge 2010). He is the 2006 recipient of a Harvard Alumni Association lifetime achievement award and was the 1999–2000 president of the American Sociological Association.

White Party,
White Government

Race, Class, and U.S. Politics

Joe R. Feagin

Routledge
Taylor & Francis Group

NEW YORK AND LONDON

First published 2012
by Routledge
711 Third Avenue, New York, NY 10017

Simultaneously published in the UK
by Routledge
2 Park Square, Milton Park, Abingdon, Oxon OX14 4RN

Routledge is an imprint of the Taylor & Francis Group, an informa business

Library of Congress Cataloging-in-Publication Data
Feagin, Joe R.
White party, white government : race, class, and U.S. politics/ Joe R. Feagin.
p. cm.
1. Political parties–United States–History. 2. Republican Party
(U.S. : 1854–)–History. 3. Democratic Party (U.S.)–History. 4. United
States–Race relations–History. 5. Racism–United States–History. I. Title.
JK2265.F35 2012
324.273089–dc23
2011041470

ISBN: 978-0-415-88982-7 (hbk)
ISBN: 978-0-415-88983-4 (pbk)
ISBN: 978-0-203-12243-3 (ebk)

Typeset in Minion
by Keystroke, Station Road, Codsall, Wolverhampton

SFI Certified Sourcing
www.sfiprogram.org
SFI-00453

Printed and bound in the United States of America
by Edwards Brothers, Inc.

Contents

Preface

During the watershed 2008 presidential campaign, the Democratic National Committee chair, Dr. Howard Dean, commented that "If you look at folks of color, even women, they're more successful in the Democratic party than they are in the white, uh, excuse me, in, uh, Republican party."[1] The Republican (John McCain) campaign pounced on this revealing political comment, calling it wrong and insulting. Yet Dean was just saying out loud what most politicians and other Americans were well aware of—that the contemporary Republican Party has to a substantial degree become the "white party" of the United States.

Clear too in the negative media reactions to Dean's comment was the fact that in this theoretically democratic country, the data on the racial polarization of the major political parties are too seldom analyzed. Indeed, a major underlying issue in recent elections has been when and how the United States can become a true multiracial democracy. This will continue to be an issue in the 2012 election and probably in many elections beyond. As the chapters that follow will demonstrate, in recent political campaigns and in much of national politics, the Republican Party has continued to be the "white party," the one most consistently or aggressively representing white interests, albeit often in disguised and euphemistic language. In contrast, as Dean suggested, and as we will also see later in this book, the contemporary Democratic Party is the political party that more often represents a greater diversity of the people and perspectives in the United States. Still, this distinctive Democratic Party diversity is a relatively recent phenomenon, for that party too was once the well-known "white party" of the United States.

Considering this bit of contemporary racial politics helps to set the stage for the many significant racial and political issues raised in this book. Here I examine in detail the relationship of the society's foundational and systemic racism to numerous important aspects of the U.S. political system, and especially to its political parties. The racial aspects of U.S. parties and politics have often been examined, but not in the depth they deserve to be. One major recent book on political scientists' efforts to deal with race and politics accents the fact that most of this research examines race as a variable in survey analysis and "proceeds as if in a historical, contextual and institutional vacuum, devoid of either a causal, constitutive or discursive narrative about racial politics or racialized development."[2] Only a few political scientists have paid much critical and thorough attention to the role of "race" in U.S. party history, and even they have usually not examined deeply the many ways in which the centuries-old system of racial oppression has fundamentally shaped U.S. political institutions.[3] In other social sciences, as well as in much humanities and journalistic analysis, similar research limitations can also be observed.

Examining U.S. politics and systemic racism means going well beyond examining a few modest political flaws, contemporary rightward shifts in party politics, or eccentric racist candidates, issues often considered in other political assessments. An accurate understanding requires going back deeply into U.S. political, economic, and social history to examine the central and ongoing social structural and institutional realities relevant to these issues. Too much past and present analysis of racial matters in North America has accented just racial attitudes or racial ideologies, and given too little attention to other important dimensions such as the concrete material realities of this systemic oppression.

Thus, in this book I use the term *systemic racism* to mean the deeply rooted, institutionalized structures of white-created racial oppression of people of color. White-on-black oppression and other white-on-nonwhite oppression have been central to this society now for four centuries. As we will discover repeatedly in the chapters that follow, systemic racism involves:

1. a complex array of oppressive racial practices;
2. the unjustly gained privileges and power of white Americans;
3. the substantial and well-institutionalized resource inequalities along racial lines; and
4. a vigorous and extensive white racial frame created to maintain and rationalize white privileges and power.[4]

Our Mythological Origins Narrative

Today in the United States, numerous political problems are blamed on ordinary Americans. The latter are commonly blamed for not turning out in high numbers for various elections, for being ignorant of U.S. political institutions and history, for being easily swayed by mainstream media, and for being poorly informed on numerous public policy issues. But such ordinary-people blaming is too easy, for many contemporary political problems have their roots deeply in fundamentally undemocratic political institutions that were created by our elite white male founders and which have, for the most part at the top, been maintained today as such by elite white men and their acolytes. Given the fundamentally flawed character of our major political and other social institutions, the often weak political commitments and inept political decisions of many ordinary Americans are not at all surprising.

Indeed, most contemporary Americans have trouble perceiving clearly or understanding well the fundamentally undemocratic reality of our major political institutions. Most have been taught, and generally accept, a substantially mythological societal and political origins narrative. This historical big-picture narrative imbeds numerous societal understandings and morals that are important to most Americans, and especially to most white Americans.

As we will soon see, these include emotion-laden stories about European American superiority, hard work, achievement, and "manifest destiny." One scenario portrays a rags-to-riches story of early English Protestant colonists, such as the Calvinistic Puritans. In these myth-filled narratives, the Protestant "settlers" came to North America with modest resources and dreams of liberty, and drew on religious faith, virtuousness, and hard work to create prosperity in a land allegedly populated by some thinly scattered and "savage" Indians. Subsequently, most white Americans, including political leaders, media analysts, scholars, and rank-and-file Americans, have portrayed the early white Protestant colonists and their slave-holding and other white descendants in the 18th century founding era as fostering the ideals of liberty, freedom, and equality that are accented strongly in the U.S. political tradition. Since the 18th century, our often slave-holding founders are said to have been highly civilized, liberty-loving, and strongly committed to equality and democracy. In this common view, the brilliant founders created a lasting U.S. Constitution that established a very democratic political system. Many Americans have also linked early Protestant religious groups and their subsequent followers to the growth of a "free market" capitalism in North America that is said to have brought significant prosperity for most Americans.[5]

Shortly after the founding of the United States, early European visitors and usually perceptive analysts like Alexis de Tocqueville described the new country as being a fine new democracy with great freedom and equality. Since that early era, the literary and scholarly traditions in the United States have frequently accented this supposed U.S. tradition of freedom and equality. This tradition also constantly celebrates the white founding fathers as political geniuses and great men. The old political institutions are often presented as more or less perfect, as is the U.S. Constitution that is viewed as generating them.[6]

Our Oligarchical Economic and Political Structure

As I will demonstrate in the chapters that follow, this standard U.S. view is often more mythological than realistic. Full of significant misrepresentations, this commonplace view ignores the negative side of the U.S. founders and the founding era. To make sense of the relationship of systemic racism to U.S. politics, we can start with certain critical elements of our still surrounding political and economic structures. One point to be clear on is that this country's political system has *never* been a real democracy in which a majority of the people have had significant and recurring input into major political decisions. From the beginning, as extensive social science research shows, much societal oppression at the hands of oligarchically organized European colonists and their descendants took the institutionalized form of anti-Indian genocide and black enslavement.[7] The new country's white elite and its acolytes created a slavery-centered economic system on much land stolen from Native Americans and with much labor stolen from African Americans. This often violent oppression soon became systemic and generated a strong societal hierarchy, extensive and unjust racial inequality, much need for violent control of rebellious oppressed populations, and extensive racial and political frames to legitimate extensive oppression. As we will see, numerous research sources show that these foundational societal developments made it impossible to construct anything resembling a really democratic political system.

Consider this reality of North American *oligarchy*, that is, rule by the few, from the earliest century to the present day. Much social science research reveals that the actual political and economic systems were substantially created and operated by a small elite of white men during the early centuries, and that powerful elite has operated in a more or less oligarchical fashion ever since. As we will discover shortly, the elite political leaders created only an imagined democratic community. Contrary to the mythology prevailing to the present day, the U.S. Constitution and other early legal documents did not create a democracy (literally, rule by the people) where most adults had the right to participate freely, regularly, and substantially in the new political institutions and the major decisions stemming from them. Although early Americans considered it "democratic," the elite founders intentionally built the political system as substantially inegalitarian and undemocratic, and most of the adult population at that time—white women, and women and men of color—had very little or no input into the shape of the new political institutions or into how top political officials operated. Most U.S. founders had no interest in establishing anything close to a real democracy where a majority had a significant and regular say in and over major political institutions. The early colonists and a few founders who sought a much more democratic political system lost out, and the country's political system was established to substantially protect elite white interests and whites' hierarchical position, which has indeed persisted from the time of the U.S. Constitution to the present day.

This country was not a full-fledged political democracy in its founding 18th century era, nor in the dramatic 1860s reform period after the Civil War. Even with the reforms moving in a more democratic direction that came later, such as in the 1930s New Deal era, this country's political system has never become such a full-fledged democracy. Indeed, it is most certainly not such a fully developed democracy today. As major researchers on the U.S. oligarchy like Philip Burch and Bill Domhoff have demonstrated, this country has long been governed at the top by a plutocratic elite in both the economy and politics, with a substantial veneer of democratic rhetoric covering up major political and economic inequalities from the 17th century to the present.[8]

As I will document later in detail, for centuries, elite white men, always a statistical minority, have sat at the top of major societal hierarchies—the racial, class, and gender hierarchies. Successive oligarchical regimes have created, maintained, or extended the important economic, political, educational, and religious institutions. In this book I emphasize the elites' major decision making power in these key institutional areas. These oligarchical elites have played the central role in generating the systemic material and other inequalities of this society.

Interestingly, scholars Jeffrey Winters and Benjamin Page have recently examined whether the contemporary U.S. political-economic system is still substantially oligarchical, using data on income and wealth to create and assess current material-power indices. An oligarchical system involves large differences in economic wealth and power being translated regularly into major differences in political power and impact. From extensive data, they show that the contemporary socio-political system is still oligarchical and that a small number of wealthy Americans "exert vastly greater political influence than average citizens and that a very small group of the wealthiest (perhaps the top tenth of 1 percent)" often have significant "power to dominate policy in certain key areas."[9] While they do not directly examine the racial dimension, their data and much other social science data indicate that the contemporary political-economic system is not only still dominated by a small oligarchical elite, but that this elite remains very substantially white and male.[10]

A Truly Democratic Future?

One of the influential political scientists of the last half century, David Easton, has offered a broad definition of politics as the process of "authoritative allocation of values for society as a whole."[11] By "authoritative" he means that people accept the legitimacy of a government authority. By "allocation" he means the distribution under that authority of important "values," by which he means tangible (for example, money benefits) and intangible (for example, rights and prestige) resources and other things that people value in society. In this book I examine many examples of this allocation of important societal resources and other socially valued items through the U.S. political system, one shaped in fundamental and foundational ways by this country's systemic racism. In addition, I extend this examination beyond the structures and decision making of the political system to broader society-wide "authoritative allocations" of important resources and other valued items. Thus, when analyzing major resources and other valued items—such as income, wealth, and even political-economic rights—one soon sees that control over their allocation and distribution oftentimes involves top decision makers in the capitalistic economic system. To a substantial degree, moreover, the economic members and political members of the oligarchical elite overlap in terms of people, organizations, or collaborative decision making.

By means of their control of the mainstream economy and the political system, the elite's principal actors have long made decisive and determining choices about the unequal allocation of major resources and other highly valued societal items. The extensive evidence presented in this book is unambiguous: The actual authoritative allocation of society's important material resources, as well as of less tangible items such as power and prestige, has been dramatically inegalitarian, massively skewed toward the elite's group interests, and aggressively legitimated by a dominant white political, racial, and class framing of society. Our examination of this country's political and economic history will show unmistakably that over several centuries, a small group of people, the mostly white and male elite, has had highly disproportionate power and authority to shape the allocation of an array of major economic and political resources, and thus the highly undemocratic economic and political institutions that control most such major allocations. Given this reality, the elite's racial and class perspectives and power have routinely shaped this society in ways that regularly go against the interests of a majority of the population—and thus against the possibility of real and sustained political democracy.

The primary purpose of this book is to thoroughly examine the oligarchical realities of the U.S. political system, and often its closely related economic system, in terms of the pervasive and ongoing impact of this country's foundational and systemic racism. Systemic racism is not the only system of oppression, but it is a very central one over the course of U.S. history and the one we will focus most upon in this book. Most contemporary discussions of numerous important societal topics—including elections, crime, policing, jobs, schools, immigration, assimilation, "cultural values," and the American dream—usually involve at some level the impact of this reality of our deep and persisting racial foundation.

If we are ever to substantially reform or even replace our highly oligarchical and quite undemocratic political-economic system, and replace its highly skewed and unjust distribution of societal resources, we must first understand its origins, history, and current reality much better than we do now. A far more accurate view of our past is necessary for us to have a much more accurate view of our present. We cannot progress if much of what most Americans believe today about our past racial, political, and economic structures was never true, and we cannot progress if what most believe about these contemporary structures is also frequently not true. Most pages in this book are not about some distant and irrelevant societal history, for the discussions there usually have major implications for a great many contemporary societal realities. Our racial, political, and economic past is most decidedly relevant to our assumed "democracy" today.

Outline of Chapters

The next two chapters (1 and 2) examine in detail some important historical background necessary for a deeper understanding of centuries of racialized development of this country's political system and its closely related economic system. Chapter 1 explores the important Puritan era, with its often dogmatic, undemocratic, and hierarchical heritage, and reviews the early development by elite whites of capitalism and the slavery system. We observe the emergence of material structures of racial oppression and an early rationalizing framing by whites of themselves as virtuous and positively racialized, and of oppressed Native and African Americans as unvirtuous and negatively racialized. These early realities of systemic racism set much of the template for later developments in our political and economic systems. Chapter 2 analyzes the impact of our racial and class heritages and foundations on the construction of the U.S. political system in the revolutionary and constitutional eras, including the specific effects of slavery on that innovative yet undemocratic political system. We explore here too some of the past and present dimensions of the undemocratic political system that emerged in this founding era and that have persisted over later centuries.

Chapter 3 assesses the intertwined racial and class dimensions of the first 140 years of the U.S. political system and its new and conflicting parties, an era that eventually sees the emergence of our two-party system with a Democratic Party and a Republican Party. From the early decades, through the Civil War and Reconstruction era, to the 1930s, we analyze the many ways in which racial and class oppression, hierarchies, and framing constantly have an impact on the developing political system and the expansion of a new nation under the continuing guidance of elite white men. We examine critical racial struggles and changes emerging during the abolitionist and Reconstruction eras, as well as post-Reconstruction Jim Crow segregation that for nearly a century essentially re-enslaved African Americans and ended the possibilities for major democratic change.

Chapter 4 moves us into the dramatic mid-20th century developments in and around our political system that again involve this country's foundational and systemic racism. From the New Deal era of Franklin Roosevelt to the tumultuous era of Richard Nixon, we discover numerous racial dimensions underlying major decisions, shifts, and changes in the U.S. political and economic system. This is the era of New Deal programs that significantly aided (yet also discriminated against) the economic progress of African Americans, of Harry Truman's desegregation of the armed forces, of Dwight

Eisenhower's reluctant role in early desegregation, and of the civil rights movement and desegregation laws of the 1950s and 1960s. It is also the period of intensive white resistance to racial change and the development of a more conservative and whiter Republican Party, one persisting to the present day. Elite Republican leaders, including Barry Goldwater and Richard Nixon, committed to a political strategy aimed at aggressively recruiting white voters, even as the Democratic Party was becoming ever more diverse, with an infusion of voters enfranchised by civil rights laws.

Chapter 5 reviews the continuing white resistance to much racial change and the hard-right political turn by corporate and Christian conservatives, including some relatively authoritarian political leaders, from the 1970s to the 1990s. In this important period, systemic racism again regularly revealed itself in the actions of major political organizations and leaders. Presidents Ronald Reagan and George H. W. Bush made explicit use of racist strategies in winning electoral victories and, later, operated out of a conservative racial framing to forestall, cut back, or end certain civil rights enforcement efforts. During the subsequent Bill Clinton era we also observe some racialized moves by Democratic leaders toward white voters; and modest progressive efforts, such as some renewed civil rights enforcement, were offset by yet more conservative Republican congressional victories, the latter again revealing the utility of southern and suburban political strategies. Then, in Chapter 6, we analyze important aspects of persisting party polarization in the era of President George W. Bush and the persisting impact of systemic racism and class stratification on the actions of Bush and his political and corporate allies operating within the larger political system. In this political-economic era we see more aggressive economic restructuring by capitalists and the important ways in which systemic racism had an impact on corporate strategies such as now infamous subprime mortgages. We also observe the impact of Bush's own racial framing, both in his administration's continuing retreat on civil rights enforcement and in his use of a few token "diversity" appointments at the top of his administration.

Chapter 7 takes us farther into the 21st century to assess the important racialized events, engagements, and conflicts of the dramatic 2008 presidential primary and general election campaigns, which resulted in the election of the first U.S. president of color. This pathbreaking event, contrary to much contemporary analysis, did not signal an end to the impact of systemic racism on the U.S. political system, although many have suggested that result. Here we examine many racial issues that arose in the presidential campaigns, including an array of racist attacks on Senator Barack Obama by ordinary white Americans and Republican operatives. We will see that individual and institutional racism constantly crashed into these revealing political campaigns; and that Democratic operatives, and even occasionally candidate Obama, operated out of a colorblind framing of U.S. society.

Chapter 8 extends this analysis and examines President Barack Obama's continuing encounters with individual and systemic racism in the years of his presidency. We evaluate the white-framed and racist political attacks on him as president and on his policies, including the rise of an often racist new "Tea Party" movement. We also scrutinize important questions that have been raised about President Obama's frequently cautious or colorblind-framed approach to various political issues, including criticisms by African American leaders of his lack of attention to the political-economic needs of communities of color.

Chapter 9 provides a concluding assessment of contemporary societal inequalities and demographic changes in light of the arguments in this book, with a specific focus on the barriers to, and pressures and possibilities for, a truly multiracial democracy for the future United States.

Author's Note to Instructors

From the beginning, I wrote this book with students, general readers, and instructors clearly in mind. One can both learn and teach much about U.S. politics and its broader contexts from the extensive material provided here on our racialized political history and linked economic history. Let me suggest several possibilities for using this book as a teaching tool.

One suggestion is to begin with a clear explanation of the concepts of systemic racism and its central white racial frame. Even much serious teaching about racial matters in the United States accents individual prejudices, stereotyping, or bigoted discrimination, while often neglecting or marginalizing the persisting reality of systemic racism. I make significant use of the concept of systemic racism early on, and one can contrast that systemic perspective with a traditional prejudice-focused approach. The history of the U.S. political system, beginning with the central role of slaveholders and slavery at the U.S. constitutional convention, provides much recurring evidence of the reality and impact of systemic racism.

A second, closely related suggestion is to employ this book to help students recover and analyze a more accurate history, to the present day, of the deep racial underpinnings of our political system and associated economic system. From my research and experience, I have observed that too much of what is provided to students about the racial dimension and associated class dimension of our political and economic systems involves serious misconceptions, myths, and omissions. Much documented material in this book—from the constitutional era, through many intervening political eras, to the presidency of Barack Obama—provides the material one can utilize to generate dialog and critical thinking among students about what these racial and class dimensions have actually been. For example, one might begin such discussions by asking questions that tie together this suggestion with the first: "What does it mean today that we still live under a

U.S. Constitution substantially influenced by slaveholders and one that protected their political-economic interests in slavery?" Or, "Why did the Supreme Court's Dred Scott decision (1857) conclude so strongly that black Americans were not U.S. citizens, and what meaning and impact did this decision have?"

In exploring our political history, one might give students the research task of comparing traditional accounts of our major political events and institutions in standard textbooks with the more critical and probing accounts of these often racialized matters in this and similar books. Another way of exploring the meaning of this history is to get students to do some original thinking about what the outcomes of hypothetical alternative histories might have been for the United States. For example, one might raise the question of what a much more democratic constitutional convention might have looked like—for example, one with significant representation of Americans of color and white women—and what that might have meant for the later course of U.S. political, legal, and economic history.

Exploring these often forgotten historical matters with more adequate conceptual tools is important because most Americans, and especially most white Americans, generally do not recognize the systemic and foundational racism that underlies our major political institutions. The famous social scientist W. E. B. Du Bois once underscored the "gift of remembrance" long offered to this country by African Americans—that is, the need to remember how the historical labor of African Americans built up a prosperous United States and how the recurring efforts of African Americans in all eras have pressed the country in the direction of full-fledged democracy. In my view, we should teach students what is really there in U.S. political and social history and help them to critically remember and analyze it.

A third suggestion for teaching is to have students explore the meanings of the racial dimension and associated class dimension of contemporary political events and actions since Barack Obama's election to the presidency, which I assess in detail in later chapters. For instance, periodically my colleagues and I have gotten students to keep regular diaries of the racial discussions and commentaries that they have had with or hear from friends, relatives, and strangers. One might thus have students keep everyday journals on political discussions they encounter that relate to racial matters. One can then ask them to reflect critically on their diaries using the data and concepts, such as the white racial frame and systemic racism, from this book or other social science sources. Such efforts by students should help them to become better at critical thinking on such political matters and perhaps to make better sense of the socio-political world around them.

A fourth suggestion is to use the material herein to get students to examine the meaning and reality of the much-heralded concept of democracy. Numerous data-based discussions in this book examine the reality and persistence over many generations of actually undemocratic political institutions. One can use these historical and contemporary materials to examine such issues as who the dominant U.S. elites are, how they have acted in their own or broader interests, what type of political institutions they have created or allowed, and why the general public has not pressed more often for a full-fledged democracy. Students might be asked to link such materials to recent political events that raise questions about the possibility of democratic institutions, such as recent ballot security and ballot restriction efforts by political activists and politicians in various states. Additionally, one can employ some materials in this book to examine what a full-fledged U.S. democracy might actually look like. One might bring the essential political issues around the 1787 constitutional convention up to the present day by having students think critically about whether the United States should now have a really democratic constitutional convention to construct the fundamentals of a much more democratic political system. Students could even be asked to hold a practice constitutional convention to explore how they themselves might assess and create such a democratic political system.

Acknowledgments

I would especially like to thank Maria Chávez, Earl Smith, Louwanda Evans, Wendy Moore, Adia Harvey Wingfield, Errol Henderson, and an anonymous reader for Routledge for careful readings of earlier versions of this manuscript. I am also indebted to an array of students and colleagues who over the years, by means of their research and intensive discussions with me, have contributed significantly to my thinking in this book. These include Glenn Bracey, Ruth Thompson-Miller, Jessie Daniels, Kristen Lavelle, Chris Chambers, Jenni Mueller, Louwanda Evans and Bernice M. Barnett. I am also indebted to Louwanda Evans for her help on this project as a library and research assistant par excellence.

1

Framing a Racist America
Puritan Inheritances and Political Framing

Over the centuries of North American slavery and legal segregation, and now decades of continuing racial discrimination, the dominant political framing of this society has contained very positive big-picture narratives of early English Puritan and other Protestant "settlers." These Europeans are said to have come to North America with strong ideals of liberty and equality, and by means of their religious faith and hard work they prospered against the Native Americans and difficult environmental conditions. These early white Protestant colonists and their descendants in the founding era are said to have generated and emphasized the grand ideals of liberty, freedom, and equality long central to the U.S. political-economic tradition. Among the questions for us to answer in this chapter are how accurate is this portrait, and what are the implications of answers to that inquiry?

In particular, we will examine how these early colonial Americans, together with their views and institutions, shaped both the political and economic institutions and the patterns of racial oppression that were emerging in North America.

Early Protestants: Dogmatic, Undemocratic, and Hierarchical

The 1830s French visitor and observer, Alexis de Tocqueville, argued that the "American" heritage was of "strictly Puritanical origin."[1] Early on, Calvinistic Protestants developed numerous communities in many areas of North America. The Puritans colonized New England areas, while yet other Protestant groups, such as Scots-Irish Presbyterians and Dutch Calvinists, established communities in other colonies. These groups generally shared the accents on relatively dogmatic religious beliefs, strict morality, and hierarchical and patriarchal institutions.

In England, groups of Puritans had sought to purify the established Anglican Church, which they saw as corrupt. One group, called the "Pilgrims," moved to North America in 1620, developing the pioneering Plymouth colony. Mostly working-class people, they came with a commitment to a Puritan covenant that tended to view all men, including elected officials, as practically equal. Over the next decade, much larger Puritan groups came and set up the Massachusetts Bay Colony. In 1630, the ship, *Arbella*, together with ten others, brought some 700 Puritans to expand the Massachusetts Bay Colony. John Winthrop, an English lawyer, was their leader and became governor. These Puritan colonists were generally from better-off groups, had more education, and had a more educated clergy than Plymouth.[2]

What are some possible social inheritances stemming, at least in part, from these famous Puritans, the Calvinist Protestants in other colonies, and their immediate descendants? One inheritance appears to be a certain dogmatism and unreflective intolerance in regard to dissenting beliefs and practices. A second inheritance seems to be a commitment to a substantially oligarchical government and political structure, yet one with a strong veneer of democratic ideals. A third inheritance has contributed to a strong commitment to social hierarchy, one accenting class, racial, and gender inequality and stratification. A fourth inheritance is clearly an emphasis on this new nation as an exceptional light to all, a Eurocentric model of virtue and democracy for others, and a guardian of democratic political values for the world. While the views and practices of these early Protestant communities were not the only sources shaping these age-old societal inheritances, they did provide an early and extraordinarily influential impact on the social and political contours of the new European American society created in North America.

Consider the first likely inheritance. The Puritans had a substantially dogmatic and authoritarian perspective that accented obedience to authority and allowed little dissent over numerous religious issues and little freedom in regard to such things as male dominance, artistic creativity, and human amusements. According to psychologist Bob Altemeyer, authoritarianism "happens when the followers submit too much to the leaders, trust them too much, and give them too much leeway to do whatever they want."[3] Many of the Puritans' community norms and laws were authoritarian and confining, as one sees in their infamous trials of "witches" (mostly women) in the Salem area. Puritan assertions of liberty and freedom typically meant some liberty for themselves (as the "saints") versus outside control, but *not* in regard to outsiders and dissidents they sought to control. Where they had power, they often denied liberty to others.[4] Later on, Thomas Jefferson also underscored the religious intolerance of the English Puritans and other early Anglo-Protestant immigrants.[5]

A second likely inheritance of the early Calvinistic groups is a socially schizophrenic view of, and practice of, political democracy that is still with us today. Contrary to commonplace contemporary notions that early English colonists emphasized a broad doctrine of "democracy," the Massachusetts Puritans were diverse and inconsistent in their support of political democracy and even of the values of political and social freedom. The Puritans did develop some more representative institutions in colonial towns than in

England, with their legislatures being elected by male voters. Puritan communities did move away from the firm aristocratic controls experienced in England, and in their churches they replaced English clerical hierarchy with elected ministers.[6] Puritan officials were often elected but, once elected, they typically viewed themselves as responsible mainly to God, and not to ordinary colonists. These men expected and got obedience to their authority. When in 1630 several ships brought many new Puritans to the Massachusetts Bay Colony, John Winthrop, their major leader, spoke onboard ship in a famous sermon for his community: "If we should change from a mixed aristocracy to mere democracy, first we should have no warrant in scripture for it: for there was no such government in Israel . . . A democracy is, amongst civil nations, accounted the meanest and worst of all forms of government."[7]

A third likely inheritance from the Puritans and other early Protestants is a strong accent on social stratification and justified inequality. The Massachusetts Bay Puritans generally exuded more status arrogance and superiority than the smaller group of Plymouth Puritans, especially in regard to nearby Native American societies and other English colonies. For them, rank and status were very important. Indeed, most early English Protestant colonists accepted and enforced a strong class, gender, and, quite soon, racial hierarchy. In his onboard sermon, John Winthrop summarized this commitment to social hierarchy and inequality: "God Almighty in his most holy and wise providence, hath so disposed of the condition of mankind, as in all times some must be rich, some poor, some high and eminent in power and dignity; others mean and in submission." Rationalizing hierarchy for the Puritans, Winthrop further accented these reasons: "First to hold conformity with the rest of his world, being delighted to show forth the glory of [God's] wisdom in the variety and difference of the creatures, and the glory of his power in ordering all these differences for the preservation and good of the whole." That is, God ordained the inegalitarian societal hierarchy. A second reason for socioeconomic hierarchy was that it enabled rich and poor to demonstrate Christian virtues—"in the great ones, their love, mercy, gentleness, temperance etc., and in the poor and inferior sort, their faith, patience, obedience."[8] Obedience to authority was central to the essentially authoritarian views of these Puritan leaders and followers.

A fourth probable inheritance from the early Calvinistic tradition is the strong accent on American exceptionalism we observe over centuries of U.S. history. A typical encyclopedia definition defines American exceptionalism as the view that the United States is qualitatively different from other countries because of its religiously fostered values of liberty, its egalitarian morality, and its democratic political institutions.[9] In a famous part of his *Arbella* speech, Winthrop made the first recorded statement about such exceptionalism. He concluded his sermon with a metaphorical assertion anticipating well the contemporary concept of America as the dominant societal model for the world: "The Lord will . . . make us a praise and glory that men shall say of succeeding plantations, 'the Lord make it like that of New England.' For we must consider that we shall be as a city upon a hill. The eyes of all people are upon us."[10] Winthrop and his fellow Puritans saw themselves as setting a spiritual and social example for "all people." Massachusetts Bay colonists and other English colonists gradually built a nationalistic exceptionalism with a distinctive "American" identity. Like many of their descendants to the present day, they saw themselves as very distinctive and "God's chosen people."[11] From the beginning, this view of America as very exceptional in comparison with other countries—part of what is sometimes called America's "civil religion"—has often been ethnocentric, Eurocentric, and, as we will see, periodically white nationalist.

Capitalism, Slavery, and the Colonists

A dramatic departure from the purported love of liberty and freedom of the early European colonists can be seen in the early development of a political-economic system that soon was centered in the coordinated operation of capitalism, genocide, and slavery. Western capitalism somewhat predated European imperialism, yet escalated and matured dramatically as numerous European countries like England aggressively engaged in overseas colonialism and imperialism. In his famous book, *Capital*, the political economist Karl Marx accented the harsh realities of the earliest capitalistic production:

> The discovery of gold and silver in America, the extirpation, enslavement and entombment in mines of the aboriginal population, the beginning of the conquest and looting of the East Indies, the turning of Africa into a warren for the commercial hunting of black-skins, signalised the rosy dawn of the era of capitalist production. These idyllic proceedings are the chief moments of primitive accumulation . . . [They all] depend in part on brute force, *e.g.*, the colonial system. But, they all employ the power of the State, the concentrated and organised force of society, to hasten, hot-house fashion, the process of transformation of the feudal mode of production into the capitalist mode . . . [C]apital comes dripping from head to foot, from every pore, with blood and dirt.[12]

Western capitalistic wealth and production thus began with the violent looting of resources and the forcible enslavement of numerous populations. This capitalism expanded, not just from the industry and hard work of a European group, but rather by that group often stealing the labor of other groups. In this process there is no market equality or equal exchange, concepts central to arguments for capitalism by early economic analysts like Adam Smith. While there were markets, the fundamental reality was one of the "violent dispossessions of a whole class of people from control over the means of production."[13] Note, too, that all these chief moments of early capitalistic wealth accumulation involve non-Europeans—*indigenous peoples, Africans, Asians, and Latin Americans*—those soon to be racialized as "not white" in the dominant racial framing of Europeans and European Americans. A key feature of European colonialism and capitalism was the turning of the actual producers—many people of color—into slave or low-wage laborers to generate much wealth for the capitalistic investors and other exploiters.

Historian James Horton has noted that the Europeans "came to what they called the New World as part of a capitalistic venture . . . From the very beginning, European colonization was very much a commercial, capitalistic enterprise."[14] Several North American colonies were set up by royal joint-stock companies to create wealth for European stockholders. The English kings gave joint-stock, individual, and group charters to exploit North American lands to various white entrepreneurs. One key royal-chartered corporation was London's Virginia Company, with its branches including the Plymouth Company and the London Company. Jamestown, Virginia, was established in 1607 by the London Company. Because there was no gold, the company turned to "tobacco farming, producing tobacco that was sold in Europe, turned out to be very valuable, very profitable. But very labor intensive."[15] There were not enough white indentured servants to meet this labor need—and Indians resisted as groups or died off from European diseases—so white planters and other whites in the North American colonies turned to enslaving Africans on an ever larger scale. As pioneering historian W. E. B. Du Bois put it, slavery was not "a plague sent from God." Instead, North American slavery arose "principally from the cupidity . . . of our ancestors."[16]

Most slavery-related enterprises in North America were very much about profit-making in this early era of world capitalism. For example, by the 1770s, slavery-centered agricultural production in the Virginia colony had made it the "most wealthy and populous of the thirteen colonies."[17] The North American colonies had developed by the mid-1700s into a slavery-centered society in which much of the economy, especially that part beyond subsistence farming, was controlled by white slaveholders and large numbers of white merchants, shipbuilders, insurance and banking firms, and non-slaveholding farmers often linked in some way to slave farms and plantations or the trade in slaves. The North American slavery system generated commodities for an ever-expanding global market, and thus created much capital that was constantly recirculated into the ever-growing Atlantic capitalistic system. In the early period of North American capitalism, important economic and social institutions became very racially encoded—thereby creating a materialistic and foundational system of racial oppression in what would soon become the United States.[18]

The White Racial Frame and the Elite

For several centuries now, a highly oppressive system of slavery, legal segregation, and contemporary racial oppression has been aggressively rationalized and legitimated by a strong white racial framing, which has been most powerfully perpetuated by the white elite. This dominant racial framing is central to our systemic racism, and it has long provided the vantage point from which most whites and a great many others have routinely viewed and interpreted this society. This *white racial frame* is much broader and deeper than just racial stereotypes and prejudices, for it includes at least the following important dimensions:

1. racial stereotypes and prejudices;
2. racial narratives and interpretations;
3. racialized imagery;
4. racialized emotions; and
5. common inclinations to discriminate along racial lines.

Early on, this dominant white frame incorporated many racial stereotypes, images, and emotions that were widely accepted among whites and essential to rationalizing and maintaining the subordination of Native Americans, African Americans, and soon other Americans of color. Also very central to this white racial frame were aggressively positive views of whites and their interests, folkways, and self-conceptions.[19]

From the 17th century onwards, in North America's new society, the early capitalist was typically a European American male. By the late 17th or early 18th century he and other powerful men were self-imaged specifically as "white" within this strong and developing white frame, and also as dominant within the often associated capitalistic and patriarchal frames central to the new society. Not surprisingly, the growing numbers of significant slaveholders and allied entrepreneurs frequently portrayed themselves as noble capitalists and patriarchs.

These capitalistic patriarchs accurately viewed themselves as powerful white "fathers" controlling not only their families but also often their communities and society more generally. For instance, in the early 1700s the powerful Virginia slaveholder, William Byrd II, portrayed himself as a biblical-type patriarch:

> Like one of the patriarchs, I have my flocks and my herds, my bondmen and bond-women, and every sort of trade amongst my own servants, so I live in a kind of independence . . . I must take care to keep all my people to their duty, to set all the springs in motion, and to make every one draw his equal share to carry the machine forward.[20]

Byrd held a religiously-tinted idea of being the master over a racialized patriarchal society. Later slaveholders like George Washington held a similar view of their farms and plantations.[21] In their domination of colonial society, slaveholding capitalists like Byrd and Washington viewed themselves as dependent on "no one but God," as they put it, and as patriarchal defenders of white homes, white-run communities, and the white "race" in an ever-expanding slavery-centered society.

Powerful slaveholding capitalists like Byrd and Washington and their economic allies, such as merchants and bankers in the South and North, were inheritors of a system of racial oppression that had been created and maintained by self-defined whites since the 1600s, and they were significant agents in its continued flourishing and perpetuation. Men like Byrd and Washington also demonstrate that the most powerful and society-determining intersectional category of the racial, class, and gender hierarchies is that of elite white men. They have long connected, directed, and maintained these major systems of oppression, systems that have long reciprocally reinforced, mutually assisted, or co-reproduced each other. These elite men have generally used their economy-based, state-based, and media-based power to maintain the deeply entrenched hierarchies and inequalities of capitalism, systemic racism, and patriarchy. For Western capitalism to flourish, it has required a total social system with racial, class, and gender hierarchies that reinforce each other in interlocking and overlapping ways, a complex ensemble of institutional relationships.[22]

Moreover, the fact that North American colonization began with these powerful men early accenting a racial framing of themselves as white and superior over those defined as not white and inferior has made a significant difference in the way these hierarchical systems have evolved and developed over time. Since they have been at the top of these hierarchies, these elite men have played the central role in constructing who is actually the truly "normal" human being against which to judge other human beings.[23] From the beginning, that most normal being has been white and male. The self-definition of white and male has explicitly included *not* being nonwhite and female, with the latter two categories being not only inferior but also carrying certain characteristics to be aggressively rejected. Thus, the dominant white male masculinity has also been heterosexist. Clearly, these elite men have long had great power to define, shape, and maintain this society's major socially constructed categories and hierarchies.

The Slavery System: A Labor Template for the Future

In my view one cannot make full sense of the centuries-old trajectories of North American political and economic history without a clear understanding of the slavery system's long-term impact. This extensive societal impact can be seen in this country's Constitution and political structures (see Chapter 2) and in its economy, popular culture, basic values, and dominant racial framing of society. Many of the country's important founders,

framers, and other major leaders were either slaveholders or heavily impli-
cated in the society's burgeoning slavery system. Indeed, over *half* of this
country's distinctive political-economic history involved a slavery economy,
many powerful and profit-oriented slaveholders, and millions of enslaved
African Americans.

Centuries of extermination of Native Americans and enslavement of
Africans in North America created a critical template for the further
development and operation of U.S. capitalism. The slave-labor system of
North American capitalism thus had a profound and far-reaching impact on
many aspects of society, including white perspectives on who was a person
and a citizen, what or who could be considered property, who does what sort
of labor, and how the country should expand territorially. For example,
much of the North American economy was grounded in the production of
major crops—such as rice, sugar, tobacco, and cotton—that were grown
substantially by enslaved African Americans. This was the basis for much of
this country's early economic prosperity and important wealth, wealth that
created prosperity in highly disproportionate ways for whites for centuries.
In addition, as Karen Brodkin argues, the enslavement of African Americans
was a "template for an enduring organization of capitalism in which race was
the basis for the organization of work."[24] As a result, the slavery-centered
economic system was soon followed by nearly a century of the near-slavery
of Jim Crow labor segregation and other legal segregation. The racial
hierarchy and racial framing created by more than 340 years of slavery and
legal segregation have long been part of a foundational "process by which
the United States continues to organize and understand labor and national
belonging." With the slavery system as the template, consecutive groups of
African, Latino, and Asian American workers "came to be treated as members of less civilized, less moral, less self-restrained races only when they were
recruited to be the core of the U.S. capitalist labor force."[25]

In addition, many aspects of the long-dominant white framing of racial
matters—including the character of racial narratives and imagery in the
media of the slavery era and in popular entertainments like minstrel
shows—were greatly and continually shaped by the same extensive slavery
system. Let us explore how this developed over time.

Extending the Great Chain of Being: European American Colonizers

Consider how the early elites and ordinary colonists interpreted and defended
the stratified society they established and maintained. The European colonists who spread capitalistic enterprises and slavery to North America came
with a distinctive hierarchical perspective like that articulated by the early
Protestant leaders. This framing envisioned an up–down ladder of superior
and inferior beings called the "great chain of being." Dating back to Ancient
Greek times, this was a view of the world held by the educated and ordinary

folks that envisioned an "infinite number of links ranging in hierarchical order from the meagerest kind of existence, which barely escapes nonexistence, through 'every possible' grade up to . . . the highest possible kind of creature."[26] Not surprisingly, European and European American colonizers firmly placed human beings at the top of the hierarchy. The higher up, the more valued a group was; the lower down, the less valued, less human, and more exploitable they were. We have seen how Puritan leaders accented the superiority of the rich over the poor. These early Protestant colonists also came with a strong patriarchal view, with men generally superior to women in this great chain of beings.[27]

As European imperialists and colonists spread across the globe, most had no misgivings about dominating other peoples. Numerous societies have attempted to dominate areas outside their own territories, but none in the modern era has done so to the dramatic global extent of Western Europeans. Most known cultures have also developed some ethnocentrism toward outsiders, but European colonizers of the Americas aggressively accented the superiority and dominance of European culture and a strongly "othered" image of the inferiority of those they dominated. The old "great chain of being" conceptualization, and its central hierarchical framing, conveniently supported an extension to a strong and dominant racial conceptualization linked to the destruction of numerous Native American societies and to the expanding slavery system focused on African Americans. The North American political-economic system was one with European American men at the top, European American women well below, and Native Americans and African Americans at the bottom. In this emergent racial system the well-framed views of those high up on the hierarchical ladder were central, while the views of those farther down were usually marginalized or excluded.[28]

European Americans as Highly Virtuous

Significantly, most of the European American colonists viewed themselves as highly virtuous Christians—Puritans, traditional Anglicans, Presbyterians, or Quakers—who were bringing advanced civilization to uncivilized territories. One aspect of this virtuousness lay in their religious and work values. The sociologist, Max Weber, famously accented the Protestant ethic of these American colonists, an ethic in his view indicating the superiority of European culture and an advance for humanity because of its supposedly universalistic character. The accent on a pro-European (soon pro-white) virtuousness was at the center of this American Protestant societal framing. As the much-cited French traveler to the U.S., Alexis de Tocqueville, put it in the 1830s, these founding colonists were that "portion of the English people . . . commissioned to explore the *wilds* of the New World."[29] That is indeed the way many of them viewed their supposed civilizing of North America.

American exceptionalism, the view of this new country as quite exceptional, was generally Eurocentric and racialized from the early decades of colonization. One key feature of European Americans' exceptionalism was an aggressively racial framing and marginalization of Americans of color, both indigenous and African Americans, who did not fit the narrative of exceptional and positive American strengths, abilities, and values. Integral to European and European American colonialism was a predatory ethic asserting the rights of European "settlers" to the land and labor of inferiorized others. Initially, this predatory ethic was dressed up in religious language. Early European Americans saw themselves as not normally possessing the negative qualities of the "creatures of darkness," the indigenous peoples of the areas they invaded. As several historians have shown, they viewed themselves as rational, ascetic, self-governing, and sexually controlled, while the Native American and African American "others" were commonly seen as irrational, uncivilized, instinctual, and uncontrolled.[30] Seeking to rationalize what they were doing in what soon became a powerful white racial frame, European Christians leading the colonization of the Americas and Africa immediately conceptualized and framed newly conquered non-Europeans as being at the bottom levels of the great chain of being, with the virtuous white European colonizers and their descendants clearly at the top.

Later on, during the American revolutionary era, both the continuation of this positive framing of whites and the impact of many decades of slavery could be seen in some of the metaphorical language white patriots used in their vigorous opposition to the British. They frequently spoke in various ways of their own "enslavement" by the British. Perhaps the most famous military and political leader of the day, George Washington, insisted "we must assert our rights, or submit to every imposition, that can be heaped upon us, till custom and use shall make us tame and abject slaves, as the blacks we rule over with such arbitrary sway."[31] Note his racial framing of whites' freedom and virtue in contrast to blacks' enslavement and lack of virtue. Many other white revolutionaries asserted it was better to be free "among the dead" than to live under British political and economic "enslavement." So much revolutionary rhetoric accented this enslavement perspective that it was clear that these white revolutionaries viewed themselves as morally superior and virtuous as compared with the oppressive "enslaving" British. They had come to view "freedom and slavery as moral values," rather than just economic or political matters.[32]

Framing Indigenous Americans as Unvirtuous

The peoples in the North American "wilds" were generally not seen as so virtuous. Surprisingly, these other peoples have often been left out of scholarly discussions of the early Protestant colonists and American colonization. For example, Max Weber notes briefly in his influential book,

The Protestant Ethic and the Spirit of Capitalism, that the American Protestants distrusted foreigners, but never analyzes any racial issues in the spread of European Protestantism and capitalism to North America. He never discusses American Indians, enslaved Africans, or white actions in regard to them.[33]

Yet, the new European American culture made significant use of a strong cultural "other" as part of the creation of a strong image of the European American self. The oppressive treatment of non-Europeans was regularly linked to the desire for European American dominance, which was gradually rationalized in a broad racialized framing. In their earliest encounters with indigenous peoples, New England Puritans and other Protestants sometimes treated Indians peaceably, especially when Europeans' environmental difficulties required that. However, their habitual practices soon changed into an instrumental type of racial oppression. They usually treated Native Americans, who were physically unlike European Americans and singled out in terms of physical characteristics, as less than fully human beings. At an early point, as historian Richard Drinnon notes, "savagery" and dark skin were "parts of a single image for the Puritans," who saw themselves as the highly civilized people. The Protestant colonists and their descendants frequently viewed North American lands they sought as "unpeopled," with Indians as the enemy. Indians were soon "wild beasts" who should be "removed from their dens" and killed. Drinnon and other social science researchers have assessed the religiously repressed nature of many colonists, with their often obsessive fears of these "dark others" and their views of the latter as highly unvirtuous and the opposite of Europeans.[34]

Early European colonization created large-scale disease, poverty, and death for a great many indigenous Americans, but these harsh realities were usually not seen for what they actually were, but were linked to the supposedly "natural characteristics of backward peoples."[35] Those Native Americans targeted, killed, or enslaved were commonly rationalized in a predatory Eurocentric frame as religiously, civilizationally, and biologically inferior peoples who could be legitimately exploited for Europeans' gain. Moreover, by the late 17th and early 18th centuries this framing of the exploited "others" was increasingly racialized.

Framing African Americans and Native Americans as Unvirtuous

The early European American view of who was truly virtuous, and who was not, was aggressively applied to the African Americans whom many white colonists enslaved in both northern and southern colonies. White Protestants who saw themselves as highly virtuous portrayed African Americans, as they had Indians, in terms of "sinful" ways of life that they felt they had given up. The virtuous European American colonist thereby created a "pornography of his former life" in his negative framing of African Americans to guarantee that he would "not slip back into the old ways or act out half-supposed fantasies."[36] David Roediger has also underscored how this accentuated Puritanical view persisted over later centuries: "Increasingly adopting an ethos that attacked holidays, spurned contact with nature, saved time, bridled sexuality, separated work from the rest of life and postponed gratification, profit-minded [white] Englishmen and Americans cast Blacks *as their former selves* . . . [R]acists still pined for older ways, and even still practiced older styles of life, guiltily."[37]

From the first century of their enslavement, African Americans have been at the core of the white-racist system of this country because they are the one racial group whose incorporation, subjugation, and framing has been given the greatest white attention among all groups of color. Whites have devoted enormous amounts of energy to oppressing African Americans—initially for their wealth-creating labor, and later for a broader range of economic, political, and ideological reasons. The first 20 African laborers were purchased off a Dutch-flagged ship by English colonists at Jamestown in 1619. African and African American laborers' numbers grew rapidly over the next century. By the time of the American Revolution, the mostly enslaved African Americans made up a very substantial fifth of the total colonial population. Early on, these profit-generating enslaved laborers were viewed in colonial laws and in most whites' everyday racial framing as personal *property*, as "ordinary merchandise" that could be bought and sold in numerous colonial labor markets.[38]

The expanding slavery system was quite significant well beyond southern areas, including in New England. And it was important in the first generations of this country's development. Around 1700, the important Massachusetts politicians and judges, John Saffin and Samuel Sewall, who were also Puritan merchants, made clear their racist framing of black Americans in their writings. They demonstrated they had a positive framing of white virtuousness and whiteness and a negative framing of black vice and blackness. Educated as a minister, Sewall was a successful merchant trading fish and furs across the Atlantic. He wrote a pamphlet that was opposed to slavery, but one riddled with antiblack imagery. Another wealthy merchant, slaveholder, and slavetrader, John Saffin, wrote a hostile attack on "negro character" that targeted Sewall's antislavery pamphlet and defended slavery.[39] In addition, leading Protestant ministers of this era, such as Cotton Mather and Jonathan Edwards, assertively rationalized the racial hierarchy. In 1706, Mather insisted whites should "Christianize Negroes," seen as "barbarians," to get them to work harder for slavemasters. Slavery was God-ordained, for African Americans were "brutish," "stupid," and "beasts."[40] In this long colonial era, the powerful white racial frame was actively spread by these economic, political, and religious elites in white-controlled workplaces, schools, and churches, as well as in the emerging print media.

By the late 1700s white-framed views of African Americans were ever more firmly enshrined in the legal and political institutions of the growing nation by the white descendants of the earlier colonists. Indeed, African Americans have long been an overt or hidden reference point for these and later whites' actions or interpretations of society. They have been central to the creation of much white prosperity, to crafting the U.S. Constitution, to economic conflicts underlying the U.S. Civil War, and to much presidential politics over centuries. Significantly, African Americans were the racial group singled out numerous times in the U.S. Constitution for enslavement and subordination within the new United States.[41] The leading theorist of that new Constitution, James Madison, often called the "father" of U.S. democracy, asserted this from his own racist framing: "Next to the case of the black race within our bosom, that of the red on our borders is the problem most baffling to the policy of our country."[42]

Madison's strong racial framing treated as very problematical the two non-European groups important in European American development for the first centuries of this country's history. In this way he made clear that whites were central to the social and political positioning of all groups in society, just as his ancestors had done. Indeed, as early as the mid-1600s, important aspects of an emerging racial framing can be seen in European American colonists' perspectives on African and Native Americans. In this colonial framing both groups are dramatically "othered" and dehumanized. There is repeated and negative emphasis on certain physical features that distinguish them from European Americans, and there is a regular linkage of their negatively framed physical characteristics to supposedly negative cultural characteristics. By the late 1600s and early 1700s, and more so by the late 1700s, European and European American physical scientists were designating and writing about dominant and subordinated groups in colonial American society as different "species" and "races." These "races" were positioned in a naturally ordered, explicitly racial hierarchy now legitimated by the emerging physical sciences, in whose development key American political figures like Thomas Jefferson were also playing an important role.[43]

Against this aggressive European American oppression and its racialization, both indigenous peoples and African Americans resisted when and how they could. For example, in August 1791, Benjamin Banneker, a free black astronomer, surveyor, and almanac creator, penned an important letter to Jefferson, then U.S. Secretary of State, in which he countered the racist framing of African Americans as lacking in virtue and humanity. He called out the "general prejudice and prepossession, which is so prevalent in the world against those of my complexion," but added that "we are a race of beings, who have long labored under the abuse and censure of the world; that we have long been looked upon with an eye of contempt; and that we have long been considered rather as brutish than human, and scarcely capable of mental endowments." Next he forthrightly urged the powerful Jefferson to recognize the "indispensible duty of those, who maintain for themselves the rights of human nature, and who possess the obligations of Christianity, to extend their power and influence to the relief of every part of the human race, from whatever burden or oppression they may unjustly labor under." Then, drawing on whites' common slavery metaphor, he cited British efforts to reduce white American revolutionaries to "a state of servitude," and suggested that there was a time when Jefferson himself had seen "into the injustice of a state of slavery, and in which you had just apprehensions of the horrors of its condition."[44]

Banneker boldly and accurately added that, even as Jefferson had articulated in a Declaration of Independence condemnations of British violations of whites' liberty, he and his slaveholding associates had also detained "by fraud and violence so numerous a part of my brethren, under groaning captivity and cruel oppression" and thus were "guilty of that most criminal act, which you professedly detested in others, with respect to yourselves."[45] In this assertive black counter-framing, which made use of some of the same "rights" language as the white American revolutionaries, black Americans were viewed as at least as virtuous and human as white Americans.

Conclusion: Persisting Neo-Puritanism?

Examining more recent political eras, a few social scientists have linked much continuing European American intolerance, racism, and authoritarianism with its common either/or thinking to the Puritan and other early Protestant heritages. For instance, researching the development of right-wing political movements like McCarthyism in the mid-1950s, influential sociologist Seymour Lipset explored in detail the impact of the long religious tradition of "puritanical morality and intolerance" in U.S. political history. He concluded from his historical review that in the contemporary era most "Americans believe that there is a fundamental difference between right and wrong, that right must be supported, and that wrong must be suppressed, that error and evil have no rights against the truth." From his perspective, such either/or Manichaean thinking is most serious, even "disastrous, in the area of foreign policy, where allies and enemies cannot be gray," and thus partly right and partly wrong, but must be clearly "black or white" in our political categorization.[46]

Over the centuries an often rigid either/or thinking and morality, an ethnocentrism toward outsiders such as new immigrants, and a stereotyping intolerance seem to have been part of the long-term U.S. sociopolitical heritage of early North American Protestantism. Social scientist Milan Zafirovski has argued that the Puritans' dogmatic "witch trials" in Massachusetts in the 1690s have had evident sequels in such later historical events as "monkey trials" over evolution in the Bible Belt and intense debates over laws prohibiting alcohol in the 1920s, and over the decades since the 1920s in various moralistic "wars on drugs."[47] Moreover, as we will see in later chapters, much either/or, exceptionalist, and ethnocentric thinking and action can be seen in U.S. national and foreign policies to the present day.

Most importantly, ethnocentric and hierarchical framing was sharply accelerated as a result of the slavery system that dramatically emerged by the early 18th century. Over this era we observe the development of the highly racist imagery and racial-category framing that for centuries now have been directed by self-defined whites at Native Americans, African Americans, and numerous other non-European groups. Clearly, whites have long been framed as much more virtuous and quite superior, while the racialized "others" have long been framed as unvirtuous and inferior. Since the late 17th century, this aggressive racial-superiority and racial-inferiority framing has persisted, and indeed periodically accelerated. The dominant white racial frame was developed in part to legitimate and enforce the racial hierarchization of Western capitalism's labor force and to explain why some workers and their families had significant liberty and others did not. But the white racial frame early on had much wider use in asserting general white superiority over other peoples and cultures, and it has functioned in that broad manner now over several long centuries.

2

Faking Democracy
Race, Class, and Our Undemocratic Political System

The influential political, literary, and scholarly traditions of this country have long accented a U.S. tradition of freedom, equality, and democracy. This mainstream tradition constantly celebrates the "founding fathers" as great men and distinctive political geniuses. The political institutions they established are popularly presented as approaching political perfection, as is the U.S. Constitution which is viewed as generating numerous important political institutions. However, as we will see later, much in the standard historical view is misrepresented or mythological. These founding fathers intentionally constructed the foundation for our actually undemocratic political system, one that has persisted over centuries now and that can be seen in the recurring operations of U.S. politics. Indeed, most of the early North American population had no direct input into the creation of these political institutions. The dramatically undemocratic features of the U.S. Constitution and of the society at the time of its creation get some selective attention in certain scholarly books in social science and legal studies, but they rarely get significant discussions in mainstream textbooks, popular books on politics, or mainstream media discourse.

We should consider for a moment how to define the concept of "democracy." In this book I do not have space to deal with the extensive discussions of this concept over the centuries, so a brief discussion will suffice for our purposes. Some researchers and analysts writing on democracy assume its definition without actually spelling one out. This includes leading books on U.S. politics.[1] For our purposes, we can start with the definition of political democracy suggested by political scientist Jim Dator: democracy is "a form and process of governance that allows each person affected by the actions of an entity, a continuous and equal opportunity to influence actions of that entity."[2] Using this reasonable definition, one soon comes to understand that the U.S. political system has never even roughly approximated this reality of a truly participatory democracy. Dator further argues that for a society to be broadly democratic such democracy should operate in all major societal "forms and processes that influence people," most especially in "economic structures, most of which are profoundly authoritarian and undemocratic."[3]

When confronted with the argument that the U.S. is not, and never has been, a real democracy in anything like the meaning just noted, many popular discussions retreat to the view that the U.S. is only a representative democracy or a republic in which the important branches of the government ultimately somehow get their political status and major power from the popular majority.[4] Yet other analysts defend the lack of real democracy by arguing that a majority of Americans today do not want a truly democratic society. Many Americans, according to political analysts John Hibbing and Elizabeth Theiss-Morse, "do not want to make political decisions themselves; they do not want to provide much input to those who are assigned to make these decisions; and they would rather not know all the details of the decision-making process." From this perspective, the majority of Americans do not want a fully active and participatory democracy; and they may not or do not participate actively, not because of the "unseemly nature of debate in Congress or displeasure with a particular public policy. Participation in politics is low because people do not like politics even in the best of circumstances." In their perspective, Americans want a visible democracy only "on those rare occasions when they are motivated to be involved. They want to know that the opportunity will be there for them even though they probably have no current intention of getting involved in government . . ."[5] Of course, one important question involves why a majority of Americans have often become discouraged in many ways from more active participation even in the limited democratic mechanisms that are available. Until one has a more accurate and detailed answer for that question, one cannot conclude that a majority of the people do not care about having a full-fledged and much more participatory democracy.

It is clear that there has never been a truly democratic political or economic structure in the United States. As we have already observed, U.S. political and economic systems have long been strikingly oligarchical. Moreover, in this book I suggest that, historically and in the present, the mostly white and male elite has been divided roughly into three political camps—a substantial conservative camp unsympathetic to populist and expanding-democracy ideas; a substantial moderate camp receptive to some populist and expanding-democracy ideas; and a small liberal group with more substantial support for populist and expanding-democracy ideas. As we will see, these three segments of the ruling elite have, over the centuries, been disproportionately represented in various regions of the country and at the top of the political system. They have also periodically found themselves in significant conflict, often over social as well as political-economic ideas and policies, and such conflict and divergence have periodically and dramatically affected the distinctive history of the United States.

The Revolutionary Era

Most of the major American colonial leaders had no substantial objections to the basic form of British government that controlled the colonies, only to the arbitrary ways in which British power was exercised. The majority of these mostly elite men would initially have been content with modest political reforms. However, once the American Revolution got heated up, certain large and more democratically oriented elements in the general population became more influential. In 1776, a more liberal, people-oriented segment of the elite played the key role in drafting the Declaration of Independence, with its dramatic declarations that "all men are created equal" and that governments "derive their just powers from the consent of the governed," as well as its statement that people have a right to abolish governments that harm them. In contrast, the elite's conservative and moderate segments mostly dominated the group that gave us a property-oriented U.S. Constitution in the late 1780s (see below).[6]

We do not know how widespread these relatively radical views in the Declaration of Independence were in the colonies, but they were sufficient to help trigger the American Revolution. Estimates suggest that at least one-third of the colonial population was opposed to the American Revolution, including many colonial officials and members of the elite. During the revolutionary period numerous colonial governments underwent significant political changes, frequently with more input from ordinary voters and a less aristocratic political framework. Colonial legislatures gained significant new powers in most colonies, with the old English idea of "checks and balances" to limit popular input being partially or substantially eliminated. Interestingly, the Articles of Confederation (1781–1788), the first constitution for the new United States, were actually more democratic in some significant ways than the later U.S. Constitution (1788). For example, they provided for a more powerful legislature, called the Continental Congress, that was unhampered and unchecked by an executive or judicial branch. Its major weakness was that its governing powers were quite limited. Much discontent with the Articles of Confederation led to the constitutional convention, whose mostly well-off members did not pursue its official charge just to amend the Articles, but instead created a new and even less democratic Constitution.[7]

Protecting Propertied Interests

Significantly, the white men at the 1787 constitutional convention did not include some of the well-known advocates of expanded political and civil rights of the general (white male) population and of popular majorities. Indeed, the more outspoken of such advocates of the era—men like Samuel Adams, Thomas Paine, and Patrick Henry—were not at this constitutional convention, and very few of the 55 men there had previously signed the more liberal Declaration of Independence. At the convention, thus, a few liberal delegates did defend the rights and needs of ordinary Americans when the constitutional discussions tilted too much to propertied interests. Numerous sections of the final Constitution were oriented to reforms rejecting certain British colonial practices and to political liberty—for example, the rejection of religious tests for office and the protection of freedom in congressional debate. Yet the dominant conservative and moderate delegates worked aggressively to protect property, including the extensive property in human beings (slavery), and to protect well-off Americans against threats they saw coming from those enslaved and the masses of ordinary white people. As a result, the small liberal group was unable even to add a strong statement on individual human rights to the Constitution. A Bill of Rights had to be added later after significant popular protest.[8]

Indeed, the broad economic and political interests of the dominant elite were intentionally placed at the heart of the new U.S. Constitution. The mostly well-off founders, a majority of whom were either slaveholders or involved as economic actors to some degree in the slavery system, viewed numerous issues of "freedom" in much the same way that those in later U.S. elites have also viewed them—that is, as centered substantially in the protection of property and property rights. The U.S. Constitution was made by these men with much thought for the economic and political interests of their dominant racial and class group, although most did not seek to directly enhance the worth of their personal financial involvements.[9] Thus, from the beginning of this country there was a direct connection between the capitalistic and other economic interests of the elite and their construction of the new U.S. political institutions, and their racial and class interests shaped what much of the political system would be like. Indeed, they substantially determined how and to what degree ordinary Americans would be able to participate in the new political system.

Unmistakably, the founders were as much "class" thinkers as was the nearly contemporary European social scientist, Karl Marx. They argued explicitly inside and outside the convention that well-off Americans had to protect themselves against the society's poor, including rebellious slaves and landless whites. In his writings during and after the constitutional convention, James Madison, the politically savvy slaveholder often considered the most influential delegate and shaper of the Constitution, openly wrote of the "class with" property and the "class without" property. In his convention notes Madison noted the inequality increasing in the United States, and indicated that he wished it to be protected. Later in the *Federalist Papers* (No. 10) defending the new Constitution, he also accented the importance of protecting private property as the most important goal of the new U.S. government.[10]

Soon after the constitutional convention a set of articles called the *Federalist Papers* were written and published in order to defend the ratification of the new Constitution. They were written by the leading Federalist advocates, Madison, John Jay, and Alexander Hamilton. In his contributions to these *Federalist Papers*, Madison indicated his fear of "impending anarchy" and the "overbearing majority" and emphasized the need for dividing the population so that the less privileged could not act as a powerful political majority. Other major framers took similar positions. The leading northern convention delegate Gouverneur Morris asserted that property is the "main object of Society." And the Federalist leader, Alexander Hamilton, aggressively pressed the convention to establish a strong central government to benefit commercial, slaveholding, and banking interests. Like numerous other founders, Hamilton felt that the "rich and well born" should not be subject to the judgments of the "mass of the people" (also termed the "great beast") who "seldom judge or determine right."[11]

A Government by and for the White Elite

Clearly, most of the white male founders did not trust ordinary (then just white male) Americans to govern themselves. Neither the creation of a "government by the people," nor the creation of a government regularly and directly responsible to the people was the goal of most of the mostly elite men at the constitutional convention. Most in the 18th-century elite felt that ordinary people were not to be trusted and that direct and participatory democracy would be dangerous to their propertied interests, and thus they made sure that the new national political institutions were as isolated as possible from direct input by the people. Evidence that they were fearful of the general public can be seen in the reality of the constitutional convention being kept very private and *closed* to that public. Their views on protecting well-off whites from the white masses—as well as from revolts of African Americans and Native Americans—were made evident in their private comments and discussions, even as they tried to sound more democratic in public declarations.[12]

To take one clear example, a major provision of the U.S. Constitution that signaled the antidemocratic inclinations of numerous founders can be seen in the great difficulties they established for amending the Constitution. The founders wanted this process to be difficult so the general public could not easily add, as Madison said, an "innovation" that might endanger elite interests. Significantly, the already undemocratic provisions of the Constitution were not enough, and the convention delegates decided the Constitution could never be modified by a direct vote of ordinary people, but only by a two-thirds vote of their representatives in both houses of Congress, plus majority ratification by three-quarters of state legislatures (or conventions). A majority of ratifiers would likely be white members of the better-off classes. Over the centuries since the Constitution's creation, numerous proposals for a more democratic political system—shorter terms for senators, specific terms for federal judges, ending the strong presidential veto, and direct election of the president—have not been implemented, in part because of the difficulties of amending the Constitution.[13]

Interestingly, in the aforementioned *Federalist Papers*, the words "democracy" and "democratic" appear just 14 times, while the words "republic" and "republican" appear more than 100 times. Frequently, these elite men are discussing what they view as undesirable direct democracy and contrast that with a much more desirable representative republic, which in their minds prevents reason from being overcome by passions of the "multitude."[14]

In *Federalist Paper* No. 10, Madison discussed "pure democracy" versus a "republic." Indeed, Madison had once said that democracy was the "most vile form of government," and in this particular *Federalist Paper* he indicated his fear of the development of "factions," such as political parties. From his perspective a pure democracy had "no cure for the mischiefs of faction." A republic was different, for it allowed a refinement of "public views, by passing them through the medium of a chosen body of citizens, whose wisdom may best discern the true interest of their country, and whose patriotism and love of justice will be least likely to sacrifice it to temporary or partial considerations."[15] Madison rejected the idea of a "perfect equality" in political rights, instead preferring the wisdom of a "chosen body of citizens," by which he clearly meant the significant propertied white men in a community.

Constitutional Protections of Enslaved Property

Since the 17th century, property in enslaved human beings had become central to the country the founders now called the United States, and the economic system that enslaved African Americans had long created significant wealth for many elite founders and other well-off white Americans. However, usually missing from the commonplace societal origins narrative is explicit attention to this political-economic centrality of the developed slavery system and of the reality that massive amounts of wealth in property in the colonies and the early U.S. were held in the form of enslaved African Americans. Recall how, from its early decades, this country's racialized oppression took the form of often violent land theft from Indian groups and then extensive African and African American enslavement to work new lands. In many areas of the country this foundational oppression created such an authoritarian societal hierarchy, such extensive inequality, such need for social control over oppressed populations, and such an extensive racial framing, that it was impossible for the founders to construct a really democratic political system in such a societal context.

At the 1787 constitutional convention in Philadelphia, the 55 framers were all white men of European origin. Their role in creating a deeply oppressive and racialized political-economic system is suggested by their occupations. About 40 percent had been or were slave owners, and many others profited as merchants, shippers, lawyers, and bankers from the trade in slaves, slave-produced agricultural products, or provisions provided for slaveholders and slavetraders.[16] The elite man who chaired the constitutional convention, George Washington, was one of the very richest Americans substantially because of the hundreds of black Americans he enslaved and worked on his farms.

Slavery was more than an extensive and dominating economic system, for it was deeply imbedded in the political and other institutional structures of this country. Central to the legitimation and organization of the North American enslavement of human beings was also the colonial and U.S. legal system, a principal foundation of the latter being the U.S. Constitution. Yet, even today, most of the debates centering on this Constitution ignore some of its most fundamental and foundational flaws. For example, the new United States began its political operation with a significant and intentional deception built into its founding document. The ever-influential James Madison successfully pressed to keep the explicit language of "slavery" and "slaves" out of the Constitution, preferring euphemistic wording to sanitize the numerous sections that were actually related to buttressing that centrally important slavery system. This was intentional deception for, as the most outspoken delegate on the immorality of slavery, Gouverneur Morris, explained: "Domestic slavery is the most prominent feature in the aristo-cratic countenance of the proposed Constitution."[17] This statement was part of Morris's condemnation of slavery as immoral, yet it was not supported by other prominent delegates at the constitutional convention. Madison him-self later made it clear that the most important split among convention delegates was not the proverbial small-state/big-state split, but rather over slavery: "The States were divided into different interests not by their difference of size but principally from their having or not having slaves . . . between the Northern and the Southern."[18]

The elite framers protected the highly racialized slavery system in at least seven major provisions of this foundational Constitution:

1. Article 1, Section 2, counting an enslaved person as three-fifths of a white person;
2. Article 1, Sections 2 and 9, apportioning by this three-fifths formula;
3. Article 1, Section 8, providing Congress authority to suppress slave insurrections;
4. Article 1, Section 9, preventing abolition of the slave trade before 1808;
5. Article 1, Sections 9 and 10, exempting slave-made goods from export duties;

6. Article 4, Section 2, requiring return of fugitive slaves; and
7. Article 4, Section 4, providing that the federal government must help states with domestic violence, including slave uprisings.[19]

As one prominent historian has recently noted, "slavery was as important to the making of the Constitution as the Constitution was to the survival of slavery."[20]

Especially important in the making of this substantially undemocratic Constitution was this famous three-fifths clause (often called the "federal ratio"), which officially counted three-fifths of all enslaved African Americans for the purpose of expanding white representation in the U.S. Congress. At the convention, southern slaveholders had insisted on counting those enslaved and thereby secured many extra U.S. House members in the new Congress, as well as extra votes in the constitutionally required "electoral college" that actually selected the U.S. president. Consider too the U.S. Constitution's requirement of a federal population census, an apparently innocuous provision, yet one insisted upon by slaveholders wanting the South's expanding white *and* black populations to be carefully counted for the purpose of increased white representation for their slave states.[21]

The undemocratic institution of an electoral college is composed of electors from each of the U.S. states (and now Washington, D.C.). The number from each state is set as equal to the number of its representatives and senators, and these electors actually select the U.S. president. Ordinarily electors vote for the candidate who got the most votes in their state, but this is not always required. As noted above, the creation of this electoral college was racialized in its origins. Its creation was linked to U.S. slaveholders' political interests, and the three-fifths clause gave slaveholding states (especially the larger ones) a significant boost in political power in presidential elections. Indeed, the famous founder and major slaveholder, Thomas Jefferson, became the third U.S. president because of extra votes he got in the electoral college from the three-fifths clause. Moreover, without the extra white southern members of the Congress, numerous nation-changing actions of early congresses and presidents would have been quite different. For example, the infamous 1850 Fugitive Slave Law would not have been enacted.[22]

The three-fifths provision regularly facilitated the expansion of the U.S. slavery system and the power of slaveholders for decades, ensuring that the system of slavery would continue to be a major part of the economic foundation of the new nation. From 1790 to 1860 white slaveholders were in control of much of the federal government. From George Washington to Abraham Lincoln, most presidents were slaveholders or supportive of slavery, and southern slaveholders also had great power in the Congress and on the Supreme Court until the Civil War. Indeed, in 1843, no less a figure than former U.S. president John Quincy Adams asserted in a famous congressional speech that the United States had *never* been a democracy because it had long been substantially controlled by a few thousand slave-holders.[23]

Significantly, the numerous *Federalist Papers* written by Madison, Jay, and Hamilton are filled with references to the "principles of liberty" and the "security of liberty," with the word liberty appearing more than 100 times. Yet, in these constitutional framers' minds this liberty was often substantially linked to property-holding and the protection of societal stability. At no point in the *Federalist Papers* is the extreme oppressiveness of the slavery system significantly discussed. There are 20 references to slave, slaves, and slavery, which mostly appear in specific discussions of the future banning of the slave trade and of the operation of the three-fifths clause. In only one article (*Federalist Paper* No. 54) does the author, who was either Madison or Hamilton, consider the reality faced by enslaved African Americans, and it simply discusses how the new Constitution "decides with great propriety on the case of our slaves, when it views them in the mixed character of persons and property." [24] This discussion of the "true condition" of enslaved African Americans, who are said to be caught between being treated as property and being considered occasionally as persons (as in the three-fifths clause), is the most significant reference indicating how these white founders viewed the Constitution's perspective on enslaved Americans. Not surprisingly, thus, there is no discussion of black freedom and equality issues in the *Federalist Papers*.

The U.S. Constitution, often called the first "democratic" political constitution in world history, created a new nation state on the backs of enslaved African Americans. The white founders knew this was the case, and thus used some significant obscuring language to hide that brutally exploitative reality. In addition, numerous white political actions during the revolutionary era made the societal conditions of African Americans worse. Thus, the powerful Madison worked to suppress efforts by African Americans to petition legislatures for their freedom, and the famous New Englander, John Adams, resisted any efforts at abolishing slavery in Massachusetts during this era. Both feared that any significant liberating actions for or by black Americans would interfere with the whites' revolutionary cause against Great Britain.[25]

In effect, the U.S. Constitution and political actions taken soon after its ratification established a "white man's republic" built in many ways on an extensive slavery system. White men, first those with significant property but soon many others, controlled the significant decisions in the new political system, although even then elite white men had by far the most political power. Moreover, for many decades a substantial majority of the U.S. population remained under a type of socio-political "totalitarianism." By definition, totalitarianism involves a society with a government controlled by a small elite with virtually unlimited power, an elite that extensively controls most areas of everyday life, both public and private. From the 17th century onward the major slaveholding areas of the colonies, and early United States, operated under a type of racially totalitarian system in regard to African Americans. Moreover, in the South, much of this racial totalitarianism persisted after slavery during the era of legal Jim Crow segregation, indeed until the 1950s and 1960s. Note too that such comprehensive oppression was also operative in numerous "reservation" areas forced upon many surviving Native Americans during the late 19th century.[26]

Protests against the Undemocratic Constitution

Not surprisingly, at the time many ordinary Americans viewed the U.S. Constitution produced by the convention as greatly favoring the few over the many. Because of the striking omission of a Bill of Rights and other undemocratic features, many Americans were unhappy with the new constitutional document, and there was much debate about it between Federalist supporters and anti-Federalist opponents in various states. The new Constitution came close to *not* being ratified, as the populations in a majority of the states at the time are estimated to have been at least half anti-Federalist in orientation. The political struggles around ratification of the U.S. Constitution were often between the well-off Federalist elite—which included "most of the public and private creditors, great landowners, lawyers and judges, manufacturers and shipowners, higher ranking civil and military officials, and college graduates"—and the anti-Federalists, who were mostly "men of moderate means, with little social prestige, farmers often in debt, obscure men for the most part."[27] Although both the Federalists and the anti-Federalists included elite men and men of modest means, the anti-Federalists were more diverse and representative of the white male population and usually took the more democratic position accenting local political and economic control and emphasizing rights for ordinary white Americans. The promise to add certain democratic rights amendments to the Constitution (the "Bill of Rights") helped to counter much opposition to the new Constitution, and it was finally ratified by state conventions. Still, the new U.S. Constitution was *never* ratified by the mass of the country's adult citizens voting in a free election. Numerous researchers' data have also indicated that, had there been such a general election, the U.S. Constitution would likely *not* have been ratified even by white men at the time.[28]

Moreover, as we have seen, the views and interests of Americans who were not white were not seriously considered by those in these major constitutional factions. By the time of the constitutional era about 40 percent of the population in numerous southern areas was black, and there were rising numbers of enslaved and free black Americans in northern states. Soon after the Constitution was ratified, in July 1788, an event took place in Providence, Rhode Island, that signaled the reaction of some free black Americans to it.

These black patriots met to assess the Constitution whose provisions they *hoped* would eventually put an end to "the trade to Africa in our Fellow-Creatures," and they called for a number of additional and very important societal changes, as reported in a local paper: "May the Natives of Africa enjoy their natural Privileges unmolested" and "May the Freedom of our unfortunate Countrymen (who are wearing the Chains of Bondage in different Parts of the World) be restored to them."[29] At the time, and later on, free and enslaved African Americans were among the most assertive advocates of greatly expanded liberty, freedom, and justice for the United States.

Our Undemocratic Political System: Limiting the Franchise

The U.S. Constitution did not create a democracy where most people had the right to vote and participate substantially and freely in major political institutions. We should perhaps not be surprised that the United States was not founded as a democratic nation, for at the time of its official creation a large percentage of the population was enslaved and had no say in the operation of any political institution. Nor did the majority of the population that was female (free and enslaved) have any significant say.

We can now examine briefly some major undemocratic and anti-democratic features of the U.S. Constitution and political system with an eye toward their racial, class, and gender biases and barriers. For example, during and after the 1780s constitutional era there were recurring debates about who should have the right to vote, and to what extent property qualifications should play a significant role in deciding who could vote. In the first decades of the new nation's history mostly only white men could vote. Yet, for a time, even these white men tended to be disproportionately from the substantial property-holding minority among all white men.[30]

The expansion of who can vote in the United States has been a slow, erratic, and often painful process. Most voting restrictions and requirements have been controlled by state and local laws. This voting group expanded from mostly white male property-holders to many white men without property in the 1830s, then (briefly) to southern black men in the 1870s, and then to white women in the 1920s. Two amendments to the U.S. Constitution broadly expanded the franchise and the right to other political participation —first, for black men in the 15th amendment to the U.S. Constitution right after the Civil War (1870); and then for all women in the 19th amendment right after World War I (1920). However, not long after southern black men got the official right to vote, during the long legal segregation era, whites barred most black men from voting with violent threats and legal mechanisms such as poll taxes. In addition, most Native Americans, Mexican Americans, and Asian Americans were kept from voting by various white-imposed legal or informal racial barriers. Indeed, not until the 1950s and 1960s was voting made possible for most Americans of color. Women, and only white women in much of the South, were finally allowed to vote in the 1920s, and in a few western areas a little earlier. The lateness of this expansion of the vote helps to explain why women have played a modest role in the long-term construction of most major political institutions, including major parties. These political institutions were well established and generally in full operation long before women became voters. For many decades, thus, systemic racism was coupled well with systemic sexism in order to ensure that the United States had elections and parties that were overwhelmingly dominated by white men. Once again, we see the harsh political realitics that the rhetoric of "majority rule" could not really conceal.[31]

In addition, not until the civil rights movement and racial desegregation of the 1960s did most black men and women, and some other Americans of color, actually get a federally protected right to exercise the franchise in much of the South. In 1964, very belatedly, a 24th amendment was finally added to the U.S. Constitution that prohibited the use of tax barriers to limit the right to vote for the president or congressional representatives, such as the poll taxes long used in southern states to block black voters. In 1965, an effective Voting Rights Act was also passed, which with other federal actions finally protected and accelerated the black vote and political participation in southern states. As a result of these electoral changes in the 1960s, and then only slowly over the next decades, the typically white political party leaders have had to pay much more attention to voters of color.

Undemocratic Political Institutions: The U.S. Congress

The elite white male founders intentionally established the U.S. Senate as an antidemocratic political institution, one designed to protect their class, racial, and gender interests. Again, the very influential founder James Madison noted that this body was designed to protect the people "against the transient impressions into which they themselves might be led."[32] Indeed, the Senate is explicitly referred to more than 100 times by Madison and his colleagues in the *Federalist Papers*' discussions and defenses of its role in the new political system. In contrast, the House of Representatives gets significantly less attention in these Federalist commentaries.

For more than a century, U.S. senators were elected, as originally specified by the U.S. Constitution, by state legislators and not ordinary voters. A major purpose was to give powerful white men at the state level more influence in the political process than ordinary white male voters—and thereby to provide additional protection for the interests of the elite. Moreover, the Constitution also specified that two senators were to be elected from each U.S. state, another antidemocratic provision that created an upper house in which people in a sparsely populated state got the *same* representation as people in a much more populated state. The Constitution also provided the senators with six-year terms, thereby allowing them to serve much longer than representatives in the more democratic U.S. House. Not surprisingly, the founders also gave this elitist Senate decisive decision-making power on certain important government matters, most especially the sole power to ratify treaties and to approve important presidential appointments such as Supreme Court justices. Such powers are firmly in the hands of the less democratic congressional branch. As a very elitist and in some ways anti-democratic institution, the U.S. Senate has protected well the interests of powerful white men over the centuries, to the present day.

In his analysis of the U.S. Constitution, the leading political scientist Robert Dahl agrees that the U.S. Senate was intentionally set up as a barrier to majority rule and that this action has been very successful over the centuries in allowing an unrepresentative Senate to ignore or trample upon the civil rights of many Americans.[33] During the slavery and legal segregation eras, southern senators frequently used antidemocratic Senate rules to block almost all important antislavery legislation before the Civil War, and almost all significant civil rights legislation between the late 1870s and the mid-1960s. In his analysis of this constitutional history, Dahl underscores how a statistical minority of southern senators in effect could veto civil rights legislation and thus be a buttress of extreme legal segregation: the "Southern veto not only helped to bring about the end of Reconstruction; for another century it prevented the country from enacting federal laws to protect the most basic human rights of African Americans."[34]

Note, too, the major racial, gender, and class bias in the demographic character of both houses of Congress for much of our political history. In the beginning, Native Americans and African Americans, as well as white women, were *completely* excluded from the U.S. Congress, and this exclusion continued until after the Civil War. Until 1868, members of Congress were only white men, and until 1916 these representatives did not include a woman of any background. The majority of adults therefore had no direct representation in Congress for a long period of U.S. history. Even after those dates of change, few men of color or women of any background served in Congress until the 1960s–1970s era. Beyond racial and gender barriers, there have also been major class barriers. Over our political history the average incomes for members of Congress have regularly been *far* above the corresponding averages for all U.S. families. Members of Congress, past and present, have mostly represented the upper 5 percent or so of families in terms of economic status. In the past and the present, the U.S. congressional structure has not been anywhere close to the truly representative democracy it is frequently claimed to be.

An Undemocratic Supreme Court

Yet another undemocratic political institution created by the white founders is the U.S. Supreme Court. Intentionally created as an unelected body with little democratic overview, over time the Court has gained even greater unsupervised political power, much of it in effect legislative. In an early and unanimous Court decision (*Marbury* v. *Madison*), the Supreme Court justices, led by Chief Justice John Marshall, decided the Court had the power of final *judicial review*, a legal theory that allows the Court to decide whether congressional legislation is constitutional, thereby allowing a few unelected justices to invalidate legislation by the more representative U.S. House.[35] The Supreme Court has the power to regularly interpret, and in effect periodically amend, the Constitution by a majority vote. In this way, the Supreme Court (and often other high federal courts) can legislate without needing the consent of the legislative branch, while the latter's legislation is subject to a judicial veto. Indeed, the Supreme Court has vetoed congressional legislation some two dozen times as unconstitutional and, even more often, interpreted congressional legislation so as to weaken or destroy the congressional intent behind that legislation. Almost all such eviscerating decisions have been made by the Court in the interests of some segment of the ruling elite. As analyst Richard Kluger has noted, across the world "no other government reserves the last word for the judiciary to pronounce."[36]

Unmistakably, the elite founders intended for most important changes in the U.S. Constitution to be in the hands of elite white men, and not even in the hands of a majority of white male voters. For much of U.S. history a majority of the Supreme Court justices were southern slaveholders, segregationists, or judges sympathetic to the latter's views. From the 1790s to the 1950s, the all-white, all-male Supreme Court was very important in protecting the extensive system of racial oppression dominating the lives of Americans of color, most especially slavery and Jim Crow segregation. We have yet to outlive the impact of centuries of foundational racial oppression on Supreme Court decisions. Even today, we can see how unrepresentative and elitist this branch of government actually is. As of mid-2011, just 112 Americans, 108 men and 4 women, have ever served as Supreme Court justices. Strikingly, more than *97 percent* have been white, and some *95 percent* have been white men, and most from some segment of the ruling white elite.

The extremely negative reality and importance of an undemocratic U.S. Supreme Court can be seen in a series of decisions on court cases involving racial issues over the last two centuries. For example, in a brutally racist *Dred Scott* v. *John F. A. Sandford* (1857) decision, seven of these elite white male Supreme Court justices, all unelected and led by slaveholding Chief Justice Roger B. Taney, declared that African Americans were inferior racial beings. In Taney's racially framed view they

> had for more than a century before [the U.S. Constitution] been regarded as beings of an inferior order, and altogether unfit to associate with the white race, either in social or political relations; and so far

inferior, that they had no rights which the white man was bound to respect; and that the negro [sic] might justly and lawfully be reduced to slavery for his benefit. He was bought and sold, and treated as an ordinary article of merchandise and traffic, whenever a profit could be made by it. This opinion was at that time fixed and universal in the civilized portion of the white race.[37]

Taney insisted that this view was shared by most in the white elite of his day. Long after the U.S. Constitution was created, well-entrenched slaveholders like Taney continued to shape U.S. legal decision making in fundamental ways, including the construction of constitutional law in federal court decisions like *Dred Scott*. Indeed, from 1788 to 1860, major decisions made by the top court almost never went against the interests of a majority of the country's slaveholding oligarchy, and even President James Buchanan (1857–1861), a northerner who preceded Abraham Lincoln, urged the country to support the extreme racist thinking of the *Dred Scott* decision.

Significantly, the continuing impact of the racialized law made before and after the mid-19th century Civil War can still be seen in numerous Supreme Court decisions handed down since that time. For example, some recent Supreme Court interpretations of the 14th amendment by the very conservative "originalist" ("strict constructionist") majority on the contemporary Court have actually ignored the *expressed intent* of the 19th-century framers of this important 14th amendment. Significantly, Civil-War-era liberal Republicans enacted the 13th, 14th, and 15th antislavery amendments to the U.S. Constitution by more than the two-thirds majority required by the Constitution, and they had also passed civil rights laws protecting the rights of freed blacks to vote and banning antiblack discrimination. Using the required constitutional mechanism, these 19th-century liberal Republicans acted to extend the U.S. Constitution's Bill of Rights actively and directly to black Americans.[38]

Yet, soon thereafter, a small group of Supreme Court justices in effect vetoed the congressional intent. Consider an 1875 *United States* v. *Cruikshank* decision by the conservative 19th-century Supreme Court judges. They ruled that the white murderers of more than 100 black southerners trying to protect their political rights in Louisiana in 1873 could not be prosecuted under a federal enforcement law. These conservative judges reasoned that Congress did *not* have the power to criminalize private Ku-Klux-Klan-type violence aimed at depriving free blacks of their rights, although criminalizing such group violence was the *expressed intent* of the Republican framers of the 14th amendment. This 1875 Supreme Court decision ignored the actual facts and thus erroneously ruled that the 14th amendment was *not* expressly intended by its framers to protect black individuals against discriminatory whites (in this case, a violent white mob) and supposedly "adds nothing to the rights of one citizen as against another."[39] Strikingly, the erroneous 1875

Cruikshank decision's reactionary white-framed phrase that the 14th amendment "adds nothing to the rights of one citizen as against another" was cited *favorably* by a conservative majority of justices on a more contemporary Supreme Court in a decision called *United States* v. *Morrison* rejecting a civil remedy provision of the federal Violence against Women Act.[40]

More recently, thus, the bloc of very conservative justices on the contemporary Supreme Court has periodically ignored the strong civil rights tradition intentionally set in place by the liberal Republican framers of the 14th amendment, and related 1866–1875 civil rights laws, in making recent decisions knocking down important affirmative action efforts and other antidiscrimination remedies. On civil rights issues, the Court's recent conservative majority has moved back to the discredited views of the post-Civil-War white justices, apparently accepting the idea that the United States is now a "post-racial society." Since the 1970s Richard Nixon era, thus, an increasingly conservative Supreme Court majority has periodically *reduced* federally protected individual rights and knocked down programs aimed at ending the reality and effects of persisting racism in the name of asserting what conservative justices view as "states' rights."[41]

As we will see in the next chapters, an aggressive emphasis on states' rights has long pervaded certain segments of the country's political elites and parties, to the present day. A common type of state-centered perspective is substantially rooted in the slavery and legal segregation eras, and not primarily in conceptions of liberty and justice for all Americans. A major early source was the slaveholders' fear, and later the segregationists' fear, that federal government agencies would interfere with their state-enforced oppression of black Americans. For centuries, whites in many areas insisted on strong white-controlled local and state governments, and a relatively weak federal ability to intervene in local decisions on issues like racial segregation and other racial discrimination. Indeed, even as the colonies came together in a new United States, slaveholders worried that local non-slaveholding officials could be a threat to their profitable slave enterprises. As a result, the slaveholding elites typically gained substantial control of their local governments.[42] Not surprisingly, thus, over time "states' rights" and other anti-federal-government views have been significant in the racially oriented political framing of many white Americans.

A Too Powerful Chief Executive?

Founders such as James Madison, George Washington, and Alexander Hamilton intended for there to be a strong central government substantially distant from, and not significantly influenced in major decision making by, most of the general public. A substantial and bureaucratic federal government with top officials typically drawn from the upper class or upper middle class, and for many decades comprising only white men, has long fit their plan. Over the centuries the operation of the U.S. government as elitist in most of its top positions and in regard to the most significant foreign and domestic policy making is in line with what most founders sought to create. A small elite of mostly well-off white men has generally governed the nation at the top from its beginning, as we can see in the occupants of our very powerful government position of president. All U.S. presidents but one (Barack Obama) have been elite white men, and not one yet has been female. All but one (John Kennedy) have been Protestants in terms of religion. Not one has been elected directly by the people, as the founders put a cumbersome organization, the electoral college, in the position of actually selecting the president. This group was put in place by the white male founders, at least in part, to further protect the federal government from more direct democratic input from the feared "masses." Indeed, in a few U.S. presidential elections, such as in the recent 2000 election, the candidate receiving a majority of the votes cast nationwide did not get a majority of the electors in the electoral college, and thus did *not* become president.

In most countries the president has modest official power; but in the United States, the president has come to be what some call "the most powerful elected official in the world."[43] Initially, the framers of the U.S. Constitution conferred on the president certain specific powers, including a powerful presidential veto. A presidential veto of congressional legislation can only be overridden by a usually difficult-to-secure two-thirds vote of both houses of Congress, yet another feature of the U.S. Constitution designed by the framers to give more control to the ruling elite. Thus, under certain circumstances, senators representing a modest percentage (as little as 20 percent, from a coalition including numerous small states) of the U.S. population can and have used their constitutional power to uphold a presidential veto that is unpopular with the general population. Significantly, over time the presidential powers have greatly expanded, with this expansion being given legal protection by vague language in the Constitution's Article II, which says "the executive Power shall be vested in a President of the United States of America." A strong presidential executive and an oligarchical Senate have frequently provided great opportunities for the U.S. elite to take aggressive action in its interests, and frequently against the wishes of the general population. From the early decades, as the scholar Aziz Rana has underscored, the oligarchical structure of a powerful president and elitist Senate has long been closely linked to American exceptionalism and the expansion of the United States across the continent and overseas. This has brought U.S. interference in the political or economic affairs of many countries across the globe, countries that often have populations that are mostly not white.[44]

We should note, too, that, over the last two centuries, U.S. presidents, other top federal executive officials, and the Congress have also had to get involved with the problems and crises of major U.S. businesses operating in a national and an international capitalistic environment. Kevin Phillips shows that, from the earliest years of the new United States, the key economic decisions made by top government officials in regard to "taxation, central bank operations, debt management, banking, trade and tariffs, and financial rescues or bailouts" have played a very important role in increasing or decreasing the extent of U.S. economic wealth, especially that held in corporate and wealthy white individuals' hands.[45] The U.S. government has long had a strong and enduring partnership with major corporations to help them prosper and expand, first nationally and then globally. Periodically, the federal executive and congressional branches have had to bail out the corporate economy from recurring economic crises. However, this bailing out periodically results in significant political and/or economic crises for the U.S. government itself, because usually it must borrow money or raise taxes as it bails out failed capitalistic firms, including financial institutions in the distant past and on the contemporary scene. This action can also severely shape and limit other actions that the federal government might consider taking in dealing with national social welfare and civil rights problems affecting large sectors of the general population.[46]

Conclusion

Initially, the dramatic imagery of America as an exceptional model and "city upon a hill" for other peoples to admire or imitate was highly religious and Eurocentric, as we saw in John Winthrop's famous sermon in Chapter 1. From the beginning, this American exceptionalism has been centered on European American culture, religion, and society, but by the late 18th century it was shifting in a more secular direction. Examining the views of our political founders and their descendants, Deborah Madsen has noted key elements of their exceptionalist views: the new United States is a model democratic nation for the world; the United States is a world guardian justifiably overseeing the conduct of other nations; and the United States is the "world's last and best chance" at salvation. In this founding era, and succeeding centuries, the religious grounding of American exceptionalism was often matched by a secular grounding, such as in a U.S. Constitution that, contrary to much contemporary sentiment, actually has no explicit references to God. Many early political leaders, as well as many rank-and-file citizens, emphasized the importance of the United States as a model of political virtuousness and a "guardian of democracy" for other countries, a view persisting to the present.[47]

Today, as noted previously, much in the standard public view of the U.S. Constitution and past and present political system is a matter of illusory belief and mythologizing about this political virtuousness of freedom and democracy, rather than a real understanding of how the U.S. Constitution and political system have actually developed over time and still operate in a frequently undemocratic fashion. As in the past, the mostly white top political leaders today play a major role in constantly circulating this illusion and mythology, as they and their predecessors have done in numerous Democratic and Republican Party platforms since the 19th century. For many decades, the party platforms and conventions have regularly proclaimed the language of freedom, justice, and democracy. Yet, the political reality over the numerous generations since 1787 has not been one of a full-fledged democracy with foundational social justice, but actually one of generating and maintaining socio-political control by the mostly white elite and the centrality of their political-economic interests and desires for present and future United States.

Interestingly, much contemporary research indicates that the 18th-century founders' plan for the class and racial elite to be dominant in a U.S. political system often claimed to be truly democratic has been very successful over these generations. Recall the findings of Winters and Page in regard to whether the contemporary political system is oligarchical. Examining contemporary data, they show well that the political-economic system is still quite oligarchical and that the wealthy few still "exert vastly greater political influence than average citizens."[48]

3
Race, Class, and Early U.S. Politics—to the 1930s

Most mainstream social scientists and political analysts accept the surrounding U.S. political system and its parties more or less as a given and view those arrangements as normal and very substantially, if not basically, "democratic." Oddly enough, however, the U.S. Constitution says nothing about political parties, and our first president, George Washington, and other prominent founders like James Madison, clearly feared the development of political "factions" as being disruptive for the new nation. Nonetheless, strong factions were already developing at that time as political groups considered more or less necessary to implement the national political mechanisms and institutions created for the new United States.[1] Indeed, the United States soon became a nation with major political parties at the national and other levels of government. Numerous political scientists and other analysts have praised political parties and argued that they are essential to our political system. Writing in the 1940s, prominent analyst E. E. Schattschneider argued that the assumed U.S. democracy would be "unthinkable save in terms of parties."[2] Today, the standard view of political parties is that they are central to the operation of what is widely said to be a strong U.S. democracy.

In conventional political analysis U.S. parties are seen as democratic intermediaries between the people and their government, like many other voluntary associations. Parties are typically viewed as groups of Americans who loosely share a set of political positions and orientations. They include elected and unelected officials, party activists and leaders, individuals and groups working on funding, and ordinary voters. Parties nominate candidates and seek to win elections, so as to implement their policy goals through governmental action and agencies. In their everyday operations U.S. political parties are seen as helping to link separate branches of government, especially the executive and legislative branches. They also assist in linking local, state, and federal political levels and bureaucracies.[3]

Yet, outspoken critics of the U.S. political system have been much less positive and sanguine about existing political parties. For example, prominent novelist and political essayist Gore Vidal has recently put it this way: parties are elite "conspiracies to gain power over the great offices of state."[4]

35

Critical political analysts like Vidal are emphasizing deeper features of U.S. society that we have unearthed in the last two chapters—the realities of a steep class and racial hierarchy and of elite white dominance in the shaping of the political system. I have previously noted the central importance of this dominant U.S. elite and its important divisions—its conservative, centrist, and liberal divisions. As we will see in this and later chapters, in various historical eras one segment (or two) of this elite has successfully vied with other segments to gain substantial power over political parties and thus the federal government and other government levels, so much so that ordinary Americans oftentimes get marginalized in this important political process.

Major Political Party Eras

Scholars have long divided U.S. political history into a series of party eras and political regimes, the earliest being called the "First" through the "Third" party systems. In fact, these historical party eras have involved more than parties, for they have also centrally involved broad politicized regimes of parties, elite ruling, and government policies and actions. The First party system, in the early U.S. era, involved two contending parties, the Federalist Party and the Democratic-Republican Party. The loosely organized Federalist Party was led by well-off founders like New Yorker Alexander Hamilton and numerous important merchants, bankers, and landowners. As we have already seen, they sought at the constitutional convention and afterwards a strong central government that would foster a property-holding, banking, taxing, and tariff system protecting the new country's capitalistic economic system. Many Federalist Party leaders and members also expressed substantial anti-immigrant sentiment with a nativistic tinge. They were concerned about supposed political radicalism among certain new European immigrants. Passed under the Federalist president John Adams, the 1798 Alien Act empowered Adams to deport immigrants considered a political and social threat to the new country. This anti-immigrant sentiment led to a significant increase in the period of residence required for U.S. citizenship. Such ethnocentric and nativistic actions were designed to limit the political power of the new European immigrants, and similarly negative actions would be seen again for yet other immigrants in subsequent party system eras.[5]

Other U.S. founders with different political-economic concerns, such as major southern slaveholders like Thomas Jefferson and James Madison, and some financiers and landowners opposed to the Federalists' policies favoring ties to Great Britain, preferred a U.S. government without certain Federalist policies and emphasized such ideas as expanding states' rights and the right to vote beyond propertied white men. They were also more supportive of the new non-English immigrants. Soon the Jefferson-Madison political faction evolved into a substantially agrarian Democratic-Republican party with activists organizing for the 1800 election, which resulted in the election of

Jefferson.[6] Significantly, this early party competition legitimated intense personal attacks and other negative tactics in party campaigns. In this era even Jefferson was accused openly of "treason" and with working secretly as a French agent. Nonetheless, in the 1800 election the Federalist candidate, John Adams, lost and the Federalist Party soon declined in influence.[7]

In addition to anti-immigrant attacks, antiblack framing and action were common in some early political party campaigns. One of the first racist campaigns by early U.S. parties took place in New York. In 1800, the Federalist Party there won an election with the help of a few free black voters. The opposition Jeffersonian Democratic-Republican party counter-attacked with the political slogan of "Federalists with Blacks Unite" and worked to end even these modest black voting rights—including using appeals to white male voters that accented the old racist stereotype of extensive black criminality.[8] Over much of the 19th century, political party appeals using such antiblack imagery and other racist framing became commonplace in various political campaigns.

The Second Party System

In the first two decades of the 19th century, with the decline of the Federalist Party, there was effectively just one major political party, the Democratic-Republicans. By the 1820s most states, under pressure from Democratic-Republicans, had opened up their voting qualifications to include white men without much property, thus greatly expanding white male suffrage and strengthening the Democratic-Republican party. Early on, U.S. elections involved party organizations mostly led by elite and middle-class party leaders, who were leading a larger group of mostly uneducated white male voters. Moreover, as we saw in the discussion in Chapter 2 of constitutional barriers such as the electoral college, the makers of the U.S. Constitution saw to it that even these latter white male voters often had only some indirect political influence over major political decision making. They did not vote directly for president, U.S. senators, or the Supreme Court. Thus, in all political party eras until the late 20th century, the major political parties—Federalists, Democratic-Republicans, Whigs, Democrats, Republicans—were normally run at the top by elite or better-off white men.

By the late 1820s, a Second party system had arisen. With the election of Andrew Jackson (1829–1837), the Democratic-Republican Party split in two. One faction representing certain major economic interests, particularly southern planters, and also many less well-off white men became the modern Democratic Party. Another faction, an overall better-off group of white men linked to other business interests, joined with others to form the short-lived Whig Party. The Democratic Party was substantially shaped by the interests of southern farmers and slaveholders, as well as by northern commercial interests opposed to the national (Federalist) Bank of the United

States. These economic interests supported state banks not connected to the national bank and were mostly opposed to substantial federal funding for public infrastructure. Nonetheless, they were committed to expanding the territory ("inland empire") of the United States. The Democratic Party was greatly influenced by the somewhat populist policies of its slaveholding President Jackson, and not surprisingly emphasized the concept of a strong presidency. In contrast, the Whig Party represented commercial capitalists interested in aggressive federal funding for public infrastructure and protectionism for manufacturing, such as U.S. textile manufacturers, as well as in supporting the national bank. They often emphasized the power of the legislative over the executive branch as well as a more cautious approach to national territorial expansion. Both political parties were thus strongly linked to wealthy economic interests. Democratic and Whig party organizations soon operated in all states, thereby creating an active two-party system, and both tried to appeal to newly enfranchised white male voters.[9]

Even considering the significant expansion of white male voters in this era, one should note that remarkably few adult Americans actually participated in most elections in the mid-19th century. Systemic racism, sexism, and classism were obvious in this political era. Given the exclusion from voting of (most) black men, black women, white women, and in some areas poorer white men—by informal means or by laws—a rather small percentage of the adult population was eligible to vote. The emergence of local party organizations that aggressively involved, or sought funding from, wealthy white men further weakened the possibility of ordinary white men having much political influence at the national, state, or local government level.[10] Still, even in the face of these undemocratic realities, political leaders loudly emphasized that the U.S. was a real democracy. In one important 1837 speech, President Jackson portrayed the country as exceptional, uniquely democratic, and free: "Never have been thirteen millions of people associated in one political body who enjoyed so much freedom and happiness as the people of these United States."[11] His phrasing echoed the American-exceptionalist and democratic imagery we observed in the sermons and speeches of the early Protestant leaders and the 1780s constitutional framers.

Over much of the 19th century, southern members of the country's elite like Andrew Jackson played an influential and dominant role in the Democratic Party. One reason for this was that the South was the most economically prosperous and politically powerful region from the mid-1700s to the 1850s.[12] Long before the Civil War, powerful white southerners, usually slaveholders with wealth made off of enslaved workers, secured disproportionate power in the Democratic Party, and these southerners had much control over the operation of the U.S. Congress and other branches of the federal government before the Civil War, and again after the brief Reconstruction era after that war. In addition, the major political parties' leaders in the 1820s–1850s era often sought to downplay in public the white disputes over black slavery in order to win a broader coalition of voters in various U.S. regions. Up to the climactic election of Abraham Lincoln, most national party leaders tried to keep significant slavery issues out of their party platforms. Various party deals and congressional compromises over slavery were also tried in order to avoid what was then termed the "racial division." Conspicuously, very few of the white creators and maintainers of the major parties cared about the voting or other civil rights of African Americans, enslaved or free, or those of Native Americans.[13]

Expansionist Actions: The Myth of Manifest Destiny

From the early 19th century to the turn of the 20th century, moreover, the heroic U.S. "freedom and liberty" narrative was greatly extended as many European Americans, including increasing numbers of new European immigrants, pressed westward across North America. A journalist, John O'Sullivan, had these immigrants in mind when in the 1840s he coined the phrase "manifest destiny" in an influential magazine article: "Our manifest destiny is to overspread the continent allotted by Providence for the free development of our yearly multiplying millions."[14] In the mid-19th century the old predatory ethic of European Americans was given this explicit "manifest destiny" name, one asserting the right of whites to expand and take lands as needed, no matter the cost to those already there. Manifest destiny mythologizers accented the need for every white man "to have his own land," an old view that entailed the idea that the way for a man to become a real American citizen was to gain some land. Becoming particularly important in the decades from the 1830s onward, this expansionist narrative yet again envisioned courageous white "settlers" fighting against the "savage" Indians to secure new and supposedly unused lands.

One central goal of elite southern advocates of U.S. expansion was to make much new land available for the growth of the existing slavery system. Indeed, a leading advocate of manifest destiny long before O'Sullivan coined the phrase was the slaveholding Andrew Jackson, who with many of his elite associates was a strong supporter of adding new territory to the south and west of what was then the United States. A top military officer, General Jackson had played an important role in U.S. expansion into Spanish and Indian lands before he became president. The land visions of many whites accelerated demands for more land for farms and plantations, and for the killing off of or displacement of Native American societies, including some in what are now the states of Florida, Georgia, Alabama, and Mississippi. As president, Jackson signed an 1830 Indian Removal Act and supported the removal of many Native Americans from their eastern lands to western territories, including armed removal of thousands along the infamous and deadly "Trail of Tears."[15]

This 19th-century drive for land had important religious rationalizations, as we see in O'Sullivan's and many others' reference to "Providence" legitimating whites' expansion. Recall that a central feature of early European colonists' view of the world was a missionary commitment to spreading a certain Protestant religion and European civilization. Certain religious aspects of manifest destiny perspectives seem to have been enhanced by the "Great Awakenings," a term for dramatic Protestant religious revivals in the 18th and 19th centuries. By the time of the American Revolution, a substantial majority of whites were connected to Calvinistic groups, and some have described Calvinism as the common faith of the revolutionary era. These rather authoritarian religious groups shared an accent on social conservatism and a strict-morality ethic, but over time there was much backsliding. By the mid-1700s, Calvinistic ministers and evangelists were holding revivals to counter backsliding and enhance piety. The first Great Awakening was a major conversion-oriented revival movement lasting through the mid-18th century, and a second Great Awakening took place in the late 18th and early 19th centuries. Both revivalist movements spread pietism and much missionary thinking and action.[16] Researchers have shown that these religious awakenings also moved several major Protestant denominations toward greater religious pluralism and certain social reforms. This could be seen, for example, in revivalists spreading support for the abolition of slavery, especially in newer denominations such as the Methodists. Still, among many Protestant groups much authoritarian religious practice continued, and the majorities in most white Protestant groups supported the great westward expansion. The Great Awakening periods especially accelerated missionary work, including much proselytizing among Indian nations, the latter often considered by whites to be godless and, thus, a "blight" on an ever-expanding Eurocentric nation.[17]

The overtly racist framing of U.S. expansion to the west and south was clear in much political commentary in this era. For example, in 1836 a Whig Party senator from Virginia, Benjamin Leigh, loudly proclaimed a racist framing of expansionism in comments in Congress: "It is peculiar to the character of this Anglo-Saxon race of men to which we belong, that it has never been contented to live in the same country with any other distinct race, upon terms of equality; it has, invariably . . . proceeded to exterminate or enslave the other race in some form or other, or, failing that, to abandon the country."[18] In his view this was a very positive feature of the white "race." Like most of his white contemporaries, Leigh was not really interested in spreading the ideals of freedom often accented in American exceptionalism to other peoples, but rather with subordinating the latter and greatly expanding the territory occupied by a great "Anglo-Saxon race of men." Note, too, that at this time such phrasing accented not just the superiority of European Americans, but especially the superiority of those white men whose ancestors had come from Northern European ("Anglo-Saxon") Protestant countries.

Not surprisingly, increasing encounters with Mexicans in southwestern areas of North America triggered a renewed accent, especially among elite whites, on the manifest destiny of the white Anglo-Saxon race to expand into these territories. United States political party leaders and government officials drew on this perspective, and in the spring of 1846 the Democratic president James K. Polk, a major southern slaveholder, adhered to his campaign promise to annex Texas and sent U.S. troops into U.S.–Mexico borderlands he knew Mexicans had long treated as their territory. White political leaders' rationalization for the resulting war was that it was indeed the manifest destiny of the Anglo-Saxon race to expand and rule over the "lesser" peoples.[19] Numerous expansionist whites interpreted the war with Mexico in this fashion. The famous Missouri senator, Democrat Thomas Hart Benton, also a slaveholder, accented the "liberty, justice, valor" that supposedly distinguished the superior "Anglo-Saxon race" wherever it went. In addition, prominent Texas leaders like the slaveholding Democrat Sam Houston described an inferior Mexican "rabble" as necessarily losing to the great "Anglo-Saxon race," given the latter's love of dominion and expansion.[20] These white-led military adventures secured huge amounts of new land for the ever-expanding nation, including for the important expansion of the slave plantation economy.

The Third Party System: New Republicans and Old Democrats

In the 1850s a Third party system arose with the decline of the Whig Party and the growth of a new national party, the Republican Party. This political division between just two major parties, a Democratic Party and a Republican Party, has persisted to the present. Republican Party officials and activists often opposed the expansion of the then dominant slavery system and emphasized the needs of northern corporate interests, such as those of the growing national railroads, and the imperative of new industrial expansion for the United States.

African American enslavement in itself was not the main cause of the Civil War, but the extensive southern economic system grounded in that enslavement was indeed a main cause. In southern and border states, slaveholders were aggressively pressing for the protection and expansion of their slavery-grounded wealth and property, including a significant westward expansion. The powerful slaveholding elite sought an agreement among the country's southern and northern elites on property rights, especially in the form of allowing enslavement of African Americans in yet more new states. One influential Kentucky slaveholder, Senator Henry Clay, accented just how central this enslaved property was to the U.S. economy in an important 1839 speech against the goals of a growing number of abolitionists. Estimating slave property then to be worth some $1.2 billion, a huge amount if translated into today's dollars, he argued that:

> This property is diffused throughout all classes and conditions of society . . . It is the subject of mortgages, deeds of trust, and family settlements. It has been made the basis of numerous debts contracted upon its faith, and is the sole reliance, in many instances, of creditors within and without the slave States, for the payment of debts due to them.[21]

Clay was a powerful border state politician, who Abraham Lincoln said had *taught* him much about slavery. Extensive investments in enslaved property explained why southern and border state slaveholders aggressively rationalized the slavery system, and important connections to the slavery economy explained why numerous elite white men across the country also supported slavery. Increasingly, however, many northern business leaders did not agree with a strong national recognition of enslaved property in all regions, nor did they want to see it expanding aggressively to western areas. The spread of slave farms and plantations was often viewed as endangering new business opportunities in the West, including the expansion of northern-run railroads serving new western farmers.[22]

The clash between two powerful economic elites and systems, one in the North and the other in the South, thus led to a major shift to a Third party system and the country's two major and lasting parties. Slavery debates destroyed the Whig Party, and in the 1850s the Republican Party emerged as an important political contender. Historian Robin Archer has shown that both the new Republican Party and the older Democratic Party involved coalitions of white ethnic and religious groups. The moral crusades of evangelical ministers and churches during the Second Great Awakening era had helped to create the Republican Party. Republicans often sought government intervention to deal with an array of societal "evils," including saloons and slavery. The new party, thus, included a heterogeneous coalition of white evangelicals influenced by the Great Awakening, some antislavery abolitionists, and numerous native-born "Anglo-Saxon" Protestants hostile to the Catholic and Jewish immigrants then coming into the United States in large numbers from Ireland and Germany.[23]

Historian Paul Johnson has shown how the Second Great Awakening had significant impacts on some white business elites and their political interests. For the key city of Rochester, New York, an inland boomtown, evangelical revivalism assisted economic expansion and worker control by the growing regional capitalist class. In Rochester and similar northern cities, revivalists and associated Protestant churches helped business executives to pressure the often immigrant working class toward hard work and temperance and away from unionization.[24] Once again, neo-Puritanism helped the expansion of capitalism and control of the working class. Clearly, the new Republican Party included northern business interests committed to much new industrial and transportation expansion, including large-scale expansion by some of the country's biggest corporations, the railroad companies. The negative view of slave labor in the thinking of many in the new Republican Party could also be observed in their slogan: "free soil, free labor, free men." Coined by Lincoln's Secretary of the Treasury, this theme signaled that Republicans did not want to see more slave-labor plantations on western or northern soil.[25]

In contrast, in the 19th century many white men opposed to certain government social "reforms" were committed to the Democratic Party, one that had northern and southern factions. As Archer notes, "To Catholics and non-pietistic Protestants in the north, the core Democratic message was that it is not for the government to decide whether drinking alcohol, and various other social and religious practices, are immoral."[26] She describes how in the industrializing North, members of liturgical churches like those of the Catholic Church typically rejected the resurgent evangelical revivalism, instead committing to traditional clergy and ritual, and they were more likely to be Democratic Party members. The view that the federal government should defer to states' rights and not intervene in debates over immorality issues, including slavery and alcohol use, was a position with which both southern slaveholders and many new European immigrants could agree.

The new Republican Party was strong in northern and western areas, and in 1860 nominated a savvy railroad lawyer with northern corporate connections, Abraham Lincoln, as its presidential candidate. The substantial growth of the Republican Party and the election of Lincoln as president soon led to southern secession from the union; this was engineered mostly by a southern slaveholding elite fearing federal intervention in the expansion of the slavery system and thus fearful for its economic and political future. As the vice president of the new Confederacy, Alexander Stephens, made clear, this Confederacy was especially "dedicated to the defense of African slavery as God's will."[27] Indeed, the new Confederate government modeled its new Constitution on the earlier U.S. Constitution, but with even more overt protection of the highly racialized slavery system.

At base, the Civil War was a clash of two economies and, more generally, two regional cultures, and the victory of the North in that war marked the arrival of northern industrialists and merchants as a dominant force in the U.S. economy and government. Not surprisingly, during and after the war, the Republicans increased protective tariffs for new manufacturers, chartered new banks, and passed a major Homestead Act opening up western lands to many Americans seeking to move west along the new railroad lines.[28]

We should also note well the impact on the Civil War of the protests and organization of antislavery African Americans and their white allies. In the early decades of the 19th century black and white abolitionists had engaged in many protest efforts against slavery and created militant antislavery organizations—thereby helping to bring about the abolition of slavery. This growth in white and black abolitionism was generated in part "by the slave unrest for which rebels and swelling numbers of runaways supplied tangible evidence."[29] Such growing slave rebellion, and the spread of abolitionist ideals in influential books like Harriet Beecher Stowe's *Uncle Tom's Cabin*, had a great impact not only in greatly increasing fears among southern slaveholders but also on the abolition efforts of a key sector of the new Republican Party. Without these important protest efforts of white and black abolitionists prior to the Civil War, efforts often funded by some northern merchants and industrialists, there might not have been the major racial and political changes seen both during and after the Civil War.

More Racialized Party Campaigns: 1860 and 1864

During the Civil War era the everyday operation of systemic racism was evident in most nooks and crannies of society, and not just in the extensive slavery system. Democratic Party leaders made clear that theirs was a strong *white man's party*, including throughout Lincoln's 1860s' presidential campaigns. During the 1860 national presidential campaign Democratic advocates aggressively attacked the Republican Party and candidate Lincoln as advocating racial equality and intermarriage. In the South and the North, newspapers supportive of the Democratic Party circulated old white racist views of enslaved or free black Americans as lazy, criminal, and violent, as well as racially stereotyped imagery of black men as a dangerous threat to white women. In response, Republican officials and Republican-oriented newspapers asserted vigorously that the Republican Party was also a white man's party, and they emphasized their own racist framing of black Americans, insisting that the latter were in no way equal to whites. Nonetheless, many individual white Republicans and Republican-oriented newspapers also expressed substantial opposition to expansion of the slavery system.[30]

Again, in the 1864 election, northern general George McClellan ran as the Democratic Party candidate against Lincoln. McClellan and numerous supporters made much use of antiblack imagery, and Democratic Party leaders and members accused Republicans of supporting "miscegenation," a new racist term coined by northern white journalists for sex and marriage involving consenting whites and blacks. Once again, many white Republicans denied allegations of being for racial integration, making it unmistakable that they too supported a white supremacist framing of society and racial inequality in society. Indeed, many white voters in the North were not sympathetic to expanding black civil rights much beyond slavery's abolition.[31]

Considered by many scholarly and popular analysts to be the greatest U.S. president, Abraham Lincoln himself held strongly racist views and took actions before and during his presidency that reflected the dominant white racist framing. While Lincoln opposed slavery and its spread, he routinely operated out of this framing. For example, in a famous 1858 senatorial campaign debate with Democratic senator Stephen A. Douglas, the Republican candidate Lincoln insisted on his white supremacist view:

> I am not nor ever have been in favor of the social and political equality of the white and black races: that I am not nor ever have been in favor of making voters of the free negroes, or jurors, or qualifying them to hold office or having them to marry with white people . . . I as much as any other man am in favor of the superior position being assigned to the white man.[32]

Ironically, Lincoln's white supremacist views would be used after his death, and throughout the later legal segregation era, by white southerners to defend the extensive legal segregation of black Americans. Note too that, before and during his presidential years, Lincoln enjoyed the public entertainment shows by white minstrels who engaged in racist "darky" and "nigger" performances. He himself used such derogatory words, viewed black Americans as racially inferior, supported racial segregation, and periodically expressed his view of the U.S. future as a white-dominant country. Indeed, Lincoln's views of African Americans were one reason he delayed their recruitment into the Union army. Pressures from black abolitionists like Frederick Douglass and some white abolitionists, and military necessity, finally got him to accept aggressive recruitment of black soldiers, who provided great military strength at a time when Lincoln badly needed it.[33]

Reconstruction in the 1860s–1870s: Radical Republicans

We can now turn to the important party developments that took place after Lincoln's death and after the Civil War ended. During the brief Reconstruction era of the 1860s and 1870s a temporarily influential group of liberal Republican members of Congress, often called "Radical Republicans," successfully sought to end black enslavement as well as some antiblack discrimination and other effects of enslavement. At an 1865 Republican convention, one courageous congressional leader, Thaddeus Stevens (R-Pa), called for taking 400 million acres from former slaveholders and providing that to freed African Americans. Another abolitionist, Senator Charles Sumner (R-Mass.), called for land grants for those recently enslaved. In the view of these liberal Republicans, legal freedom alone would not eradicate the "large disparities of wealth, status, and power."[34] Unfortunately, these courageous efforts at land redistribution were unsuccessful. However, as we saw in Chapter 2, these liberal Republicans did play the central role in putting major (13th, 14th, 15th) amendments into the U.S. Constitution, ending slavery and expanding certain civil rights for African Americans.

Significantly, after the Civil War state Republican parties became very influential in southern party politics because of the disenfranchisement of elite whites who led southern secession, because of newly enfranchised black voters, and because of non-slaveholding whites in numerous southern areas who had opposed the Confederate secession. In the South, some 17 African Americans were elected as Republicans to Congress (two to the Senate) and more than 2,000 African Americans were elected as Republicans to local and state political offices, as were the even more numerous non-slaveholding whites, with this latter group substantially controlling all state governments during Reconstruction. In the southern Reconstruction era, local and state Republican Party efforts brought significant reform to southern states, including modern state constitutions, prison reform, and public schools.

Meanwhile, the Democratic Party had been seriously weakened by the Civil War, most evidently in the (temporary) elimination of the old slave-holding oligarchy from the southern political scene, but also in the weakening of Democratic Party leaders in numerous northern areas. One reason for these party difficulties was that in many northern voters' minds the Democratic Party was strongly associated with treasonous southerners and the rise of the Confederacy. Nonetheless, in the first national election after the Civil War in 1868, northern Democratic Party officials persisted in antiblack rhetoric. Now, however, northern black voters had increased significantly in number, and some of the conventional antiblack rhetoric of Democratic officials was replaced by the language of "states' rights" and "laissez-faire" government, the often coded racial language that has persisted in U.S. politics for many decades now.[35] For a relatively brief period before and after the Civil War, antislavery efforts and some efforts at expanding black civil rights in the South had significant northern white support, but soon many whites there tired of Reconstruction difficulties, debates, and costs—not least because a great many northern whites were as racist in their negative framing of black Americans as white southerners. Moreover, as noted previously, the actual implementation of the extraordinarily important 14th and 15th constitutional amendments and related civil rights laws was soon substantially blocked or weakened by racially reactionary Supreme Court justices not long after they had been added to the constitution. As a result, the possible society-changing option of U.S. liberation from extreme racial oppression at this time was thereby destroyed and would not be renewed for yet another difficult century.

Resurgence of the Democratic Party and Jim Crow

After former general and Republican Ulysses Grant's two terms as president (1869–1877), the Democratic Party was gradually restored to significant political power nationally. In a very contested 1876 presidential election the Democratic Party candidate, Samuel Tilden, won the popular vote with the help of violent white Klan-type groups that suppressed the black Republican vote in the South. Yet Tilden lost out then in a political deal that gave the presidency, through the electoral college, to conservative Republican Rutherford Hayes in return for withdrawal of the modest numbers of federal soldiers remaining in the South, and for cutting back other federal Reconstruction efforts. The white conservative Republican leadership had sold out their loyal black supporters. Once northern troops were gone, and with continuing antiblack terrorism from white supremacist groups, the whites who had been central to southern slavery, especially the old elite, soon retook political control of most southern areas as members of the resurgent Democratic Party.[36]

In national presidential elections from 1880 to 1908, the white southern-voter majorities went for the Democratic Party, with northern voters still substantially going for the Republican Party. Under this renewed two-party system, white Democratic Party officials aggressively sought an end to black political power in the South. Many from the old slaveholding elite regained political power and successfully worked to disenfranchise mostly Republican black voters, reduce the number of black elected officials, and re-establish the Democratic Party's power lost during Reconstruction. From the 1880s to the early 1900s, racial segregation was extensively developed across southern and border state areas by Jim Crow laws, all of them passed by elite and middle-class whites. Over the long Jim Crow era, indeed up until the 1960s, the lives of black Americans there were highly restricted and regimented by extreme segregation laws, including those mandating racially segregated schools, workplaces, restrooms, drinking fountains, telephone booths, and even courtroom Bibles. By the early 1900s, intensely authoritarian white Democratic Party regimes dominated southern states, strongly enforcing segregation laws. The successful establishment of extensive and extreme segregation for black Americans was a major political coup for a supposedly defeated oligarchical elite, and the near-slavery of legal segregation meant that the federal government had not really "freed" black Americans after slavery. Gradually, too, southern white Democrats also regained substantial power in national political institutions, especially the very undemocratic U.S. Senate. From this renewed position of power they set up major roadblocks to congressional attempts to end racial segregation and expand, even modestly, civil rights; this went on until the 1960s.[37]

In southern and border areas ordinary white farmers and workers played a critical role in enhancing and maintaining this elite-created system of legal segregation, as well as in the de facto racial segregation in northern areas. The white working and middle classes provided the lower-level southern and border state officials who routinely kept black Americans racially subordinated. In the U.S. racial hierarchy, no matter how economically deprived many working-class or middle-class whites might be, there were always millions of black people below them who were mostly in worse shape. Sociologist W. E. B. Du Bois developed the concept of the "public and psychological wage" of whiteness to describe the compensation that ordinary whites got from the white elite for siding with the latter on critical political and economic issues, including not organizing with black farmers or urban workers to protest their exploitation by that elite. In compensation, the members of the white working class:

> Were given public deference and titles of courtesy because they were white. They were admitted freely with all classes of white people to public functions, public parks, and the best schools. The police were drawn from their ranks, and the courts, dependent upon their votes, treated them with such leniency as to encourage lawlessness. Their vote selected public officials, and while this had small effect upon the economic situation, it had great effect upon their personal treatment and the deference shown them.[38]

There was also an important deflection of real white working-class interests. As Michelle Alexander has more recently noted, Jim Crow segregation was "part of a deliberate and strategic effort to deflect anger and hostility that had been brewing against the white elite away from them and toward African Americans."[39] As a result, the segregated racial hierarchy and other segregation were routinely reinforced by ordinary whites operating out of an openly supremacist racial frame; this included mob violence and other overt aggression targeting black Americans.

Ironically, the system of Jim Crow segregation also had a significant negative impact on ordinary whites. As Du Bois noted well, they received public and political rewards from segregation, but their often poor economic situation relative to wealthy whites did not improve as much as it might have without that highly authoritarian segregation. In addition, *white* conformity to the oppressive social system was generally required, and this usually meant a suppression of white political dissenters and liberal reformers even on non-racial matters. The end of postwar Reconstruction, as Du Bois has shown, "established fraud and oligarchy in the South," and "Democracy was largely prevented in the South, and much art and literature was stunted." Significant cultural and moral loss in the South stemmed from the extensive segregationist propaganda and mythology, especially from what Du Bois called the white "lying" in the racist framing of black Americans.[40] Racist propaganda and mythology about both blacks and whites became central to the segregationists' racial frame. This deep racist frame has helped to keep the South, and indeed much of the United States, from full freedom of thought and discussion about the realities of racial oppression and inequality from the end of Reconstruction to the present day.

Political Party Shifts: 1880s–1890s

By the 1880s and 1890s, for complex reasons we do not have space to examine here, some northern banking, railroad, and other corporate executives had shifted their political allegiance and funding from the Republican Party to the resurgent Democratic Party. This business coalition sought lower tariffs and emphasized the importance of the gold standard for U.S. currency. Openly antiblack rhetoric was still strong in this eras' Democratic Party campaigns. In 1884 the Democratic Party succeeded in electing Grover Cleveland for the first of two terms as president, yet he was one of only two Democrats to serve as president in the long era of mostly Republican presidents from 1860 to 1932. Business backers of the Republican Party during the Cleveland years included a coalition of other railroad executives, merchants, and bankers who mostly supported higher tariffs and pressed for a bigger navy and aggressive overseas imperialism. Given this well-organized and well-funded Republican opposition, and Cleveland's inability to end an 1893 depression, the Republican Party soon came back into national power with landslide presidential victories in the mid-1890s and mostly remained in power until 1932. Indeed, this long era of Republican domination is called by some the Fourth party system.[41]

Nonetheless, this national dominance by the Republican Party did not signal similar political changes in the South. In the late 19th century, the Democratic Party continued its political resurgence in the South. The remaining black voters had no place but a weak Republican Party, and legal segregation soon ended voting for most. As a result of this extensive segregation, and contributing to it, national Republican officials quit referring to civil rights in party platforms and major speeches. The Republican Party remained very influential outside the South, continued to grow as the party of a new industrializing economic system, and thereby dominated politics at the national level from the late 19th century to the early 1930s. Significantly, too, a series of important Republican presidents—Robert Taft, Theodore Roosevelt, Herbert Hoover, Warren Harding, Calvin Coolidge—took openly racist and segregationist positions in regard to the societal conditions faced by black Americans. They had shifted dramatically from the views of the "Radical Republicans" of the Reconstruction era.[42]

Political Parties and Progressive Movements: 1890s–1910s

By the late 1890s and early 1900s, major organizational and communications changes had come to an ever-expanding U.S. capitalism. More large-scale bureaucratized corporations developed around farm products, railroads, coal, steel, and the new automobile manufacturing. Increasingly, corporations collaborated and colluded with each other in monopoly and oligopoly arrangements, often with government assistance. New or enhanced communications technologies, such as the telegraph and telephone, and faster ships and trains, greatly facilitated large-scale corporate mergers and collaborative developments. Given these trends, public resistance to this great corporate dominance and to corporate exploitation of farmers and workers also increased. In this era there was significant expansion of progressive activism and movements seeking to deal with the often tough economic times faced by ordinary Americans as a result of these large-scale economic changes.

For instance, the late-19th century Populist Party, a radical agrarian political party (1891–1908), was one of several movements in this era that involved some white and black farmers in the South and/or some white farmers in the Midwest aggressively protesting decreasing prices for agricultural products and exploitative economic actions by banks, railroads, and grain companies. In the 1896 election the Democratic Party split significantly over key economic issues. The more populist wing, representing small farmers and ordinary workers, pressed for important government reforms and restrictions on, or nationalization of, big businesses affecting ordinary farmers and workers. However, big silver-mining companies also aggressively supported the Democratic Party, seeking to influence government policy toward their corporate goals. These corporate interests more than offset the influence of the populist farmer–worker organizations. William Jennings Bryan was nominated by the Democratic Party, and also got the official support of the Populist Party. Focusing too much campaign rhetoric on monetary issues (such as silver versus gold), Bryan lost the election to Republican William McKinley, and the Republican Party mostly controlled the presidency from this 1896 election until the Great Depression of the 1930s.[43] Even with this loss, significant pressures for some anti-monopoly government action still came, not just from small farmers and organized workers, but even more importantly from many smaller business owners. Given these continuing anti-monopoly pressures, some political progressives could be found in both major parties, including the Democratic Party (for example, Bryan and Woodrow Wilson) and in the Republican Party (for example, Theodore Roosevelt). These progressives often supported breaking up certain huge corporations and trusts, the creation of some workers' unions, the creation of certain public welfare programs, and an end to conventional political corruption.[44]

Significantly, too, in this progressive era several attempts were made to create permanent labor or labor–populist parties. Workers in numerous other Western countries were successfully creating labor-based political parties that assisted greatly in the development of social welfare states benefitting ordinary workers. Yet the U.S. attempts were unsuccessful. One reason was substantial government repression of union protests with local police and state or federal soldiers. Another was that union leaders feared that by getting involved with a new labor-based party, they would alienate union members already in the well-established Democratic and Republican parties, many of them for distinctive religious or racial-ethnic reasons.[45]

In this period, religion and political parties were intertwined, as they have often been from the country's beginning to the present. Recall that in the 1830s–1860s era the Democratic Party and emerging Republican Party had different religious factions and ethnic groups in them. Native-born white southerners and new European immigrants gravitated to the Democratic Party, with native-born northern and western whites gravitating to the Republican Party. Crusades of evangelical ministers and churches against saloons and slavery had helped to create the Republican Party in the 1850s. Not surprisingly, during the last decades of the 19th century and first decades of the 20th century, religious and racial-ethnic concerns and ties continued to shape most Americans' political party allegiances more so than their class interests. Historian Robin Archer has argued that most voters of this era were concerned with their class interests, yet the majority still mostly followed the lead of their party leaders and platforms and voted in line with their religious, racial, and/or ethnic interests.[46]

Very important too in this connection is the "psychological wage of whiteness" accented previously. This psychological wage can be seen in operation not only in the South but also in other regions. The great racial divide in the U.S. working class meant that whites in all regions had a large group below them on the racial hierarchy, and could thus "feel better" about their often inadequate economic conditions. In this era such a large racial division did not exist in most of Europe, where the working class was a racially homogeneous group at the bottom of the economic ladder and thus was able to organize strikes and unions more successfully. This huge U.S. racial division helps to explain the great and continuing strength of aggressive U.S. capitalism in regard to workers and the continuing weakness of unions in these decades and later on. In the U.S. case the class relations of capitalistic production have often been so fully racialized that working-class unionization has been much weaker as white men refused to organize effectively with workers of color because of their racist framing of the latter.

In the decades from the Civil War to the early 1900s, yet another factor weakening the development of labor and left parties was a dramatic strengthening of the individualistic achievement perspective. With aggressive industrialization came what Du Bois called the distinctive "American assumption" of individualism. Long part of a dominant Calvinistic work perspective, individualism in this era developed into a yet more aggressive and often secular form—with the assumption that personal success and wealth were the result of an individual's own achievements and "that any average worker can by thrift become a capitalist."[47] This accentuated individualism was central to the national political framing of individual and society in this era, and especially among white Americans. Ever since, ordinary Americans of various backgrounds have been greatly pressured with what is in fact a mythology perpetuated by the country's top leadership: a neo-Calvinistic mythology of "bootstraps individualism" being the major and sure way to significant societal success.

Only occasionally is a significant collective counter to this dominant individualism generated among white Americans, especially on a large scale. In contrast, because of facing the structural barriers of racial oppression for centuries, a majority of African Americans have long had a counter-frame to this white racial and political framing of society—a counter-framing that accents, much more so than for white Americans, the reality of major structural constraints and pervasive societal barriers that greatly and routinely block significant individual efforts. Indeed, this age-old and well-developed black counter-frame is likely what helped Du Bois, an African American, to name and assess this turn-of-the-century individualistic "American assumption" so well. Such counter-framing has also long accented the great importance of *collective* organization and resistance to racial and other societal barriers.[48]

Racialized Manifest Destiny: Late 19th and Early 20th Centuries

Over the 19th and early 20th centuries, the U.S. government's territorial expansion in North America and imperialism overseas dramatically increased, for the most part with leadership from the country's top white politicians, party leaders, entrepreneurs, and intellectuals. In a famous paper on the "significance of the frontier" in U.S. history, the intellectual Frederick Jackson Turner accented a continuing manifest-destiny framing of territorial expansion, thereby helping several generations of whites and others to rationalize the advance of Western "civilization" against "uncivilized peoples" in Indian territories and in various countries overseas.[49]

Beginning in the 1890s, U.S. imperialistic operations expanded greatly. In the decade of the 1890s alone, the U.S. military defeated the Spanish in the Spanish American War, and the U.S. government added Cuba, the Philippines, and other areas to a burgeoning empire. Once again, the country's white leadership, and especially party leaders and officials, aggressively framed these victories as indicative of white superiority and the destiny of the "Anglo-Saxon race" to expand. The Spanish American War involved the first major expansion by the federal government into the sphere of overseas imperialism like that of European governments. Soon, there were many more U.S. military and economic interventions in Latin America in the name of whites' manifest destiny. These imperialistic ventures were increasingly facilitated by the concomitant growth of very substantial U.S. military and other government bureaucracies, and such ventures were often undertaken in ways that kept the general public uninformed.[50]

Most of those colonized in the new U.S. expansionism were people of color, including the substantially black population of Cuba. Given this reality, most in the oligarchical elite routinely viewed these acquired areas as uncivilized and peopled by those racially inferior to the "white race," "Anglo-Saxon race," or "Aryan race." The persisting racial framing of the dominant white group as virtuous and master organizers of the world could be seen in many comments by influential whites in the government, political parties, and corporations. For instance, in 1898 one U.S. congressional representative described the U.S. annexation of Hawaii as yet "another step in the onward march of liberty and civilization" and as the "conquest of the world by the Aryan races." He later added that the "reign of the Aryan" will "penetrate to every nook of the habitable globe" with its lofty values of "justice, enlightenment, and liberty."[51] The supposed "Aryan" race's spread and dominance were viewed as consistently good and unstoppable.

After returning in 1900 from a new U.S. possession, the Philippines, prominent Republican Party leader and senator Albert Beveridge aggressively accented the theme of a racialized American exceptionalism:

> God has not been preparing the English-speaking and Teutonic peoples for a thousand years for nothing but vain and idle self-contemplation and self-admiration. No. He made us master organizers of the world to establish system where chaos reigned . . . And of all our race He has marked the American people as His chosen nation to finally lead in the redemption of the world.[52]

Famous for these imperialistic views and for strong support for an expanded navy, the influential Beveridge also asserted the common white racial framing that "we are a conquering race" with a "blood" right to occupy new lands and markets as "part of the Almighty's infinite plan," one that would mean the disappearance of "decaying races before the higher civilization of the nobler and more virile types of man."[53]

In 1912 the powerful Republican president William H. Taft, later also a Supreme Court chief justice, declared strongly that "The day is not far distant when three Stars and Stripes at three equidistant points will mark our territory: one at the North Pole, another at the Panama Canal, and the third at the South Pole. The whole hemisphere will be ours in fact as, *by virtue of our superiority of race,* it already is ours morally."[54] Again and again in U.S. history, we observe this great insistence on U.S. exceptionalism, which provides the elite with an excuse to be "master organizers" and exploiters of the globe. For the most part, overseas imperialism was not viewed by the white elite or ordinary whites as morally or politically problematical. One reason was that the colonized "decaying races" overseas, just like those people of color oppressed within North America, were not deemed to be fully adult human beings, but to be inferior childlike beings dependent on "civilizing" white actions.

New Immigrants and Political Party Nativism

In the 1880s, more than half of all white Americans still had significant British ancestry, and most of the rest had substantial Northern European ancestry. This changed dramatically with the great Southern and Eastern European migrations of the late 19th and early 20th centuries. Many of these immigrants came into cities, and those who became citizens, together with their citizen children, were often successfully recruited into the Democratic Party's urban political organizations, often called "political machines." The local Democratic Party organizations were very important in orienting new immigrants to the United States and in helping them find jobs, housing, and other life necessities.

This new urban immigration and its political impacts in the cities stimulated a strong negative reaction from many native-born Americans. Nativistic members of Congress like powerful Republican senator Henry Cabot Lodge, an English American, were fiercely determined to combat alleged immigrant "threats" to the social fabric of the country. These nativists contended that admitting more Southern and Eastern Europeans (who were often not Protestants) would destroy the "superior race." For example, the very influential Northern European intellectual, Madison Grant, claimed, like many white intellectual and political leaders of the day, that interbreeding with inferior European "races" would lead to mongrelization of the Northern European "race." Grant was an influential Republican intellectual and leader who played an important role in eugenics and anti-immigration organizations. Even political party progressives were *not* progressive on numerous racial and ethnic matters. Prominent progressives, such as Republican (later Progressive Party leader) Theodore Roosevelt, strongly expressed racist theories of Anglo-Saxon superiority. Roosevelt articulated a version of scientific racism in his view of immigrants, setting up an immigration commission that agreed with him about the superiority of immigrants from Northern Europe and the inferiority of immigrants from Southern and Eastern Europe, with the latter viewed as racially inferior. Many white political leaders in both major parties were eugenicists who thought, often accurately, that their anti-immigrant views were supported by the racist science of their day.[55]

Even the more progressive party factions were frequently populated with Protestant reformers with nativistic inclinations, who frequently sought to reform what they saw as corrupt urban Democratic Party organizations.

And they did succeed in lessening the role of these urban machines. In addition, native-born Northern European Americans formed anti-Catholic, anti-immigrant organizations like the Immigration League and the American Protective Association, which frequently worked in collaboration with Republican political leaders, as organizations like them had before the Civil War. While some Democratic Party leaders played a role in certain anti-immigrant efforts, the Republican Party and its leaders were the most central to the era's anti-immigration movement, what some have termed a "Republican crusade." By the 1910s, anti-immigrant activism had fueled much pressure for new legislation, which was strongly supported by Republican political leaders; legislation that would discriminate substantially against immigrant groups not from Northern Europe. One bill restricting some immigration was vetoed twice by Democratic president Woodrow Wilson, but was finally passed in 1917.[56]

The nativistic pressures continued to build for yet more extensive legislation, especially in nativistic organizations and Republican Party circles. A mostly Anglo-Protestant Congress, led by the nativistic Republican representative Albert Johnson (Washington) and Republican senator David Reed (Pennsylvania), succumbed to this pressure and overwhelmingly passed a strong 1924 Immigration Act. This aggressive legislation set discriminatory immigrant quotas that sharply reduced the number of immigrants from Southern and Eastern Europe and Asia—discriminatory quotas that for the most part lasted several decades until the 1965 immigration reform legislation. Racist framing was intense in the party and congressional discussions of European immigration. Representative Johnson, chair of the House immigration committee, spoke about the need to stop a "stream of alien blood," and when he put his signature on the legislation Republican president Calvin Coolidge said that now "America must remain American." Such racialized political action has had very significant societal consequences, as in this case it has over the last century made the U.S. population far more Northern European, much more Protestant, and much less Catholic and Jewish than it might otherwise have been.[57]

The New Immigrants and Systemic Racism

Over these early decades of the 20th century, and in spite of this nativist sentiment, numerous U.S. corporate executives actually sought out new immigrant workers. Although these corporate executives often viewed the immigrant workers as racially inferior, that was not a serious problem because immigrant workers typically provided cheaper labor than that of native-born white workers. Not surprisingly, this corporate recruitment of immigrants created significant political tensions inside the Republican Party, as has frequently been the case with such immigrant issues to the present day.

The head of U.S. Steel, among other major industrialists, fought against congressionally legislated quotas for the Southern and Eastern European immigrants. These immigrants, as well as new black immigrants fleeing the Jim Crow South, allowed such corporate executives to implement a type of "divide and conquer" approach to control of their diverse workers. By the 1910s, for instance, an ever-expanding Ford Motor Company was hiring workers from numerous racial and ethnic groups, including large numbers of white immigrant workers and black workers. Ford managers played off one group against others in order to control a diverse workforce. Significantly, the father of a new discipline of "scientific management," Frederick Taylor, saw the business utility of racialized competition of workers in his implementation of new management practices in various businesses. Yet, this new scientific management perspective was heavily infected by the old white racist framing of society. In the dominant white framing, as well as in the new management perspective, both Southern and Eastern European workers and black workers were viewed as inferior "races" with poor work habits and other cultural inclinations. The prevailing perspective of U.S. and other Western capitalists has long had this white superiority versus others' inferiority dimension. Moreover, white managers and owners in industrializing companies often aggressively communicated their racist stereotypes and framing of black Americans to the new European immigrants and their children, so that the latter too would view black workers as quite inferior racially. In this way workers could be more easily divided and controlled. Historians Elizabeth Esch and David Roediger have demonstrated how the new scientific management experts were expected "to know and develop 'the races' not only for the purpose of accumulating capital but also for the organisation of modern production through the first decades of the twentieth century."[58] However, after a generation or two, the once racially inferior Southern and Eastern European Americans were allowed by older white groups to become fully "white."

Some white political and economic leaders exported this racialized perspective on labor management from the United States to other countries. No less a figure than Herbert Hoover, later a U.S. president, was a consulting engineer who carried his intensively racialized perspective on mining management to Africa. In South Africa he wrote reports "judging the relative efficiency of African, Chinese and white miners" and liked to calculate "productivity by weighing 'coloured shifts' and 'coloured wages' against the white" counterparts.[59] Honed in U.S. workplaces, the use of white racist framing to manipulate diverse worker groups became an important export carried by U.S. corporate executives, engineers, and other professional advisers.

The White Racist Frame: U.S. Presidents through the 1920s

In the three decades after 1900, major party leaders and leading politicians from both major parties utilized and emphasized a strong pro-white and antiblack framing of society. They also espoused openly racist views of other Americans of color, including Mexican Americans, Asian Americans, and Native Americans. For instance, not only did the Republican progressive Theodore Roosevelt adopt strong anti-immigrant attitudes, but he publicly praised white supremacist Madison Grant's highly racist book, *The Passing of the Great Race* (1916), for its "grasp of the facts our people need to realize."[60]

In addition, President Woodrow Wilson, one of the few Democrats in a long Republican-dominated series of U.S. presidents, was a southerner and a Jim Crow segregationist who praised the Ku Klux Klan, and he increased the racial segregation of black workers in the federal government.[61] (Adolf Hitler, among others, later said he was influenced by both Grant's and Wilson's racist writings.) After Wilson, the next president, the Republican Warren G. Harding (1921–1923) had personal links to the Ku Klux Klan, and he openly rejected any "suggestion of social equality" between whites and blacks. After Harding came Republican president Calvin Coolidge (1923–1929) who had penned a piece in a major magazine asserting that "Biological laws tell us that certain divergent people will not mix or blend. The Nordics propagate themselves successfully. With other races, the outcome shows deterioration on both sides."[62]

Clearly, the most powerful white leaders in both political parties, including famous presidents, openly operated out of an aggressive racist framing of U.S. society and, in most cases, of the entire globe. Their frequent speeches, comments, and actions in the 1900s–1920s era periodically reflected the reality of, and likely the impact of, nativistic, anti-immigrant, and white supremacist groups such as the then politically very influential Ku Klux Klan. These well-organized right-wing groups provided a resurgent organizational base for the many native-born white Americans seeking to subordinate not only African Americans but also the recent Catholic and Jewish immigrants, and thus to preserve what they often framed as the "Anglo-Saxon race."[63]

These right-wing organizations, as Allan Lichtman has accented, were overwhelmingly and aggressively white, Protestant, and Northern European in ancestry—that is, they held to the old white ideal of the United States being centrally a white Anglo-Saxon Protestant nation. Clearly, the *contemporary* right-wing approach to limiting or encouraging federal government intervention on societal issues has significant antecedents in this earlier political era. Thus, arch-conservative views were articulated vigorously during the 1920s and 1930s by white leaders and members of organizations like the Ku Klux Klan and Daughters of the American Revolution; their views then signaled very strong opposition to labor unions, immigrants from Southern and Eastern Europe, homosexuality, and the Darwinian theory of human evolution.[64] We can see, quite clearly, that such socio-political issues are by no means new in U.S. politics.

Conclusion: The Persisting Undemocratic Framework

A clear lesson from the data examined in this chapter is that in its foundation the political party system is profoundly flawed. All political parties have developed within an essentially undemocratic political framework. The mostly well-off white men who made the Constitution set up our political institutions in part to prevent or slow down numerous popular-majority sentiments and preferences from being implemented politically.

As we have seen, in early party struggles party leaders have usually been in tune with the white male elite's class and racial interests. Whether in the past or present, the Democratic Party and the Republican Party have typically operated as organizational variations of one dominant "property party." Political parties are thus not independent political organizations seeking only to bring out to vote a large number of ordinary voters. Party leaders are often more concerned with building up their party's economic resources by getting major financial and other support from what Thomas Ferguson has termed their political "investors," the important economic blocs that seek to shape the important decisions and actions of parties and, thus, of local, state, and federal governments. Philip Burch has made a similar argument with much historical data on the economic and social blocs linked to the political elites in various presidential eras.[65] Contrary to the conventional U.S. view of political parties and citizen voters, who are seen as directly and greatly influencing "democratic" elections and public policies this investment theory of politics argues that the views of the majority of voters on numerous government policy issues are regularly trumped by the interests and actions of powerful business groups and other elite groups working in and behind the political parties and other political institutions.

The elite groups are those with the wealth, clout, and networks to influence candidate choices, elections, and the government policies advocated and implemented by political parties. Since at least the era of French commentator Alexis de Tocqueville in the 1830s, numerous analysts of U.S. society have accented the central importance of powerful networks, associations, and interest groups in shaping parties, elections, and government policies.[66] In the earliest decades, as we have seen, much wealth and national political control were firmly in the hands of the slaveholding oligarchy of southern and border states. Almost all presidents from George Washington up to Abraham Lincoln were slaveholders or supportive of the slavery system. Indeed, until 1860 over half of the wealthiest Americans resided in the South, and their wealth gave them tremendous power in Congress, the presidency, and other important political and juridical institutions.[67] In this 1790–1860 era, the important politicians in the major parties in the First, Second, and Third party systems typically had close ties to some mix of plantation, textile, banking, railroad, shipbuilding, and other major business leaders.

For centuries now, in our substantially business-controlled political system, the conventional election contests have been rather different in reality from what is suggested by standard U.S. democratic theory. In effect, political party leaders and politicians often operate as allies and supporters of their elite business backers and other wealthy funders, if they are not elite business leaders themselves. Party leaders, typically influenced by well-off party funders, directly and indirectly shape who party candidates are, and these candidates often become presidents and members of Congress, as well as state and local government officials. For the most part, major state and national candidates who are elected, as well as those who are appointed to top political positions, are from the mostly white, upper 5 percent or so of the population in terms of socioeconomic status—and are not, as a group, anywhere close to being representative of the general population.[68]

Since the Abraham Lincoln era, on economic and political issues of greatest concern to most major business leaders and their political blocs, the two major parties' policies have often not differed much. However, where major business blocs do differ on important government policies, because of divergent economic or other societal interests, the major political parties linked to particular business blocs may differ in their support of particular government policies. Sometimes, one business bloc will contend with another by helping to pit one political party against another. We saw this in the party conflict over the Bank of the United States in the Andrew Jackson era, as well as in the party conflict over expansion of the slavery system between southern planters and northern corporate interests in the early days of the Third party system.[69]

Historical and contemporary research has shown that the business investors in U.S. politics and their political allies have often preferred to change the political subject from their underlying economic interests to deflection issues such as patriotism, the family, immigrants, alcohol, or abortion. They may also focus on making certain groups—such as "alien" immigrants or blacks—the scapegoats for economic difficulties whose real causes lie in the malfunctioning of the capitalistic system. Over the centuries such strategies have taken many voters' eyes off the deep economic interests of the business blocs that contradict ordinary workers' interests. Even in political or economic crises, most voters have been pressured to view the political and economic worlds from social perspectives and framing long socialized in them by parents and teachers, peers, or the media. Often limiting their information sources to mostly elite-controlled sources, ordinary Americans have been handicapped by having limited data and inadequate conceptual frameworks to make sense out of difficult societal problems. While the various media have sometimes been critical of elite political blocs, especially in times of societal crisis, these typically business-controlled media have generally operated from a perspective similar to that of the business political blocs. That means that they have only occasionally carried out in-depth, substantive analyses that examine the deeper political-economic reasons for numerous major societal crises.[70]

As a result of this oligarchical control over several centuries, most social, political, or economic information that U.S. voters and others get has been uncritically delivered, if not intentionally misleading. For centuries, most major policy presentations by establishment politicians and commentators have been designed to draw from or feed into an elite-provided framing of society, including the white racial frame, the capitalistic frame, and the patriarchal frame. In the past and present, those population groups with relatively little power—such as poor whites, black Americans, other Americans of color—have rarely gotten significant and sustained media coverage reflecting well their economic and political views and interests. Moreover, social science researchers have shown that in all party eras voter ignorance has been very significant, and some social science analysts have argued that such voter ignorance is essential for our undemocratic political-economic systems to work. Indeed, in this society one has had to have substantial economic resources to get out serious political or economic interpretations of society to be considered by the general public, so that most voters and others are not likely to encounter much in the mainstream media in the way of in-depth critical interpretations on most societal issues.[71] We will return to a more detailed look at these issues in Chapter 8.

Nonetheless, we should underscore the fact that over the course of U.S. history this oligarchical control has, on occasion, been vigorously contested. From the beginning, the European American men who controlled the colonies and early U.S. states overtly feared recurring racial, class, and gender challenges from ordinary Americans. The U.S. Constitution and numerous early laws and presidential decisions reflected significant concern over the challenges and rebellions of ordinary Americans in various walks of life. Over several centuries, a major countering force to the elites' undemocratic domination of U.S. politics and the economy has been people's movements—including early farmers' movements, slave rebellions, worker organizations like unions, the abolitionist movement, civil rights movements, and women's movements, among numerous others. These people's movements have frequently sought, and occasionally brought, progressive changes in our relatively undemocratic economic, political, and other social systems. Indeed, over the centuries they have provided major pressure keeping strong ideals of people's democracy very much alive in this country.[72]

4

Race, Class, and U.S. Politics
1930s–1970s

The National Democratic Party and the New Deal

The Great Depression of the 1930s brought another major party shift, this time to a more progressive Democratic Party and a soon-to-be-powerful president, Franklin Roosevelt. He won four terms as president, which began the era of a strong Democratic Party. During his administration the harsh economic trials of many Americans finally came to be viewed by many men inside the elite's moderate and liberal segments as important for federal government action. The New Deal era eventually became one involving major new federal programs to resolve serious economic crises and to provide expanded social welfare programs. In this era the Republican Party also became ever more linked to certain major business interests, which generated much organized opposition to numerous new federal programs.

This shifting party system involved the development of a strong New Deal Democratic coalition of voters, including the Southern and Eastern European immigrants and their children, especially in cities, who were now voting in large numbers for Democratic candidates. Generally, white union workers and many other white workers became very important in the Democratic Party. During the 1930s and early 1940s large numbers of workers engaged in a great array of union organizations and protests, in perhaps the most significant increase in worker organization in U.S. history. By the late 1930s, union organization had substantially increased, and broad unions like the Congress of Industrial Organizations (CIO) had become more willing to engage aggressively in party politics. This increase in unionized workers' political power played a key role in Roosevelt's political victories and his willingness to undertake numerous social reforms that significantly assisted ordinary workers and their families. Moreover, during the 1930s many black voters in the North shifted to Roosevelt's Democratic Party. Although the New Deal's employment programs usually operated along Jim Crow lines in many areas, they did put many black job seekers back to work, thereby offering significant economic support in the 1930s Great Depression. As a result, many northern black voters shifted from their support of the Republican Party in 1932 to strong support of the Democratic Party in 1936 and numerous subsequent elections.[1]

Historically, large-scale working-class organization—including unions, populist groups, and civil rights groups—has been home-grown. According to David De Leon, we find the "spirit of our radicalism not in Lenin but in [Eugene V.] Debs . . . in the Populists . . . Our radicals have concentrated on emancipation, on breaking the prisons of authority, rather than on planning any reconstruction."[2] Thus, the increasingly organized U.S. workers in this era, and indeed subsequently, were clearer in their minds about what types of economic exploitation they opposed than about the type of economic system they would like to see replace the existing one, but the majority did see the New Deal economic efforts as a significant move in the correct political direction.

Many political analyses accent Roosevelt's assertive personality or his coalition of people's groups for the great success of Roosevelt's New Deal. While acknowledging the importance of these factors, we should note the great importance of the powerful political coalition of businesspeople underlying the Roosevelt years. Thomas Ferguson has argued, with sub-stantial evidence, that more important than this coalition of ordinary workers and other modest-income Americans was a distinctive coalition of high-tech companies, multinational corporations, and investment banks that Roosevelt and his advisers constructed as his base of political investors. Many older and nationally focused companies tended to stay with the Republican Party, but numerous capital-intensive firms with a growing multinational orientation gradually moved to the Democratic Party. By the mid-1930s these important multinational corporations were joined in support of the Democratic Party by the expanding and internationally oriented investment banks, and were further buttressed by the growth of internationally focused media such as *The New York Times*. Under the influence of this multinational corporate umbrella, a strong free trade position and significant involvement in international monetary matters were adopted as strategies by the Roosevelt administration. Moreover, given growing pressures from the better-organized union movement, by the mid-1930s important pieces of social welfare legislation—for example, the Social Security Act and the National Labor Relations Act—were passed by the Congress.[3]

Segregation and Other Discrimination: The New Deal Era

The New Deal's dramatic expansion of economic and social support pro-grams during the Great Depression was very important in moving the United States in the direction of an expanded social welfare state like those in Europe. Significantly, too, black Americans were included in these critical support programs, yet these programs did not come close to ending anti-black discrimination. African Americans continued to suffer much racial discrimination at the hands of whites, especially in the South, including those white officials working in expanding New Deal agencies. Federal relief programs tended to provide black workers with lower pay and less-skilled jobs than whites, and black workers were often employed only after whites were hired. New housing programs increased racial segregation by allowing federal home loans only in racially segregated areas and by racially segregating new public housing. In addition, Roosevelt himself was unwilling to seek any anti-lynching legislation, fearing powerful white southerners in Congress might block his other important legislation.[4]

Nonetheless, organized political and civil rights actions by black Americans, especially in the expanding civil rights movement of the 1930s and 1940s, did force a reluctant President Roosevelt to take some action against legal and de facto racial segregation. Under pressure from A. Philip Randolph and other black leaders threatening antidiscrimination marches, Roosevelt issued a pathbreaking fair employment executive order reducing discrimination in wartime employment and setting up a Fair Employment Practices Committee. Roosevelt also called for some new civil rights legislation. Black voters in the North had grown greatly in numbers since 1920, and this was one reason for the pro-civil-rights positions of Roosevelt, as well as of subsequent Democratic presidents. Since the 19th-century Reconstruction era ended, the first presidential attempts to put civil rights issues back on the national political agenda came during this Roosevelt era. "People were no longer infinitely discardable, and the New Deal of Franklin Roosevelt became the first national administration to treat black Americans as recognizably human."[5]

Toward the end of Roosevelt's long service as president, the pressures from labor and civil rights groups, his experience with desegregating New Deal programs, and his experience dealing with the racist extermination of Jews by German Nazis likely contributed to his increasingly public concern with the expansion of civil and economic rights for ordinary Americans of all backgrounds. Labor and civil rights leaders had pressed hard for expanded rights since at least the late 1800s, but the moderate and conservative segments of the elite had long fought to keep the status quo on the expansion of civil and labor rights. Indeed, only in the 1960s were civil rights movements able to move the legal system dramatically in the direction of protected civil rights for Americans of color. Even then, no economic rights were added to the U.S. Constitution. Yet, in a little known but prophetic 1944 State of the Union address an eloquent Roosevelt assertively pressed for a major "Economic Bill of Rights."[6] This expanded U.S. bill of rights must include, he argued, broad economic and social rights for all regardless of racial, class, or religious characteristics. Without full respect for the diversity of individuals, communities, and cultures, there could be no authentic U.S. democracy, as he stated the matter.

Yet one more sign that the United States today is not the comprehensive political democracy often celebrated is the fact that the U.S. Constitution has not yet been amended to include President Roosevelt's important economic bill of rights. Moreover, while numerous reforms and executive orders during Roosevelt's era did further democratize the United States, they did not do away with basically antidemocratic institutions such as the electoral college and its power to put candidates into major political office without a majority of the popular vote or the power of a minority of U.S. senators to block treaties and major presidential appointments and filibuster and kill important legislation. The New Deal actions also did not reform the congressional committee system with its ability to routinely perpetuate the power of corporate executives in usually getting legislation in their interest passed, even against the views and interests of a majority of the population.[7]

Attacks on the New Deal: Deep Roots of Contemporary Conservatism

A common interpretation of the great conservative wave of the last few decades is that it has been to a significant degree a white resistance ("backlash") to the 1950s and 1960s civil rights, women's, and anti-war movements. This is only partially true, for several social scientists have shown that a powerful white conservative backlash against early incarnations of these movements began much earlier, and also in reaction to the social, economic, and civil rights reforms and changes of the long New Deal era.[8] The relatively progressive eras of Roosevelt and his successor Harry Truman brought economic and social welfare reforms, an increase in labor unions, and a Keynesian approach to government stimulation of an economy oriented to consumers. Yet, neither Roosevelt nor his advisers saw themselves as a threat to U.S. capitalism. As propertied men, they viewed their efforts as trying to save the country from major upheavals that threatened its capitalistic and associated political structures. Indeed, the greatest pressures for change usually did not come from these elite men, but from reform organizations and protests of ordinary Americans, including union strikes and civil rights demonstrations. Grass-roots pressures succeeded in gaining new rights for unionizing and protections for workers in terms of safety and health in workplaces, minimum wage laws, and working hour limitations. New laws created the Social Security Program and other social support programs and greatly increased government regulation of employers.[9] Many other New Deal programs also substantially assisted the unemployed, such as employing them in numerous public works projects, and expanded some rights for black Americans.

Yet the many New Deal interventions in the depressed capitalistic economy triggered a major and often militantly conservative response. Within two years, a group of very powerful capitalists created an organization, the American Liberty League, designed to fight those New Deal programs viewed as limiting their formerly freewheeling economic operations. Funded by a few dozen wealthy manufacturing, banking, and other corporate capitalists, the arch-conservative League began a series of highly politicized attacks on the Roosevelt administration as dictatorial and a great threat to private property. Unions and union rights were major targets for their attacks. The National Association of Manufacturers became a major player in the attacks on the Roosevelt administration. Some associated company executives even stockpiled tear gas and weapons to fight a feared major uprising of U.S. workers.[10] Out of these arch-conservative organizations, and often led by powerful white men associated with them, came numerous postwar organizations that laid the groundwork for the later expansion of contemporary conservative political movements.

The Democratic Party and Civil Rights: The Truman Era

In a recent opinion piece in a major business newspaper, "Whitewash: The Racist History the Democratic Party Wants You to Forget," Bruce Bartlett, a former adviser to Republican president Ronald Reagan, vigorously criticized the Democratic Party for its long white-racist heritage. Most Democratic Party leaders were "openly and explicitly for slavery before the Civil War, supported lynching and 'Jim Crow' laws after the war, and regularly defended segregation and white supremacy throughout most of the 20th century."[11] As we have seen in previous chapters, there is much truth to his assertion about some historical whitewashing, especially if one focuses on Democratic actions before the party's 1960s shift to the support of civil rights and desegregation. Even so, the phrase "most of the 20th century" is an exaggeration, for numerous Democratic Party leaders began to break significantly with its segregationist past during the Roosevelt administration and the 1945–1953 administration of Harry Truman, formerly Roosevelt's vice president.

Significantly, many decades of difficult civil rights protests and legal action by black Americans preceded, encompassed, and followed the New Deal and World War II era. The increasingly important National Association for the Advancement of Colored People (NAACP) had been founded in 1909, and its activists and lawyers had worked for decades to end racial segregation. Other black protests against discrimination increased significantly in this era. Moreover, this was a time when certain liberal and moderate segments of the white elite agreed to some important changes in the U.S. system of racial discrimination. World War II had an impact too, for Americans were contending with a highly racist German government. As a result, some limited progress in reducing segregation in the workplace and expanding political rights occurred between the 1930s and early 1950s.

During the Roosevelt era changes in the system of racial oppression came slowly, often because of intense opposition from white southern senators.

For example, in 1942 the House actually passed a Roosevelt bill to end the racially discriminatory (voter) poll tax, but a filibuster by southern senators stopped it from passing in the Senate. The political scenario of southern senators killing poll tax legislation after it passed in the House was repeated in 1945, but this time with Truman as president. Truman pursued legislation ending some forms of discrimination. Late in 1946, he issued an executive order establishing a President's Committee on Civil Rights. Executive Order 9808 asserted that civil rights were constitutionally guaranteed and necessary for domestic peace and democratic institutions. Soon, in 1947, his Committee conducted major hearings and put out an important government report, *To Secure These Rights*, which asserted that all Americans had basic civil rights to be protected and called for federal protective action on civil rights. Truman drew on its findings in his special civil rights message to Congress, as well as in his important executive orders to desegregate the U.S. armed forces and the civil service system.[12]

In 1948, in a major special message to Congress, Truman proposed ending the poll tax and racial discrimination in education and public accommodations (stores, hotels, etc.), with enforcement of these laws by a new Department of Justice Office of Civil Rights. He also pressed for a law against lynching crimes. Still, no such legislation was passed, in large part again because of opposition from openly white-supremacist southern senators. Even with majority support for his legislation in the North, and in the U.S. House, these arch-segregationist Democratic senators blocked the legislation. The founding fathers had "armored the Senate," to use Robert Caro's apt phrase, in order to block significant legislation if a powerful minority of the elite desired such action.[13]

Until the 1940s, only Republican Party platforms had mentioned racial matters and civil rights. Truman's support for a significant civil rights plank in the 1948 Democratic Party platform led to the creation of a major party spin-off called the States' Rights Party, one established by white supremacist leaders such as South Carolina's famous Senator Strom Thurmond. These former Democrats, often called "Dixiecrats," bolted from the Democratic Party out of fear of federal action knocking down southern segregation. During the 1930s and 1940s these southern segregationists had tried, mostly unsuccessfully, to build political alliances with whites of similar persuasion in the North, explicitly arguing that white supremacy could be a true national identity.[14] Thus, the angry Dixiecrat abandonment of the Democratic Party signaled that some moderate and liberal elements in the white elite were gradually coming to view segregation in the South as no longer essential to maintain their power and privilege in society. In addition, the long trek out of the South by millions of black Americans to northern cities where they could have more freedom and a vote was having a significant political impact. Numerous white Democratic politicians in northern cities owed their political positions in part to growing numbers of black voters, and increasingly they supported an end to southern racial segregation out of concern for these voters.[15]

Republican Dwight Eisenhower: The 1950s and the *Brown* Decision

By the mid-1950s the growing black civil rights movement had created an ever more critical legitimation crisis for this white elite. Increasingly, the U.S. elite faced much national and international questioning of its social and political legitimacy in face of growing rights protests from African Americans. Assessing the 1950s racial situation, W. E. B. Du Bois underscored the considerable impact of African Americans' organizing over previous decades against Jim Crow segregation: "Slowly they beat upon public opinion and then entered the courts. The courts dodged and evaded with every subterfuge, but they faced inevitably clear decisions unless the principle of democratic government was to be completely surrendered in the presence of world war in which we claimed to lead democracy."[16] Important to success in the desegregation efforts in the 1950s and 1960s were both the black activist organizations and the reality of wartime eras during which the ideology of democracy was increasingly heralded by U.S. government officials at home and overseas. Large-scale wars like World War II, the Korean War, and the Vietnam War also required substantial mobilization of much-needed black workers and soldiers for U.S. success in these national efforts.[17]

Legitimacy on the international scene was a growing concern for many in the ruling elite, and by the mid-1950s its moderate and liberal segments were increasingly willing to abandon Jim Crow segregation, thereby facilitating and generating the unanimous Supreme Court decision *Brown v. Board of Education*, which ruled that "in the field of public education the doctrine of 'separate but equal' has no place."[18] Under international pressure, the U.S. Department of Justice had submitted a supportive legal brief in the *Brown* case citing the need for the United States to look good on the international scene by removing "existing flaws in our democracy" like racial discrimination. Numerous other key officials made similar pronouncements about the need to counter the Soviet Union internationally by improving the U.S. civil rights situation. During the 1950s, 1960s, and early 1970s, federal courts ordered substantial desegregation in U.S. institutions. As the leading constitutional scholar Derrick Bell has long argued, such examples indicate a relatively rare *convergence* of certain black and white interests. That is, historically, white elites act to improve the conditions of black Americans only when they themselves can benefit significantly in the process.[19]

Nonetheless, the white elite's support for even this limited racial change was often not enthusiastic. This was an era when neither most of them nor most rank-and-file whites could envision a racially inclusive society, with fully inclusive schools, workplaces, churches, and political institutions.

Indeed, a great many whites argued that the racial desegregation sought by black Americans conflicted with white employers' and other whites' property rights. As researcher Nancy MacLean has put it, in this era "resurgent corporate political power brought renewed popular white support for private property rights over human rights."[20]

Not surprisingly, thus, the *Brown* decision was reluctantly supported by Republican president Dwight Eisenhower (1953–1961), who expressed privately his own racist views and moral support for the antiblack "concerns" of white segregationists. In addition, the dramatic *Brown* decision precipitated an extreme reaction from numerous openly white supremacist members of Congress. One official response came from white southern congressional leaders in a "Southern Manifesto," a statement signed by almost all southern senators and House members, all of whom were white Democrats.[21] The manifesto shouted that "The unwarranted decision of the Supreme Court in the public school cases is now bearing the fruit always produced when men substitute naked power for established law." These elite politicians argued that Jim Crow inequality in school facilities "is founded on elemental humanity and commonsense, for parents should not be deprived by Government of the right to direct the lives and education of their own children."[22] Clearly, they were speaking unreflectively out of a strong white framing, for indeed they meant *white* parents and children. At that time, of course, a great many southern parents and children were African Americans, but their family and educational interests were not to be seriously considered by these "elected" congressional leaders.

The Supreme Court's 1954 *Brown* decision was not the only major factor in generating the renewed white resistance to racial change that also helped to stimulate a vigorous white conservative resurgence over the next decades. In September 1957, nine black students attempted to enroll in historically white Little Rock Central High. In response, Arkansas governor Orval Faubus used the state National Guard to block the students' entrance. Several weeks later, President Eisenhower reluctantly put in a U.S. airborne division and federalized (took control of) the National Guard, and the black students were finally admitted. After much white protest against desegregation, Faubus closed the Little Rock high schools, which remained empty for a year. Finally, in August 1959, the high schools reopened.[23] Faubus received hundreds of thousands of letters and telegrams from whites supporting his aggressive opposition to the federal courts and the president's actions on racial matters, and in a Gallup opinion poll, this outspoken segregationist was later chosen as one of the country's *most admired* men. His conflict with the federal government over racial desegregation made Faubus a national political star for a great many whites.[24]

New and younger white segregationist leaders were becoming important. Joseph Lowndes has underscored the rise in this era of new arch-conservative leaders in the South, who often developed a renewed language of violence for what they saw as a new "racial political order." One leader was Asa-Earl Carter, a white supremacist organizer of anti-segregation protests and one-time speechwriter for George Wallace. In his inflammatory speeches, Carter played up racist imagery such as the alleged threat to white women from black men, a very old theme from the still-dominant white racial frame.[25]

In spite of major political losses from actions such as the Supreme Court's *Brown* decision and Eisenhower's intervention in Little Rock, leading white segregationists still held significant political influence and power. For example, in 1956–1957, the U.S. House managed to pass a civil rights bill banning Jim Crow segregation in schools, parks, hotels, theaters, restaurants, and voting, with strong enforcement provisions. While the bill passed the House, it was summarily killed in the Senate by the segregationist senators. Two relatively weak civil rights bills did pass, one setting up a U.S. Civil Rights Commission and another establishing court-appointed referees to protect some black voting, but with weak enforcement provisions. Significantly, these civil rights policy efforts were made under a mostly moderate Republican administration, and in the 1960 election the Republican Party platform still asserted the Republican Party's commitment to desegregation and other civil rights issues. At this point in time, the Republican Party did not seem a likely place for openly racist arch-conservatives to turn. Significantly, the 1960 Democratic Party platform also took a strong position on civil rights issues. However, once elected, President John Kennedy decided to move very slowly on civil rights reforms. Only in 1963, his third year in office, did he send a major civil rights bill to Congress, and a compromise version of that bill was passed in the relevant House committee just before Kennedy was assassinated late in 1963. Nonetheless, the start on civil rights reform by President John Kennedy would soon become a major political effort of the next Democratic president, the Texan Lyndon Johnson.[26]

Barry Goldwater: A "Southern Strategy"

Republican Party leaders were very concerned at the loss by their candidate Richard Nixon to John Kennedy in the 1960 presidential election, and some thus decided to recast themselves. After 1960, influenced by Senator Barry Goldwater and southern white Republicans, some party leaders developed "Operation Dixie," a program strongly advocating for "states' rights" and Jim Crow segregation and seeking party candidates with such views.[27] Recall from Chapter 2 that an emphasis on the barely coded racial language of "states' rights" has long pervaded the racial and societal frames of many in the white elite and their constituencies. For centuries, whites in many geographical areas have insisted on white-controlled local governments and a weak or nonexistent federal ability to intervene against such discriminatory realities as local racial segregation. Starting in earnest with the 1964 presidential campaign of Goldwater, conservative leaders increased their power in the Republican Party, marginalizing the East Coast's more moderate Republican elite over the following decades, and largely abandoning black voters. As a result, since the 1960s the Republican Party has drawn rather small percentages of black voters in most national elections.

Instead, since the 1960s the Republican Party has developed a strategy to secure replacement voters, what has been called by many academic and media analysts a "southern strategy." However, the use of this phrase without the adjective "white" is a misnomer for what has in fact been a "white southern strategy." "Southern strategy" is a misnomer because an often large percentage of southerners were (and still are) not white, depending on the geographical area being considered. In many areas where conservative political appeals were made using overtly or covertly racist language, the intention was only to attract white voters. Some Republican pioneers working for this important white strategy have been forgotten. For example, conservative Texas senator John Tower, one of the first Republican senators in the South since the 19th century and a major player in the making of the contemporary Republican party, was a leader in pro-white voter campaigns in the South and nationally. Serving in the Senate from 1961 to 1985, Tower was an overt segregationist who opposed the 1954 *Brown* decision and the 1960s civil rights acts.

Over time this pro-white strategy emphasized the interests of whites in southern states, as well as in much of suburbia in all states, with influential and widely used codewords like "states' rights," "busing," "racial quotas," and "crime in the streets," all of which explicitly or implicitly referenced antiblack images, stereotypes, or narratives from an old white framing of society. While the development of the so-called southern strategy is typically linked to the political efforts of Richard Nixon in the late 1960s and early 1970s, in fact this strategy was developed and used well in the 1964 campaign of Senator Goldwater, an Arizona Republican who took pride in the right wing's increasing control of the party. His famous phrase "extremism in the defense of liberty is no vice" and his vote against the 1964 Civil Rights Act made very clear his arch-conservative orientation. While Goldwater spoke occasionally and generally about racial integration being preferable, he was adamantly opposed to the federal government doing anything significant to end segregation and related racial oppression. Some analysts have described Goldwater as "neither racist nor segregationist," but rather an advocate of "racial policy conservatism" that sought to end New Deal-type government intervention on racial matters.[28] However, such analysts miss the key point that Goldwater, like a great many other whites, only viewed society from a white racist framing that prized existing racially oppressive institutions that greatly benefitted whites. Nothing about racial segregation and other racial oppression was so serious for Goldwater, and for many other white conservative leaders in this era, as to necessitate viewing the oppressive racial world empathetically from a black point of view—and thus to necessitate working aggressively to change its extraordinarily brutal and oppressive features.

Goldwater's very conservative orientation in regard to much government action and other matters disturbed some Republican moderates still in the party at this time. The major Republican figure, George Romney, a moderate governor, privately faulted Goldwater for adhering to a "Southern-rural-white orientation."[29] Nonetheless, Republican conservatives were on the ascendance, and the 1964 Republican platform was brief and much weaker on civil rights issues than the Democratic Party platform; this time, the Republican platform espoused the view that the "elimination of discrimination was a matter of heart, conscience and education." We should note too that the new Republican political strategy included some attempts to reduce voting by black and Latino voters, as Republicans feared such voters of color would increasingly go for Democratic candidates. Prior to the 1960s, such attempts to block black and Latino voters had mostly been carried out by Democratic Party operatives, especially in the South. However, by the early 1960s the Goldwater campaign was actively engaging in voter restriction activities, actions later adopted by Republican operatives working for the Richard Nixon campaign.[30]

Although the Republican Party lost the nationwide race for president in 1964, the pro-white strategy did work well regionally in capturing a majority of white voters in *five* traditionally Democratic southern states and gaining those states more or less permanently for the Republican Party. Political scientists Edward Carmines and James Stimson argue that one cannot overestimate the great shift that took place with the Goldwater campaign: "Before Goldwater, the Republican Party was dominated by candidates and party leaders committed to racial progressivism."[31] There was indeed a major political shift with Goldwater, but this statement exaggerates the past Republican reality because, for instance, President Eisenhower and some of his cabinet members were well known for their overtly racist views and sympathy for white segregationists fighting change. Still, the Republican Party was more moderate on matters such as civil rights before 1960 than it was after the right-wing Goldwater's run for the presidency in 1964.

Lyndon Johnson and the Civil Rights Era

Lyndon Johnson's landslide victory over Goldwater in the 1964 presidential election encouraged the new president to propose, and a now more liberal Congress to pass, numerous pieces of social reform legislation, including new programs in urban development, health care, environmental protection, education, and especially civil rights. What made these political actions both more likely and more effective were some underlying demographic and organizational shifts in this country, most especially among African Americans.

As we have observed previously, during World War I and World War II, and continuing into the 1950s and 1960s, much of the U.S. black population greatly expanded its visibility and political clout by moving out of the rural South to southern cities and, more dramatically, out of the South to many northern cities. This migration away from Jim Crow segregation helped to expand northern black incomes, and thus black support and funding for the southern civil rights movement. In the early 1960s, black civil disobedience demonstrations targeting racism further increased. One Greensboro, North Carolina sit-in by black students at a segregated lunch counter triggered many similar protests. Black and white freedom riders tested federal court orders desegregating public transportation. New organizations pressing for significant black political and economic power were created, including the Student Nonviolent Coordinating Committee and the Black Panthers. Gradually, protests against various types of racial discrimination moved to the North with boycotts in Harlem, sit-ins in Chicago, and numerous demonstrations in other cities. Antidiscrimination groups engaged in school boycotts against discrimination and in picketing discriminatory construction sites.[32]

As it had in the 1950s, the expanding 1960s civil rights movement continued to generate a serious legitimation crisis for the white elite. Significant pressures from civil rights organizations helped to secure the passage of major legislation prohibiting discrimination in employment, voting, and housing. Doubtless, without this constant pressuring from organized black Americans, the moderates in the white elite, including those then in the U.S. Senate, would not likely have continued to move toward expanded civil rights and racial desegregation. In addition, these civil rights movement pressures were made more significant by other factors cited previously, including the pressures from the Cold War with the Soviet Union. Given the great array of black protests, the international publicity given to southern segregation and civil rights movements by the Soviet Union, the national need for black workers and soldiers, and the era's significant economic growth, yet more northern and national Democratic leaders moved to support legislative and court actions directed at liberating the country from legal Jim Crow segregation.[33]

These particular Democratic officials were themselves supported by some powerful white executives in certain major corporations who decided to provide the civil rights movement with funding and to support some Democrats in Congress in their efforts to pass civil rights laws. For a time, the white elite's liberal and moderate factions provided support for civil rights efforts through funding from certain corporate sources, including key foundations. Some in the elite temporarily invested in aspects of the civil rights movement, and many of these were linked to multinational corporations—that is, some of the corporate interests that supported the Democratic Party and President Lyndon Johnson at this time. One reason that this shift in support by some elite whites for strong civil rights laws and enforcement was more possible in the 1960s than previously was likely the relative weakness of the Republican Party after the Goldwater debacle in 1964. The Republican loss to the Democratic candidate, John Kennedy, in 1960, and the huge Republican loss to Democratic candidate Lyndon Johnson in 1964, significantly weakened the Republican Party politically. According to political scientist Paul Frymer, only in specific periods where one U.S. political party is seriously weakened—such as during the Reconstruction era (when the Democratic Party was weak) and during the mid-1960s civil rights era (when the Republican Party was relatively weak for a few years) –could significant black needs and interests be taken into serious account by the other major political party.[34]

Responding to these various pressures, President Johnson and Congress passed two very important civil rights laws, the 1964 Civil Rights Act banning discrimination in employment and public accommodations and the 1965 Voting Rights Act protecting voters of color from some voting discrimination. Johnson pressed for the passage of the 1964 civil rights bill that had been initiated by President Kennedy. Given his knowledge of the Senate as a former Senate leader, President Johnson was able to get the bill past the southern senators' filibuster. Clearly now, the white southern Democrats in Congress were in the minority on numerous civil rights matters, and the majority of the Democratic Party's white officials had shifted in the direction of support for at least certain desegregation and civil rights policies.[35]

Two years later, in 1966, Johnson and his allies proposed yet another important civil rights law banning housing discrimination. This time the civil rights legislation passed by a narrower margin in the House. In the Senate the Republican senators voted nearly two-to-one to support the southern filibuster against the legislation, which was successful in blocking its passage. Extending civil rights legislation to northern areas, and to housing there, garnered significantly less support in both parties, and especially in the Republican Party, than did previous civil rights laws that especially targeted Jim Crow segregation and other southern racial discrimination. Eventually, in 1968, some housing discrimination legislation was barely passed, but the difficulty showed a significant growth in resistance to national desegregation and antidiscrimination efforts.[36]

The Democratic Party's more prominent leaders for a decade, including Johnson, Hubert Humphrey, George McGovern, Walter Mondale, and Jimmy Carter, publicly supported a commitment, as the 1972 Democratic Party platform put it, to "resuming the march toward equality . . . to bringing a more equal distribution of power, income, and wealth . . . and equal and uniform enforcement in all states and territories of civil rights statutes and acts." This 1972 statement was the most progressive one on racial and other societal change made by any political party in this era.[37]

The three major civil rights laws of the 1960s, as well as the favorable orientation of the Democratic Party to expanded civil rights since this era, have had significant positive results on U.S. politics over the last few decades. One dramatic effect was on black voters and the Democratic Party. During and after the 1960s there was a major increase in the number of black voters, and a strong orientation to the Democratic Party on the part of many. Democratic Party reforms of the late 1960s further helped black voters and black officials to gain some power within the Democratic Party, although there was a significant retreat from these party reforms after the Republican Richard Nixon's major win in the 1972 presidential election. Additionally, since the 1960s the black vote has continued to greatly favor the Democratic Party. Data on presidential elections from the 1940s to the present show that a key voting differential—the percentage of black voters voting Democratic minus the percentage of white voters voting Democratic—has increased to a large positive percentage. The voting change came most dramatically in the 1960s, rising from a 23 percent differential in 1960 to 56 percent in 1968 and 57 percent in 1972. It has remained high since that time—for example, at a very substantial 52 percent for the 2008 election that Senator Barack Obama won. In addition, the percentage shift since the 1960s has been accompanied by much larger absolute numbers of black voters casting votes for numerous Democratic candidates in local, state, and federal elections.[38]

Urban Black Revolts and White Reactions

While the major 1960s civil rights movement and consequent civil rights laws and reforms had important and positive effects on the political and economic rights and opportunities for black Americans, they also had dramatic effects on the reactions and attitudes of many white Americans. As we noted previously, one common interpretation of the great conservative wave since the 1960s is that it began with a white backlash reaction to the civil rights and other people's movements of the 1960s. While it is true that some white conservative opposition to racial reform and social welfare programs began in the Roosevelt and Truman eras, contemporary racialized conservatism is also substantially a result of much negative white reaction to the 1960s civil rights movement, laws, and advancements made by African Americans and other people of color into major institutions, including political institutions, from which they were once excluded.

Well into the civil rights movement era, in the mid-1960s, much more aggressive protest by African Americans further stirred up conservative white reaction and resurgence. By the middle of Johnson's presidential years the anger of urban black Americans over continuing discriminatory and impoverished conditions was increasingly being expressed in urban rioting in northern cities like Los Angeles, Detroit, New York, and Washington, D.C. From the mid-1960s to the early 1970s, thousands expressed their anger against racism and poverty in hundreds of riots in or near the country's poor and racially segregated urban communities. As a result, in 1968, President Johnson established an important National Advisory Commission on Civil Disorders to investigate the causes of these urban black revolts. The mostly accurate, data-filled report of this commission concluded that the United States was "moving toward two societies, one black, one white—separate and unequal" and explicitly asserted that "white racism" was substantially responsible for an "explosive mixture" in U.S. cities.[39]

Influenced by examination of the field research data gathered by their well-qualified staff, the mostly white commissioners argued for an end to institutional discrimination and for considerable expansion of government programs for poverty-stricken urbanites. Clearly, the report's research-based view of the impact of persisting discrimination was accurate and was heralded by civil rights leaders like Dr. Martin Luther King, Jr. Not surprisingly, it was considered too radical by most white leaders in both political parties, white media commentators, and most ordinary whites, and its major recommendations were rejected by President Johnson. Indeed, a common white response to these urban black revolts was that of prominent Los Angeles police chief and conservative Republican William Parker. In a 1965 Los Angeles riot, black anger over deteriorating living conditions, high unemployment, and police brutality had triggered a week of large-scale urban rioting. Yet Parker and most other local white officials ignored the underlying socioeconomic and policing conditions leading to the rioting, and Parker insisted on his unreflective racial framing of "ghetto riots" as mainly being caused by black "criminals." In addition, like many others, Parker somehow linked in his mind the urban riots in the North and West to the nonviolent black civil rights movement in the South, which he also condemned.[40] In his earlier 1964 campaign Senator Barry Goldwater had already articulated elements of this criminalizing perspective and tried hard to link the black civil rights movement, civil disobedience, and assertions of equality to "black crime" and "violence in the streets." In Goldwater's view these black efforts for civil rights and justice required a tough "law and order" response by government authorities.[41] This "law and order" theme was one which Republican officials increasingly used to attract white voters and to counter the goals and actions of the spreading civil rights movement of this era.

Remarkably, the often courageous efforts of black Americans to free themselves from centuries of extreme racial oppression, which was "legal" in the South because of whites' political dominance there, were intentionally being distorted into the opposite of the freedom-seeking and justice-seeking efforts they really were. By the late 1960s, thus, opinion polls showed that the overwhelming majority of white Americans felt that "law and order" was indeed breaking down in the United States and had to be reimposed by get-tough measures. Additionally, during the Johnson era many white members of Congress, mainly conservative Republicans and southern Democrats, tried to link parts of Johnson's "Great Society" civil rights and social programs to the generation of crime "by the eroding of the work ethic and fostering black laziness."[42]

Criminalization of black Americans in white minds did *not* begin in the 1960s. Indeed, in the 1930s and 1940s white southern Democrats and northerners opposed to expanded civil rights had frequently linked what they then called the "Negro problem" with the "crime problem" in their racial framing, as whites had done for generations. Members of the elite and other whites did not racialize a "crime problem," but criminalized the "race problem"—that is, the civil rights protests of this era. In the 1940s, many whites in the North and South had already come to view efforts at racial desegregation as threats to societal stability and their social status.[43] Later on, in the 1950s and 1960s, many whites, especially in southern areas of the country, continued to accelerate this portrayal of black rights activists as criminals to be processed by the criminal justice system. A great many viewed real integration as bringing significant impacts on formerly white public spaces, and many in and out of Congress fulminated against racial integration as making more of the formerly segregated public world "unsafe" for whites.

Later on in the 1970s and 1980s, as we will assess more fully later, this constantly reiterated criminalization perspective made it easier for elite white officials to develop, and the white rank-and-file to support, an expanded U.S. prison–industrial complex that in effect created a new type of "Jim Crow" segregation for much of the ostensibly free black population.

The White Conservative Reaction: Fear of "Big Government"

During this late 1960s and early 1970s era the renewed white accent on local "law and order" and criminalizing of the civil rights movement were just two aspects of the conservative white pushback against the black liberation and other people's movements of this era. Significant too in the adverse reaction was then, as now, a deep and abiding concern with losing the status and privileges of being white. The possibility or reality of significant government civil rights enforcement in workplaces, public accommodations, and other settings brought much white fear of losing significant racial privileges. Recall the deal white workers had long ago made with the white elite to the effect that they would get a public and psychological "wage of whiteness" in return for accepting substantial elite political-economic dominance. Yet, this privileged position for ordinary whites began to break down by the 1960s, as black workers and other workers of color pressed for better job opportunities and workplace climates. Many whites felt they were losing their advantaged "labor aristocracy" position, an attitude which often fueled their increasing support for the Republican Party, then and later on.

In addition, federal enforcement of civil rights laws and decisions led to desegregation of public schools and public accommodations. The enactment and enforcement of the 1965 Voting Rights Act brought a substantial enfranchisement of African Americans in southern and border state areas, which in turn had negative effects on whites who often feared the black vote. Then, as now, many whites were also fearful of expanded black political power and black elected officials at local and state levels.

Not surprisingly, thus, a very important dimension of many whites' reaction to racial changes in this era was a renewed accent on the supposed perils of "big government." Indeed, since the 1960s an anti-federal-government perspective has been central to much of the conservative movement's political and racial framing. Because the federal government under Johnson had moved to end Jim Crow, pass civil rights laws, and institute some affirmative action regulations, many whites came to associate, more than in the past, much federal government ("public") action with black Americans and, in their view, as action against white interests. In this era it was indeed African Americans who aggressively pressed for the federal government to protect their civil rights and expand their freedom. Sometimes the federal officials did in fact expand civil rights and freedoms, and this government-action imagery captured many a white mind. Thus, for decades survey researchers have found a strong association between the antiblack views espoused by whites and certain anti-federal-government views.[44]

Many whites even developed the view that much of the federal government was somehow under the control of African Americans, other Americans of color, and certain groups thought to be allied with them (for example, "the Jews"). Since the mid-1960s or so, much domestic public policy and government action have come to be seen as somehow black-linked in many white minds. Drawing on his substantial research in Alabama, sociologist Randolph Hohle calls this the public-equals-blacks political theme. Thus, a great many whites in local areas in the South developed a strong and influential "language of privatization that degraded all things public as 'black' and inferior and all things private as 'white' and superior."[45]

Moreover, while often honed in southern areas, this racialized perspective on much government action was actually national in scope, and this reality helped to accelerate and buttress the support of whites in all regions, and especially in the white middle class, for the elite's privatization efforts. Over the next few decades, the neoliberal political coalition moved even further away from government social welfare and support programs to an array of privatization efforts, such as the privatization of public schools under pressure of desegregation. Because of this powerful and somewhat disguised public-equals-blacks and private-equals-whites language, conservative Republican appeals to white voters have been less overtly racist and can use recurring attacks on "big government," with a wink to white voters who understand that the implicit referent is often public policies seen as benefitting black Americans, other people of color, or poor people generally.

White Reactions: Racialized Suburbanization and Privatization

Across the country, with the creation of exclusively or predominantly white suburbs in the decades from the 1950s to the 1980s, and thus with white flight from central cities on a large scale, came an aggressively conservative political framing that emphasized property rights, the privatization of public services, and a strong anti-government attitude on many issues. Large-scale suburbanization became a successful strategy that worked intentionally or unintentionally against much racial integration, one pioneered by whites dealing with the official end of legal segregation in southern and border cities. Part of this success involved whites convincing the federal courts and other federal officials that this suburbanization strategy was not motivated by white racist inclinations, but was about other factors such as economic issues, affluence, or new metropolitan sprawl.[46] Social scientists like Kevin Kruse have shown that white southerners fighting school and other desegregation fought for their "right" to "select their neighbors, their employees, and their children's classmates" and the "right" to do what they wanted with their property. Most importantly, they insisted on their "right" to get away from what they viewed as "dangerous encroachments" by a federal government seeking to enforce civil rights laws in housing, employment, and voting. Using data from the Atlanta area on white flight and suburbanization, Kruse has shown that the racialized actions of Republican political operatives in this era were often undergirded by these much deeper socioracial realities of segregative suburbanization and local privatization.[47]

In the Georgia area that Kruse researched, as well as in numerous other states, the older white conservative hostility toward certain federal actions—in regard, for example, to civil rights, labor rights, and business regulation—was accelerated. Added to that old hostility were new elements, including an accent, in particular, on the privatization of public services such as the local schools, which also could bring sharp reductions in local government taxes. These strong views were often to be found among white southerners opposing racial desegregation before they became as important in numerous other geographical areas. Yet large-scale white suburbanization became a successful anti-integration strategy utilized by non-southern whites to counter black migration to their cities, especially central cities. When school desegregation efforts moved more aggressively to big cities in the North in the 1970s, this further accelerated white flight to suburbs and private schools. In the North and the South, this was not just a matter of a few scattered suburbs but of many whites in many suburbs.[48] In many of these cases the strong white framing of public-equals-black and private-equals-white helped to legitimate major neoliberal privatization projects in which mostly white entrepreneurs could make much money off the privatization of what was once public, such as in the "construction of a publicly financed private school system that emerged from the struggles to fight school desegregation."[49]

As I have discussed elsewhere in this book, there is much contradiction and irony in most whites' anti-government views and actions. For example, it was major federal programs, such as the extensive highway funding programs and the large-scale tax benefits for homebuyers, that made possible the many expanding white suburbs. Note too that many whites have been committed to numerous other large-scale government actions, such as those in regard to the U.S. military and social security programs at the federal level, and those relating to numerous major government programs at local and state levels that provide public services they enjoy. Only certain "big government" efforts have actually been included in this negative political framing of government.

Richard M. Nixon and the Successful "Southern Strategy"

We have already seen how the "southern strategy" targeting white voters in the South and in the suburbs was developed by Barry Goldwater and his white conservative allies in the early and mid-1960s. While the Republican Party lost in 1964, a similar strategy was used by Richard Nixon's political team in 1968 and 1972 to capture more white voters, especially but not only in southern and border states, and this helped Nixon win the White House twice. Indeed, some political strategists, such as Kevin Phillips, argued that in this era the "emerging Republican majority" among voters meant that the Republican Party did not need "urban Negroes" and certain other "vested interests" to win nationally, but could successfully focus on white voters. Among these white voters those in the burgeoning suburban areas were especially important.[50]

In this era, much pressure on the Republican Party and Nixon was coming from the racist right. For example, in 1968 the segregationist southern governor, George Wallace, ran a racialized campaign as the presidential candidate for the American Independent Party, campaigning against racial desegregation. In his previous 1964 primary campaign within the Democratic Party and in this 1968 national campaign Wallace garnered millions of white votes nationally, in both northern and southern states. While Wallace is remembered as a famous southern segregationist, he played an important political role nationally in helping to focus and shape the strong combination of white racial fears of the civil rights movement and enforcement, white longings for a less diverse country, and right-wing "free market" thinking into the white conservative resurgence. Most significantly, perhaps, Wallace's great successes with white voters in various areas added substantial pressure on Republican candidate Nixon to use more thinly disguised racist language in his own political efforts.[51]

Not surprisingly, the 1968 Republican Party platform was relatively conservative on racial matters, and did not even mention support for the new civil rights laws passed in the 1960s. It had only one brief sentence on civil rights. In 1968 speeches and commentaries Nixon too made increased use of subtle and covert racist appeals ("states' rights," "law and order," and "crime in the streets") to attract a great many whites from the Democratic Party to the Republican Party. Contrasting himself with his more liberal Democratic opponent, Hubert Humphrey, Nixon succeeded by relating to white discontent with the civil rights movement, North and South, that had been more openly expressed in the Wallace campaigns. Nixon also forced very conservative Republicans to accept a more moderate candidate than Goldwater, as Nixon still articulated support for certain government social programs. In the 1968 campaign Nixon claimed to be a political moderate and often seemed moderate in public.[52] He won in a close election, in part because of substantial support from many voters in the burgeoning white suburbs across the country.

In his first two years as president, Nixon's actions sometimes did suggest he was a political moderate, at least in appearance. For instance, he supported some significant civil rights policies, including one important Philadelphia affirmative action plan. This Philadelphia plan required contractors to hire workers of color on federally funded projects, but white-controlled craft unions were known to be very opposed. However, several researchers have shown that Nixon's public support of the plan was designed in part to divide the Democratic Party—that is, to pit white union workers who voted Democratic but opposed job desegregation against black workers who voted Democratic and benefitted from such desegregation plans.[53]

Moreover, President Nixon moved to a more conservative white-oriented strategy by the middle of his first term. He made increasingly evident his goal of weakening government pressure for racial desegregation. He had welcomed Strom Thurmond as a member of the Republican Party, and now he nominated southern racial conservatives for the Supreme Court and reduced federal efforts to desegregate schools. He was also good at using codewords with strong racial overtones. He continued to present "law and order" speeches to numerous political groups. He used phrases like "silent majority," "forgotten Americans," and "middle America," terms then increasing in popularity. Thus, he spoke about the needs of the "great silent majority" in a 1969 speech that was negatively alluding to those protesting against societal oppression, and which phrase was taken by many to mean the white majority of Americans. Analytical treatments of Nixon's early actions, including revealing accounts of his close political advisers, accent his zigging and zagging on racial and other issues.[54]

Nixon regularly indicated that he operated from a strong white framing of politics and society. His private and backstage actions, only later revealed, signaled his deeper views and aggressive use of the old white frame and its blatantly racist imagery. According to his close advisers, Nixon frequently used racist words like "nigger," "jigaboo," and "jigs" in phone calls and other discussions. Privately, he said to associates that certain government social programs could not benefit black Americans because they were "genetically inferior to whites."[55] Moreover, Nixon's chief aide, H. R. Haldeman, kept detailed diaries of his many interactions with Nixon. Made public on a *Nightline* show, one important April 1969 diary comment on President Nixon went as follows:

> President emphasized that you have to face that the whole [welfare] problem is really the blacks. The key is to devise a system that recognizes this, while *not appearing to*. Problem with overall welfare plan is that it forces poor whites into the same position as blacks . . . Pointed out that there has never in history been an adequate black nation, and they are the only race of which this is true.[56]

In March 1970, Nixon and Vice President Spiro Agnew performed a piano duet at a local celebrity dinner. After jokes were made about Nixon's southern strategy, Nixon and Agnew played two pianos there. Nixon asked Agnew, "What about this 'southern strategy' we hear so often?" In counterpoint, Agnew answered in mock black dialect, "Yes Suh, Mr. President, ah agree with you completely on yoah southern strategy." The heavily white audience of the Washington, D.C. elite laughed loudly at these racialized performances.[57] In addition, Earl Butz, a powerful Secretary of Agriculture under Nixon, and the next president, Republican Gerald Ford, made jokes about what the Republican party could offer African Americans—with the racist punchline being that all a black man really wants is loose shoes, warm toilet facilities, and sex. As we have seen, Nixon himself engaged in racist commentaries and joking, according to his closest advisers. Clearly, Nixon and some advisers and cabinet members fostered a racist climate in certain very important political spheres both inside and outside Washington, D.C.[58]

Nixon's political actions spoke even louder than his harshly racist language. His most important appointment to the Supreme Court, William Rehnquist, was well known for his previous opposition to school desegregation; Rehnquist would later become Chief Justice and guide the high court in an ever more arch-conservative direction from 1986 to 2005. By the end of his first term, Nixon brought in numerous conservative officials to weaken enforcement of school desegregation and pressed the FBI to go after civil rights leaders and groups. While Nixon sometimes supported important civil rights measures and periodically courted some moderate black leaders and voters, by the early 1970s he was working harder with Republican operatives to cast the Democratic Party as the party of black issues and to buttress the political strategy of securing white voters in the South, and white voters in suburbs across the country. In his memoirs Nixon asserted that he did not especially seek out southern whites' votes and did not use an explicitly racialized campaign strategy, yet the overwhelming evidence previously discussed shows that he really did.[59]

Recall that in the 1972 election the percentage of black voters voting Democratic minus the percentage of white voters voting Democratic reached a very high 57 percent, up from a 23 percent differential in 1960. President Nixon was indeed helping to reconfigure the national political terrain on racial issues, including accenting the implicit messaging on law and order issues, for a more conservative and white-oriented Republican Party. In this regard he was clearly pressing the more liberal Democratic Party hard from the right. Yet in some other policy areas he supported the continuing expansion of the federal government started under Johnson. In a split government situation, he found himself working with a Congress controlled by the Democratic Party and periodically collaborated with them in expanding important programs for older Americans, such as social security and the Supplemental Security Income program, and in expanding some important regulatory efforts, including the new Environmental Protection Agency. Thus, the powerful movement to societal reform begun in the mid-1960s did not end abruptly with Nixon; the radically conservative shift away from this more moderate perspective on these particular government programs was yet to come for the Republican Party.[60]

Elite Leaders of the Conservative Resurgence

Overall, the late 1960s and early 1970s Nixon era revealed the divisions within the white elite becoming sharper and more evident. Certain moderate and liberal segments had recently accommodated or supported many societal reforms of the Roosevelt to Johnson eras, including a commitment to civil rights laws. In contrast, the more conservative segment of the white elite mostly did not accept many of the governmental reforms, especially in regard to expanded civil rights, the social welfare state, and labor unions.

By the late 1960s and early 1970s the Republican Party of Abraham Lincoln, which had supported civil rights for African Americans, was becoming not only whiter but also the party of former segregationists. A fair number of members of the white southern elite were moving into the resurgent racially and socially conservative Republican Party. Moving into the party, for example, former Democratic senator Strom Thurmond helped it capture politically much of the white South, and neither he nor most other Republican Party leaders seem to have viewed his former rabidly segregationist role as problematical.[61] Others with ties to the white South's segregationist past moved easily into the Republican Party. Another key former segregationist, Jesse Helms, also a former Democrat, was elected a Republican senator for North Carolina in 1972. In his campaigns, Helms received the open support of the Ku Klux Klan, which he had defended in the 1960s as being as legitimate as the black civil rights movement. Even in the 1970s he did not reject their overt political aid.[62] Nonetheless, most of the Democratic senators in the South stayed in the Democratic Party through the 1960s–1970s era, for seniority and other reasons, yet when they retired they were usually replaced by Republicans.

We should also note that in southern (and border) areas it was not just some older white segregationist leaders and voters who were moving in ever larger numbers to the Republican Party in the 1970s and later; many younger white conservative leaders and voters in the growing white-collar (for example, clerical, professional, managerial) groups in the rapidly expanding suburbs of the southern cities were also joining the ranks of those opposed to the racial and other social programs of the Great Society era. As we will observe in the next chapter, numerous contemporary conservative Republican leaders have come from these expanding suburban areas.

In addition, intensive opposition to racial desegregation and Great Society programs was also led by important conservative segments of the white elite and affluent middle-class groups in northern and western areas. Numerous conservative media outlets like the *National Review*, located in New York, opposed what they and others sometimes called "integrationist policy." Editorials in the *National Review* strongly condemned the *Brown* school desegregation decision. A major Republican figure in the arch-conservative expansion, William F. Buckley, was a founder of the *National Review* and a strong advocate of racial apartheid in South Africa, as well as in the United States. Reflecting paternalistically on southern desegregation, he said he prayed "every Negro will not be given the vote in South Carolina tomorrow. The day after, he would lose that repose through which . . . some of the decent instincts of the white man go to work, fuse with his own myths and habits of mind, and make him a better and better instructed man."[63]

Examining these decades after World War II, Allan Lichtman has detailed the role of numerous important right-wing political leaders and activists. Important arch-conservatives included not only Thurmond and Buckley, but now a few female leaders like Phyllis Schlafly, money men like J. Howard Pew, and the savvy organizer Richard Viguerie. Much of their concern too was over government desegregation efforts and related social changes taking place since the 1950s and 1960s, including those brought by the civil rights movements and by the increased immigration of people of color that was occurring since the ending of racist immigration quotas in 1965.[64] These right-wing thinkers and organizers were joined by many white corporate and other business leaders moving to more aggressive support of the Republican Party and significantly away from support of 1960s civil rights and social welfare programs. Indeed, on key political issues many moderates in the white elite were now moving in the direction of the perspectives of the increasingly more conservative Republican Party.

Conclusion

Sociologist Seymour Lipset once suggested three important explanations for the rise of the very conservative political and social movements in the 1950s:

1. one group's fear that another group will take away some of its status and privileges;
2. the lack of a substantial tradition of intergroup tolerance and civility in the United States; and
3. the reality of "Americanism" being constructed in terms of the dominant ideology.[65]

The expansion of the arch-conservative movement since the 1950s–1960s era has indeed reflected these elements. We have seen the importance of white reactions to the end of much segregation and white fears of losing status and privileges in the face of increases in black political and economic power, as well as the absence of a strong and institutionalized U.S. tradition of intergroup tolerance and fully protected civil rights before the late 1960s. We have also seen the recurring tensions over what "real Americanism" should be and who should determine that.

We should emphasize that the conservative resurgence in the late 1960s had broader roots than just the large-scale white pushback against the civil rights movement and civil rights laws of this important era. The rise of the new Republican right was also in part a backlash against the anti-war movements and other people's movements of that era. Still, these other people's movements were not isolated from the black civil rights movement, for they were often triggered by, or at least significantly shaped by, the goals and efforts of the civil rights movement. Indeed, other 1960s movements often learned protest strategies and tactics from the experiences of that civil rights movement.[66] Reviewing this era, sociologist Bill Domhoff has accented the accumulating factors:

> The changes forced on the white South and the northern white working class by presidential executive orders and congressional legislation in the first five years of the 1960s, along with divisions over the Vietnam War, were the main factors in the initial rise of the right, which appealed to racial resentment and super-patriotism to gain support.[67]

These important racial and anti-war factors gradually helped to generate a resurgent and very conservative coalition of southern whites, white northern workers, and white evangelicals in all regions, as well as many white corporate executives and other white elite leaders. Racial, religious/cultural, and economic reasons undergirded this shift.

5

Race, Class, and U.S. Politics
1970s–1990s

The Hard-Right Corporate Turn in the 1970s–1980s

The investment theory of politics suggests that major U.S. political parties are linked closely to powerful blocs of businesses. Over U.S. history the mostly white-run business blocs have risen and fallen in political power and influence; they sometimes shift from one party to another depending on their needs and the circumstances of the national or global economic systems. Beginning in the mid-1970s there was a major move to the Republican Party by certain multinational corporations' executives. Up through the 1960s, the U.S. corporate sector had been dominant in much world trade. However, by the 1970s and 1980s greatly increased international competition from businesses in the then rising economies of Asia and the recovered economies of Europe were reducing or threatening U.S. corporate profits. The massive U.S. recession in 1973–1975 has largely been forgotten, but this economic crisis helped greatly to further move many business executives' support from the Democratic Party to the Republican Party. Numerous multinational and other business leaders, who had once been relatively supportive of the Democratic Party in the 1930s–1960s era, increasingly shifted funding and other support to the ever more conservative Republican Party, substantially because their international business climate had changed dramatically and because of the expansion of business regulation during the presidential administrations of the 1960s and early 1970s.[1]

As we observed in prior chapters, U.S. corporate and other business interests have always had significant and organized influence in political parties and elections, and likewise on many government policies. That was the case in this era too, only this time with dramatic acceleration and organizational development. Corporate political action committees working to elect corporate-friendly politicians increased substantially, as did corporate political contributions made through various means. More conservative, mostly white politicians were elected in many geographical areas. During this era of right-wing resurgence, corporations greatly expanded lobbying efforts in Washington, D.C., in order to end or reshape government policies. The number of corporate public affairs offices in the capital city increased dramatically—from about 100 to about 500—in the decade between Nixon's election in 1968 and the late 1970s. Even more strikingly, the number of registered corporate lobbyists increased from a mere 175 in the early 1970s to about 2,500 at the beginning of the Reagan administration in the early 1980s. Memberships in national business organizations like the Chamber of Commerce more than doubled.[2]

In addition, right-wing think tanks like the American Enterprise Institute and Heritage Foundation expanded and received major infusions of money from wealthy corporate executives and business owners seeking to promote very conservative views about ending or restructuring U.S. government policies. Prior to the late 1970s era a majority of experts consulted by government officials and drawn on by the media came from centrist or liberal think tanks. However, in this era, wealthy white corporate and small business conservatives began to fund heavily existing right-wing think tanks and create new ones. They also sought to expand their influence over the views expressed in university policy institutes and graduate programs and in the mainstream media. As a result of such efforts, over recent decades they have gotten many right-wing experts into mainstream media presentations and other public discussions and debates; and they have been very successful in conservative campaigns aimed at shaping public views on a great many important social and political issues.[3]

Unsurprisingly, this substantial corporate right turn and its impact on Congress meant much less support for expanding social support programs and meant that moderately liberal Democratic officials such as President Jimmy Carter (1977–1981) had less support and federal funding for important domestic programs. In addition, the shift in the corporate elite's international and political concerns increased pressures on the federal government for military intervention on behalf of U.S. corporations trying to increase profits globally. This in turn meant considerably increased military expenditures by the federal government. Given declining profits, major tax increases on corporations could not be accepted by the elite for this military expansion. Yet the federal government was saddled with high military expenditures and, thus, recurring budget crises, indeed to the present day. Since in the 1970s and early 1980s the Republican Party had no large popular base that, unlike the Democratic base, was frequently in an employment or other economic crisis, the Republican Party more easily took up the platform of major cutbacks in government social-support spending, of increased military expenditures, and of corporate tax cuts. In contrast, the Democratic Party increasingly became a political party of oscillating political contradictions, sometimes obviously supporting multinational and other capitalists' business interests, while at other times trying to work more aggressively for the essential employment, economic, and other social needs of ordinary Americans, including in regard to the issues of health, aging, and the environment.[4]

An Uneasy Republican Coalition: Corporate and Christian Conservatives

As a result of these corporate and other organizational developments, over the last decades of the 20th century and into the 21st century there has been a significant increase in U.S. political party differentiation and polarization. Before and during this era of the major corporate right turn, there was also a conservative turn by a significant number of whites, one often generated or facilitated by certain media efforts and other corporate actions. For some time, as we have seen, whites, especially in the South and in conservative Christian groups, had already been reacting negatively to the 1960s civil rights movement and the cultural liberalization generated by that and other people's movements in the 1960s and 1970s. For racial, religious, and other cultural reasons, many whites were gradually or rapidly moving from political support of the Democratic Party to more frequent support of the Republican Party. Since the 1970s, thus, the Republican Party has increasingly involved a coalition of white corporate and other business leaders and white evangelical and other social conservatives. Over these recent years, the more business-oriented Republicans and the Christian conservatives have joined together in numerous political campaigns, though there have been persisting intragroup tensions. This important Republican coalition and its divergent interests must be taken into serious consideration when analyzing the major conservative political developments over recent decades.

Many corporate and other business Republicans seem to worry more about such issues as government business regulations, government rules about unions, and taxes on profits and wealth. These Republicans are often more fiscally conservative than religiously conservative. In contrast, those on the Christian right are often not as centrally concerned about such business issues, but rather are social conservatives who are more concerned with so-called "culture wars." The latter's concerns especially target groups thought to be "immoral," people said to be violating certain religious norms and cultural values. These include people having abortions and gay people, especially those trying to get married. Conflict over "cultural issues" has also included such hotly debated issues as affirmative action, gun control, separation of church and state, feminism, evolution, and (mainly in the South) such white traditions as flying the Confederate battle flag. Many white social conservatives have thus portrayed themselves as "victims" of government action, including on racial matters such as affirmative action and school desegregation. By incorporating and emphasizing such cultural issues, a more business-oriented Republican leadership has been able to attract many white evangelicals and other social conservatives to Republican candidates who publicly adopt a socially conservative perspective. Clearly, white Christian conservatives have become a very important part of the Republican Party coalition since the 1970s.[5]

The contemporary white Christian right signals a new intensity in orga-nized authoritarianism—organization that frequently attempts to impose its authoritarian views on the larger society, an issue we review below. The influence of this Christian right on the modern Republican Party has been so great that the influential political commentator Kevin Phillips has argued that these religious conservatives have turned the contemporary Republican Party into the "first religious party in U.S. history," and one that he even views melodramatically as a "theocratic" threat to the future United States.[6]

Interestingly, historian David Courtwright has noted that much of the cultural issues agenda of the Christian right, such as abolishing abortion, has not yet been accomplished.[7] However, in contrast, the corporate conser-vatives have gotten much of what they have sought over recent decades as part of this important Republican coalition. Since the 1980s they have gotten less government in the form of major tax cuts for corporations and well-off Americans generally as well as some major reductions in federal regulations. Significantly, too, the same corporate conservatives who have said they are against big government have eagerly pressed for federal business subsidies and valuable federal government contracts. Note again that many ordinary right-wing activists and voters have not supported a limited federal govern-ment when it comes to social matters they want the government to actively regulate such as abortion, or programs that older Americans among them rely upon, such as Social Security.[8]

The Contemporary Christian Right and Authoritarianism

In some of its views and inclinations the contemporary Christian right in the Republican Party appears substantially neo-Puritan. Recall from Chapter 1 the early Puritan colonists and their emphasis on adhering strongly to established doctrine and obeying established and traditional authorities. Their worldview often involved an authoritarian framing of society, in which there were strong authority figures who sought to be followed by relatively obedient followers. This perspective has been adopted by many in other European American groups over the centuries since the initial colonization. From the first centuries, too, this authoritarian framing of society was often closely linked to a white racial framing of society. As noted previously, this country began with a strong racial hierarchy linked to the foundational oppression created by European colonists in the 17th and 18th centuries, initially in regard to subordinated Native Americans and African Americans. Ever since, societal arrangements of authoritarian leaders and obedient followers have been commonplace. Indeed, much literature on the contem-porary Christian right neglects the early and important authoritarian framing that many contemporary Americans have inherited. Moreover, while many prominent U.S. founders did not seek the close ties between Christian religion and the government that are sought by many today in the

Christian right, in other ways the latter are similar to the founders who worked hard to keep their dominant authority at the top of the country's socioeconomic hierarchy. Indeed, in the 18th and early 19th centuries, many of the famous founders were authoritarian slaveholders and leaders who made sure that, politically and legally, most Americans were generally submissive to their authority.

Researchers Marc Hetherington and Jonathan Weiler argue there has been an evolution in political worldviews over the last few decades, one in which the Republican Party has become a much more authoritarian party and the Democratic Party has become much more of a non-authoritarian party.[9] However, the contemporary authoritarian approach to society and politics is *not* really new, but substantially a repackaging and reassertion of an old authoritarian framing of this society that has been significant since at least the 17th century. The intensive accent on following authoritarian leaders and accepting traditional ways of doing things, as well as on punishing those who deviate from traditional ways, has been passed along over the generations. Today, a strong orientation to following traditional authorities is commonplace and imbibed by a great many people. Considering the contemporary Republican Party, both the business conservatives and the Christian social conservatives commonly emphasize important aspects of a relatively authoritarian framing, including routine and often uncritical respect for certain political authorities and traditional folkways, although the Christian right members of the Republican coalition are the most likely to translate their authoritarian views into strong support for socially conservative political policies on such matters as abortion, same-sex marriage, and the death penalty.[10]

The Contemporary Authoritarian Frame and U.S. Politics

I suggest the term "authoritarian frame" to make sense of numerous contemporary socio-political issues associated with authoritarian approaches and ideas. Such a conceptual frame involves principles of selection and presentation and is "composed of little tacit theories about what exists, what happens, and what matters."[11] The authoritarian frame collates and shapes ideas, thinking processes, and what people see and do. People operating from a strong authoritarian frame tend to view the social world in terms of "either/or," and not in terms of "both/and." And they commonly have difficulty in seeing shades of gray on scores of important societal issues. Those with very authoritarian views typically have a different cognitive style from those who are not very authoritarian. They accent the importance of conservative authorities, and they are more likely than others to rigidly accent the maintenance of certain social and cultural orders.[12] In addition, this authoritarian framing of society includes an array of important emotions and narratives about authority, obedience, and tradition, as well as conventional images of what is social success and failure. Consciously or unconsciously, this authoritarian frame regularly affects perceptions and actions in everyday life in obvious and subtle ways.

Consider three central dimensions of the frame—authoritarian submission, strong adherence to certain traditional folkways, and aggression toward selected unvirtuous outgroups. One key metaphor in a common authoritarian frame depicts society as necessarily a ladder, as a social hierarchy with powerful leaders at the top and weaker followers down the ladder toward the bottom. People strongly committed to, and operating out of, the authoritarian frame tend to be much more oriented, cognitively and emotionally, to certain prominent authority figures and expect them to maintain the societal status quo. Moreover, a strong tendency toward submission to selected authorities is frequently associated with a significant lack of critical thinking and some anti-intellectualism. The evangelical Christian historian, Mark Noll, opens his book on contemporary evangelicals by asserting that the "scandal of the evangelical mind is that there is not much of an evangelical mind." He argues there is much oversimplification of issues and anti-science thinking among contemporary white evangelicals. Anti-intellectualism and oversimplification frequently incline many people to accept the arch-conservative political thinking of their chosen leaders.[13]

Another major feature of a typical strong authoritarian frame is its accent on conforming to a certain traditional social order and a willingness to be aggressive toward those perceived as bringing disruptive or immoral social changes. Most people come to the authoritarian frame in the normal ways, through adaptation and conformity in their everyday environments, including the family and peers. Thus, the famous theorist, Erich Fromm, noted that a strongly authoritarian person is a conformist, a sort of human chameleon who prefers to conform to normative surroundings. Those holding to a strong authoritarian framing of the world usually encounter little in the way of recurring contradictions to such framing—such as being in groups or knowing people well who violate the valued traditional rules of society.[14]

Yet another common dimension of a strong authoritarian frame is hostility toward certain outgroups, including certain racial or ethnic outgroups in the U.S. case. The contemporary right-wing resurgence has meant a new intensity in a type of organized authoritarianism, which frequently attempts to impose certain authoritarian views on the larger society, especially its discontent with supposedly deviant outsiders who are viewed as menacing the status quo and a particular established authority. Thus, white right-wing authoritarians have usually viewed straight white Christians as the most virtuous Americans and the standard for social desirability and standard morality, with the outsiders and enemies often including black Americans and other people of color, immigrants, gay Americans, or feminists. This dimension of the authoritarian frame usually has a high emotional valence, as it is linked to such emotions as hostility, anger, fear, or a sense of threat. Studies of authoritarianism have often noted the role of threat in an authoritarian framing of the world that, often without difficulty, links to right-wing political action.

In recent years psychologist Bob Altemeyer has resurrected research on contemporary authoritarianism. His innovative survey scale of attitudinal items measuring "right-wing authoritarianism," which in his view assesses personality traits and not directly a person's politics, includes distinctive survey items like these:

1. "Our country desperately needs a mighty leader who will do what has to be done to destroy the radical new ways and sinfulness that are ruining us";
2. "The only way our country can get through the crisis ahead is to get back to our traditional values, put some tough leaders in power, and silence the troublemakers spreading bad ideas"; and
3. "God's laws about abortion, pornography, and marriage must be strictly followed before it is too late, and those who break them must be strongly punished."

People who agree strongly with the views expressed in survey items like these, Altemeyer argues, reflect right-wing authoritarianism that is imbedded in their personalities. One sees in the measured items the key dimensions of authoritarian submission, authoritarian aggression, and acceptance of selected traditional ways that have been accented since the earlier social science work of the 1940s.[15]

For decades now, social scientists have found many close ties between the authoritarian orientations of whites and their negative and hostile attitudes toward specific racial and ethnic outgroups. In their famous 1940s study of authoritarianism and personality, T. W. Adorno and his social science colleagues argued from their psychological data that people with intense hatred of other groups, such as they found then for many white Americans in regard to black Americans, typically differed from more tolerant people in regard to central personality traits—that is, they tended to show "authoritarian personalities." These researchers found that those with more authoritarian socio-political views differed from those with less authoritarian views in their greater willingness to submit to authority, their tendency to be fearful of and stereotype others, and their great concern for social ranking and the status quo. They also connected people's strongly authoritarian and stereotyped views to deep internal and personal psychological problems, arguing for a Freudian-type interpretation of externalization. That is, strongly authoritarian people are viewed as projecting some personal fears and unacceptable desires onto other people, often those considered inferior, because they cannot accept those particular fears and desires as their own.[16]

In contrast, much recent psychological work views authoritarianism as a personality disposition that is usually more a matter of conformity and socialization than of externalizing specific personal psychological crises. From this more collective perspective, most people learn important frames, such as the strong authoritarian frame and the often closely related white racial frame, from implicit and explicit socialization at home, school, and church, as well as from much of the mainstream media. As with the right-wing authoritarian frame, conformity is very important in how people come to adopt the commonplace white racial frame. People adopt both strong authoritarian views and racially prejudiced and stereotyped views in conforming to expectations of reference groups such as important relatives and friends. This is true for authoritarian leaders and authoritarian followers. Social psychologist Thomas Pettigrew has noted that authoritarianism can be a significant early personality orientation and also be amplified by significant situational and conformity dimensions that kick in later on: "Authoritarianism begins early in life as a personality orientation that later typically leads to a particular type of political ideology. In addition, just because situational and societal factors influence authoritarianism, this does not mean it cannot be considered a personality variable."[17]

Historically and today, a strong authoritarian framing of society is not necessarily linked to or coterminous with a politically conservative framing, but over the decades of the late 20th and early 21st centuries the two societal frames have frequently been closely intertwined and linked. (Left-wing authoritarianism appears to be rare today.) Among whites, these frames have also been commonly intertwined with a strong white racial framing of society. Clearly, both a strong authoritarian framing and a white racial framing accent dominant and subordinate groups, acceptance of certain traditional societal folkways, and some aggression toward selected outgroups. Both are deeply imbedded in the minds of a great many whites today, as they seem to have been now for centuries. These frames are recurringly operational in everyday life and regularly shape many aspects of mainstream politics and of numerous other societal operations and institutions.

Authoritarian Political Action: Politics, Media, and Religion

In the contemporary United States right-wing authoritarianism has typically involved religious and politicized framing, a collection of beliefs "a person uses as a guide to interpret the world" and a framing that is closely linked to a "visceral sense of right and wrong."[18] Contemporary authoritarianism thus often links to a very conservative political framing. In making full sense of contemporary authoritarianism, one can distinguish between the different roles of authoritarian leaders and followers. In this society, as in virtually all societies, some people greatly desire to dominate other people, and succeed in that effort. Many others are willing to more or less be the followers of the powerful leaders. Some research data on U.S. political leaders reveal that many regularly operate out of a strong authoritarian framing of society. For example, a survey of several states' legislators by Altemeyer found that the members of Republican caucuses in state legislatures generally averaged significantly higher scores on his authoritarianism scale than did those in the Democratic caucuses. The numerous Democratic caucuses of state legislators were more diverse, with average caucus scores on the authoritarianism items ranging considerably but with frequent middle and lower averages, while the averages for the numerous Republican caucuses were mostly clustered toward higher-end scores, thus indicating significantly stronger support of Republican legislators for authoritarian attitudes and ideas.[19]

Politicized authoritarianism is not limited to political leaders. Numerous conservative media and religious figures with social and political influence, most with Republican inclinations, have operated out of an aggressively arch-conservative, often authoritarian framing of society. These include major Republican figures such as right-wing talk show host Rush Limbaugh, who became influential among conservatives by the late 1980s. In recent decades, an array of far-right television and radio commentators have gained many devoted conservative followers who accept their often politically authoritarian views.

Also consequential in the conservative political and social resurgence of recent decades have been the activities of numerous right-wing religious leaders. One key example is Reverend Jerry Falwell, a central political figure of the Christian right and co-founder of the influential conservative Moral Majority organization in the late 1970s. Prior to his work in building Christian right politics in the 1970s and 1980s, Falwell had been a white advocate of black racial subordination and had taken strong segregationist and other racist positions in his numerous white-framed commentaries and sermons. In the late 1950s, for instance, he had strongly opposed the 1954 *Brown* v. *Board of Education* decision on segregationist grounds: "If Chief Justice Warren and his associates . . . had desired to do the Lord's will, I am quite confident that the 1954 decision would never have been made. The facilities should be separate. When God has drawn a line of distinction, we should not attempt to cross that line."[20] He easily mixed strong authoritarian and white-racist frames. The old racist hierarchy was divinely ordained, and the Supreme Court had violated God's racist law. Falwell, like many other Christian conservatives, advocated and funded private segregated Christian academies for white children as a bold privatization response to the civil rights movement and government desegregation efforts.[21]

During the 1960s Falwell preached strong sermons from a extensive white-racist framing. He preached against the civil rights movement and the black ministers who were leading it. In a famous sermon on "Ministers and Marches," Falwell attacked the "sincerity and nonviolent intentions of some civil rights leaders such as Dr. Martin Luther King, Jr., Mr. James Farmer, and others, who are known to have left wing associations."[22] Falwell condemned them for their involvement as religious leaders in secular political matters—a view he himself later violated dramatically in his own political activities. Like many white religious leaders in the South, he condemned the 1964 Civil Rights Act and even invited segregationist politicians like Lester Maddox and George Wallace to the *Old Time Gospel Hour*, a religious television program.[23] Very evident in Falwell's extensive activities is the dramatic intertwining of evangelical religion, support for antiblack racism, and political activism against integration and other progressive social changes. As it had for centuries, conservative religion again often backed conservative political-economic perspectives and actions.

Most strikingly, perhaps, Falwell's Moral Majority organization sought to Christianize a fallen America with substantial political action, especially on religious-right "pro-family" themes. Other Christian right activists, like television evangelist Pat Robertson, likewise worked hard to get Christian right voters to support conservative politicians. Together with other religious conservatives, Robertson created the important and influential Christian Coalition in the 1980s. Hundreds of thousands of mostly white conservatives joined in extensive political activities of various Christian right groups, including voter registration, posting signs, and circulating information on political candidates in churches. They began to have great influence in Republican organizations. Over the decades, they have had a significant influence on most Republican state committees, controlling more than half of them at certain points in time. These Christian right groups have indeed played a major role in the conservative resurgence that has taken place since the 1970s, including the strong conservative control of much of the Republican Party. During the late 1970s and 1980s, moreover, they were very important in getting out white evangelical and other conservative voters for Republican candidates like Ronald Reagan and George H. W. Bush.[24]

In addition to "pro-family" and "pro-life" themes, these groups have frequently emphasized other political themes, including renewed negative attacks on big government, with its often thinly disguised racial meanings, and strong positive assertions about "free market" capitalism. As historian Kim Phillips-Fein has suggested from her data, the Christian anti-government crusade has repeatedly been "bound up with some sense of protecting a world ordered by divinity. The market and the church are close companions in a single vision that reviles any conscious, collective effort to shape society. Back in the 1970s, Jerry Falwell could quote [right-wing economist] Milton Friedman as comfortably as the Bible."[25]

Some Sources of the Conservative Resurgence

Commonplace in the Christian right movement and the conservative revitalization more generally have been recurring signs of considerable white racial anger, resentment, and fear, which are commonly part of a deeper white racial framing of society. We have previously noted the emergence of the strong reaction against the civil rights movement and government efforts at racial desegregation. Based on many hours of interviews with Christian right leaders, attendance at worship services, and listening to their radio programs, Max Blumenthal has demonstrated that these deeper racial issues undergirded much conservative political thinking and activism by the growing Christian right in this era. By the 1970s, as many whites abandoned Jim Crow and much of its more overt segregationist discourse, the deeper racial resentment and fears that many whites felt, including Christian right leaders, were just below the surface and often shifted into what Blumenthal calls the "more palatable moral crusade" of political conservatism.[26] As we have already seen, and will observe again, much of this more recent racial framing and fear was not really new but a continuation of old racial framing and fear of racial change.

While the relationships and interactions of most white and black Americans did change with the end of Jim Crow segregation, albeit most evidently in the public sphere and to varying degrees depending on the region, a majority of whites were unwilling to give up their still significant white privileges and power in most major institutional areas. Recall from Chapter 4 that much white conservative political activity in this particular era was energized by white bitterness about the civil rights movement and government actions bringing changes in traditional white privileges and patterns. After Jim Crow's demise, the dominant white racial framing in most areas of the country was altered in some ways—such as by softening some old racist imagery, at least as presented in public, or by emphasizing notions of equal opportunity as the supposed new societal reality. Yet many of the essentials of the old white racial frame remained, if somewhat disguised in public with codewords such as "big government" and "property rights" that we noted previously. A majority of whites in this 1970s–1980s era, as well as later on, still opposed or begrudged the racial desegregation and other changes stemming from civil rights efforts, including their often disruptive impact on white status and power in society.[27]

A great many whites acted politically on their racial resentments and fears. Since this 1970s–1980s era, the Republican Party has become a party heavily dominated by white Christian right conservatives and other white conservatives. Republican liberals, and even moderates in most areas, no longer have much of a political home there. Republican Party leaders and activists have frequently moved to articulating assertively the barely disguised racial framing and coded language of whites who fear major institutional integration and other significant changes in traditional white status, privileges, and power. In addition, these leaders have mostly abandoned serious efforts to recruit many African American voters, and certain other voters of color, into the Republican Party. Not surprisingly, as we have seen, African American voters moved to yet stronger commitments to the Democratic Party and many of its political candidates.

The Ronald Reagan Campaigns: Shifting Racial Strategies

After Richard Nixon was forced to resign in disgrace in 1974 because of his felony involvement in the election break-in at the Washington, D.C. Watergate complex, his vice president Gerald Ford became a relatively moderate Republican president. During Ford's relatively brief term, the former actor and California governor, Ronald Reagan, became ever more politically visible and a key contender for the Republican nomination for president in 1976.

Reagan was often given to grand political speeches that captured attention, many of which called up old nationalistic themes. Thus, at a 1974 conservative conference Reagan gave a speech explicitly underscoring the age-old American exceptionalism:

> Standing on the tiny deck of the *Arbella* in 1630 off the Massachusetts coast, John Winthrop said, 'We will be as a city upon a hill.' . . . Well, we have not dealt falsely with our God. . . . We cannot escape our destiny, nor should we try to do so. The leadership of the free world was thrust upon us. . . . And we are today, the last best hope of man on earth.[28]

Recall from Chapter 1 the early idea of the new America being exceptional and a God-ordained model for all people to admire. Over the centuries this religiously tinted view has regularly been seen in many politicians' portrayal of U.S. society as exceptionally virtuous in comparison to other nations, which was Reagan's periodically expressed view of American exceptionalism. Central to his essentially authoritarian political and racial framing was the idea that the United States had a God-ordained role to be the world's dominant nation and spread its elite's ideas about liberty across the world. As with earlier versions of this exceptionalism, some enemies were required, as exemplified by a Soviet Union periodically called by Reagan the "evil empire" when he became president in the 1980s. In his commonplace political view the world was quite Manichaean—a world of good versus evil, of "good guys" versus "bad guys."[29]

Later on, campaigning against Gerald Ford for the Republican Party nomination in 1976, Reagan conducted an arch-conservative and racist campaign. Following the lead of former segregationists like George Wallace, and courting Wallace's dedicated white voters, Reagan pressed for a constitutional amendment that would end desegregation by means of school busing and also for an end to government affirmative action. He appealed to many whites' fears and their concerns to return to certain traditional racial folkways and patterns. Clearly reflecting the interests of whites opposed to much of the Johnson era's racial and other social reforms, Reagan regularly used mythological stories of "welfare chiselers" and similarly coded racial language that called up in many white minds images of undeserving blacks. At one point, Reagan's white supporters circulated material suggesting that President Ford would put a black Republican on his ticket as vice president, at the time an idea very disturbing to many white Republicans. Moreover, by his often racialized political tactics, Reagan helped to drive out many of the modest number of black Republicans still remaining in the party and to bring in yet more white voters who were angry about past and continuing changes in U.S. racial patterns.[30]

These strategies were not new. When Reagan had run for governor of California in 1966, he had made clear his opposition to laws protecting people of color against housing discrimination, and he won a major political victory. Moreover, when Nixon decided to run for president in 1968, his main Republican rival was Reagan, and even an internal memo of the Nixon campaign noted "Reagan's strength derives from personal charisma, glamour, but primarily the ideological fervor of the Right and the emotional distress of those who fear or resent the Negro, and who expect Reagan to somehow keep him 'in his place' or at least to echo their own anger and frustration."[31] At that time, and later in the 1970s, Reagan was a master of white framing and, thus, of barely disguised racial codewords for black Americans and anti-civil-rights views, not only "welfare chiselers" but also the language of "law and order" and "get tough on crime." Reagan also openly misrepresented the character of racial events in the 1960s, with comments that during that time a virtuous "white community hasn't lifted a finger against the Negroes,"[32] even though in that era many black civil rights leaders and protesters had been injured or killed by white officials and white mobs.

After losing to Ford in 1976, Reagan came back in 1980 to run again for the U.S. presidency. During and after his successful campaign for president, he again sent many racial signals to white voters in all class groups. He famously began his presidential campaign by asserting strongly a "states' rights" doctrine, and for this provocative statement he intentionally picked Philadelphia, Mississippi, a town where civil rights workers had been lynched by white supremacists in the 1960s. Reagan's intent was evidently to make a symbolic and coded appeal to conservative whites. In this way he had shifted somewhat from his earlier political tactics. Now in 1980 he mostly made racial political appeals without using explicit racist language or imagery and usually avoided bringing up civil rights issues unless asked.

Soon after Reagan was elected the key Republican political operative, Lee Atwater, explained this new strategy and its white-framed codewords:

> You start out in 1954 by saying, "Nigger, nigger, nigger." By 1968, you can't say "nigger"—that hurts you. Backfires. So you say stuff like forced busing, states' rights, and all that stuff. You're getting so abstract now you're talking about cutting taxes, and all these things you're talking about are totally economic things, and a byproduct of them is blacks get hurt worse than whites.[33]

Interestingly, too, in his 1980 campaign Reagan made occasional attempts to at least appear in public as moderate on poverty and race issues by meeting with a few black leaders, speaking to the National Urban League, and visiting one impoverished community in New York City. This last event took place right after his famous Philadelphia, Mississippi speech. Yet, during this visit an angry group of black New Yorkers argued with candidate Reagan and, as one political analysis notes, "probably helped him shore up his support with the white backlash, since television captured Reagan yelling at poor blacks in anger."[34] By these various actions Reagan more or less protected himself against direct charges of a personal racist orientation, and thereby succeeded in appearing relatively moderate on racial matters, at least to much of the white population. Later, in his second (1984) presidential campaign, Reagan mostly abandoned this pretense of political moderation on civil rights and made no significant attempts to court black voters. By then much of the black population had become upset with his administration's backtracking on civil rights matters, and many were supporting the first strong black Democratic candidate for the presidency, liberal Democrat Jesse Jackson. The success Jackson had in several Democratic primaries further disturbed many white voters, and the Republican Party again took advantage of this new political reality.[35]

Clearly, in his 1980s presidential campaigns Reagan and key members of his political team decided to appeal mostly in a less overt way to the racist framing in the minds of much of the white electorate in the South and the North, and to implicitly link that framing to such influential conservative political themes as states' rights, lower taxes, and big government. His conservative team effectively used the "southern strategy" of Barry Goldwater and Richard Nixon by targeting southern and border state whites. In his 1980s elections Reagan won the electoral votes of southern states in part with thinly concealed appeals to many whites' preferences for more traditional racial patterns and to their concerns over desegregation and other racial changes. In addition, Reagan and many of his supporters periodically tried to link the Democratic Party to direct responsibility for U.S. "racial problems."[36]

Between the Reagan 1980s and the present, many working-class and middle-class whites, particularly in southern states and various suburban areas, have moved to firm support of the Republican Party at least in part for an array of reasons growing out of racial desegregation and related racial changes in the 1960s–1980s period. Indeed, it appears that in many white minds the Democratic Party was becoming too black-oriented in its party inclinations and positioning in the U.S. political system.

The Reagan Administration: Weakening Civil Rights Enforcement

In January 1981, with Reagan's inauguration, a much more conservative political era made its official debut. Once in the White House, President Reagan and his many conservative white (and some other) colleagues there and in Congress generally operated from a white-suburban or other white-enclave approach emphasizing a distinctive white political framing. Although as California governor and president, Reagan had sometimes said he opposed discrimination in principle, he also strongly opposed much civil rights enforcement in practice, including aggressive enforcement of the major civil rights laws on employment, voting, and housing. In effect, Reagan operated like Nixon "in constructing a politics and a strategy of governing that attacked policies targeted toward blacks and other minorities . . . a conservative politics that had the effect of polarizing the electorate along racial lines."[37] During his administration the assertive racial framing, including the racial resentment and fears, of many whites often got translated into political action.

During the 1970s and 1980s the increasingly numerous Republican-oriented political organizations and think tanks worked aggressively in pressing the White House, Congress, and the courts to weaken or eliminate antidiscrimination programs, affirmative action programs, and other state and federal government programs designed to help those who were racially and economically oppressed. Not surprisingly, President Reagan was frequently receptive and worked with his Republican subordinates, some recruited from these conservative organizations, to weaken federal civil rights enforcement and investigation agencies, including the U.S. Commission on Civil Rights and the Equal Employment Opportunity Commission (EEOC). In a book on his Reagan years, one important Reagan cabinet member, moderate Republican Terrel Bell, reported that at major White House meetings he sometimes pressed for equal opportunity and strong enforcement of civil rights, but *never* got any support from other members of the administration in the White House or the Department of Justice.[38]

Key white advisers in the Reagan White House sought to bring several black conservatives into the administration, in large part to buttress their anti-civil-rights efforts. Soon after Reagan's election in 1980 a conservative think tank, the Institute for Contemporary Studies, organized a San Francisco conference that was attended by leading black conservatives, including Clarence Thomas, and that tried to generate enthusiasm for Reagan-type "free enterprise" solutions to black problems and thereby to counter the goals of major black civil rights leaders. Edwin Meese, a major Reagan adviser and later Attorney General, was a key player in this important event. Moreover, near the beginning of his second term Reagan called together about 20 black conservatives again to counter the black civil rights leadership's usually critical assessments of Republican actions on civil rights.[39] Over recent decades other Republican political officials have attempted to do the same, though it is important to note that one recent analysis estimates the percentage of conservatives among black leaders to be only about 2 percent.[40]

Reagan also appointed a few black conservatives to non-cabinet administrative positions, including Clarence Pendleton as the controversial head of the U.S. Commission on Civil Rights. The new conservative black head of the EEOC, future arch-conservative Supreme Court justice Clarence Thomas, supported lawsuits there for victims of individual discrimination, but moved the agency away from the important class-action lawsuits seeking redress for extensive institutional discrimination in U.S. workplaces. The new administration weakened or eliminated other antidiscrimination programs, affirmative action programs, and school desegregation efforts, doubtless with an eye to pleasing white voters. Federal agencies such as the FBI were used to police and reduce some voter registration efforts and turnout campaigns aimed at voters of color. Initially, Reagan opposed a federal holiday honoring Dr. Martin Luther King, Jr., and an extension of the Voting Rights Act, which he had once described as "humiliating to the South," although he eventually signed the legislation. Reagan also supported significant tax exemptions for the many private all-white schools that were clear examples of the use of privatization strategies to destroy or counter public school desegregation. Moreover, in the late 1980s Reagan vetoed new U.S. civil rights legislation and also legislation imposing economic sanctions on South Africa's white-run apartheid government, both of which vetoes were so extreme that they were overridden in rare legislative procedures by Congress.[41]

The Reagan White House was well known for an openly racist climate. A major Chicago newspaper noted that Michael Deaver, a major Reagan adviser, had a "penchant for telling racist jokes about blacks" and that these "jolted associates and members of the White House press corps."[42] Other White House aides liked racist jokes, and some referred to Dr. Martin Luther King, Jr., as "Martin Lucifer Coon" and to Arab peoples as "sand niggers." In his important book on his sometimes difficult time in the administration, Terrel Bell reported encountering such racist commentary among important Reagan aides. In addition, James Watt, Reagan's Secretary of the Interior, was forced to resign from his position because of mocking comments he made about having "a black, a woman, two Jews and a cripple" on a leasing panel.[43] During his last week in office in 1989 President Reagan also showed off his personal white framing in barbed comments about black civil rights leaders: "Sometimes I wonder if they really want what they say they want, because some of those leaders are doing very well leading organizations based on keeping alive the feeling that they're victims of prejudice."[44] Echoing comments often heard on the racist right to the present day, outgoing President Reagan was of course talking about some black men and women who had devoted their careers, and sometimes risked their lives, to end the institutional racism that was still widespread in U.S. society.

The totality of Reagan's and his subordinates' white racial framing and associated administrative efforts was catastrophic for the interests of African Americans and other Americans of color in regard to civil rights enforcement and the country's previous, albeit slow, movement to reduce racial and class inequalities. As the Citizens' Commission on Civil Rights put it, Reagan caused "an across-the-board breakdown in the machinery constructed by six previous administrations to protect civil rights."[45]

In addition, by the mid-1980s the conservative Republican appointments to federal courts were having a major effect in further weakening the impact and enforcement of the 1960s civil rights laws and other antidiscrimination regulations. During and after the Reagan presidency numerous conservative, mostly white, federal judges ruled that group-remedy programs for racial discrimination violated the Constitution, which they asserted only recognizes *individual* rights to not face discrimination. For example, in 1989 a relatively conservative Supreme Court, with seven Republican and only two Democratic appointees, produced *City of Richmond, Virginia* v. *J. A. Croson Co.*, a major ruling that knocked down a Richmond city government program designed to remedy massive past discrimination against businesses run by people of color by offering modest government contract set-asides for the latter.[46] The white court majority naively ruled that the city government had not demonstrated that there was enough significant antiblack discrimination there to set up a modest set-aside program, although local officials had presented substantial statistics showing that, in a city that was 50 percent black in population, less than 1 percent of government business went to black firms. In this era the conservative, mostly white justices on the Supreme Court intentionally limited the enforcement and impact of several 1960s and later civil rights laws by rejecting the legal relevance of plaintiffs' arguments showing institutional and systemic racism. The Court's lack of fair representation of people of color in its membership in this era doubtless had a negative impact in numerous decisions affecting racial discrimination.[47]

The Reagan Era: Government Cutbacks and Privatization at All Levels
While the heavily white Republican engineers of the 1980s conservative resurgence often claimed they were colorblind and that their conservative actions in regard to various government programs had nothing to do with

the country's racist history, in fact their approach to numerous local, state, and federal government programs did frequently reflect their white racial backgrounds, concerns, framing, and interests. Not only did they usually have a religious-like faith in the superiority of the "free market," but those working at the federal level were frequently from white suburban areas and often had significant hostility to important concerns of central city residents, especially those who were poor, working class, or not white, as well as to numerous urban-oriented government programs put into effect since the 1960s. Not surprisingly, they often accented private enterprise approaches to urban issues and supported the weakening of progressive government reform programs. We have already observed some of this approach in their cutting back or weakening of civil rights enforcement and affirmative action programs.

One observes an anti-labor, free market approach in the way that Reagan, and his Republican successors, packed the National Labor Relations Board and other labor-related federal agencies with mostly business conservatives. As a result, these Republican-influenced government agencies often worked against the organizing and other rights of labor union members, who were increasingly workers of color. Numerous labor laws were unenforced or weakly enforced. In this era private corporations had increased their power relative to that of ordinary workers and labor unions.[48]

The fact that many influential Republican leaders in the federal government have come from historically white suburban areas, especially those of southern and border cities, suggests that their typically conservative, often dogmatic or authoritarian perspectives have probably been influenced, at least in part, by years of white resistance efforts to the desegregation of public schools and other public facilities, as well as to government and other residential desegregation efforts.[49] Consider for a moment the importance of this racial and spatial background. For many decades, racially segregated housing patterns and the government institutions that maintain them have been a spatially revealed example of white privilege. Under pressure to desegregate, whites have generally worked hard to keep the privileges that segregated housing areas have brought to them for generations. This residential segregation prized by so many whites has long generated de facto segregated schools, recreational facilities, and other public services. From the beginning of the 1960s' desegregation movements many whites joined in organizing against school and other desegregation because they sought to maintain their numerous white privileges, including the better government services they often got in their heavily white residential areas, public services frequently unavailable to or less adequate for black Americans or other Americans of color in other residential areas.[50]

Thus, the 1970s and 1980s white resistance to the civil rights movement and further desegregation involved not just a fearful racial framing, but also a deep concern to protect ongoing material and spatial privileges. Indeed, one study of white support for local and state anti-busing and anti-tax movements over several decades by Clarence Lo found that whites "sought to maintain advantages for their racial or ethnic group in the consumption of government services" and were fighting to keep the "customary patterns of residential segregation and school policies that sent white, middle class children to the white school in the white neighborhood."[51] Even in states like California the government efforts at reducing overt housing discrimination were periodically knocked down by coalitions of mostly white homeowners and realtors who worked aggressively to pass state ballot initiatives designed to veto fair housing legislation.

Where whites have not been able to prevent significant school and other types of public desegregation, they have often moved to the privatization of important public services like public schools. Recall Randolph Hohle's showing that in reaction to the civil rights movement in southern areas many white conservatives developed a public-equals-blacks political perspective that involved "a language of privatization that degraded all things public as 'black' and inferior and all things private as 'white' and superior."[52] Never just southern in appeal, this perspective accenting privatization's superiority, and the often associated public-equals-blacks theme, has characterized much of the contemporary conservative approach to numerous government programs since both the Nixon and Reagan presidential eras. Indeed, there is a specific historical linkage of the southern privatization approach to Reagan himself. After running his own surprisingly strong presidential campaigns in the 1970s, Alabama's former segregationist governor, George Wallace, helped to reinforce at the national level a racialized privatization approach to public schools and other public programs, which he strongly supported, when he dramatically appeared on stage with Reagan at the latter's famous Philadelphia, Mississippi speech in 1980.[53] Clearly, the impact of local and state privatization efforts in regard to threatened or actual desegregation had proceeded well beyond southern areas to influence actions in other regions. Apparently, this vigorous privatization approach also influenced the Reagan administration's privatizing, reducing, or defunding of various important government social programs, including important civil rights programs and agencies.

Moreover, since the 1960s and 1970s, as George Lipsitz has shown, many whites' segregated suburban neighborhoods and social networks have continued to provide the "main sources of mobilization for tax limitation, defunding the public sector, and denying social services to minorities and immigrants."[54] Some California research shows that heavily white areas that are well segregated from people of color are the most likely to support state ballot propositions aimed at repealing fair housing, limiting taxes, and targeting undocumented immigrants. Once residential housing is racially segregated, whites in the middle- and upper-class suburban and other residential areas have over time been able to keep themselves mostly isolated spatially from Americans of color, and they can maintain their racially hierarchical position in part through politically enforced and racialized land use and discriminatory real-estate policies. Over time these whites' accumulating racial privileges get translated into spatial and geographical realities and enable them to claim they are just "racially unremarked homeowners, citizens, and taxpayers whose preferred policies just happen to sustain white privilege and power."[55]

Certain of their racial privileges are regularly translated into material and spatial realities that do not appear on the surface to be racially rooted or connected. These material and spatial privileges, in turn, enable these more affluent whites to have much greater political influence at the local, state, and federal government levels in regard to cutting back or defunding government social programs that they view as not benefitting them and to reducing taxes on themselves as well-off Americans. We should note too that given the persisting and strong segregated ecology of everyday living, most whites spend very little time interacting with blacks, especially on an equal-status basis. The absence of significant equal-status experiences with black families and peers because of intentionally segregated neighborhoods and communities contributes greatly to unfamiliarity with African Americans. Most whites' framing of African Americans, thus, usually reflects the centuries-old white racist framing. Not surprisingly, residential and other spatial isolation constantly reinforces this racist framing for a great many white Americans, including those who serve at high state and federal government levels and frequently have substantial power to take government action greatly affecting the lives of black Americans, as well as other Americans of color.

The Reagan Administration and Criminalization of the Black Population

Very important to the Reagan administration was the famous "war on drugs." By the early 1980s the Reagan administration had moved federal employees working on white-collar crime to this new drug war, which accented drug use and selling in communities of color and not in white middle-class communities. There were also large increases in funding for drug programs, and local police departments could now aggressively expand their personnel and equipment with huge amounts of federal money flowing to them. Aggressive media promotion of the new "war" was greatly encouraged by the Reagan administration. Significantly, too, this drug war expansion coincided with some economic interests seeking to expand the U.S. prison complex. Beginning in the 1970s a loose coalition of corporate interests and local real-estate, other business, and political interests were working to create an expanded prison complex, mainly for profit and local economic development reasons.[56]

Even though at the time most Americans showed in opinion polls little concern about drug issues, the Reagan administration still accelerated its efforts because, as legal scholar Michelle Alexander suggests, this drug war "had little to do with public concern about drugs and much to do with [white] public concern about race." She adds that the appeal of Republican officials was successful in showing that ordinary whites were again "willing to forego economic and structural reform in exchange for an apparent effort to put blacks back 'in their place.'"[57] The current system of racial oppression, including that imposed through our often segregated and racially discriminatory prison system, does indeed put a large percentage of black Americans back in their subordinated racial "place," one that has numerous parallels to old Jim Crow segregation. As noted previously, many whites in the South and elsewhere were encouraged to be, and were, very concerned about the black population set free by the end of legal segregation. Many in the elite and general public were upset with the racial realities generated by the 1960s–1970s civil rights movement and the remedial enforcement and affirmative action government efforts for African Americans and other Americans of color. Numerous white members of Congress who had voted *against* civil rights laws also pressed for anti-crime legislation focusing on drug crimes and other urban street crime. Moreover, in this era survey researchers discovered that whites' racial attitudes, and not actual crime rates, were the significant factors in whether whites supported aggressive anti-crime measures.[58]

In Chapter 4 we saw the close connection between the negative white reactions to the civil rights movement and the way in which black protesters have been criminalized in white minds for decades. Recently, researcher Naomi Murakawa has strongly underscored the point we made previously that many whites, especially white elites, had in their minds already criminalized black Americans and their civil rights protest movements in the 1940s and 1950s, well before the 1960s white concerns about supposed black criminality.[59] Actually, one can find such racist framing of black Americans even centuries earlier. For example, a 1690s preamble to a South Carolina colony's slavery law conspicuously reveals the white elite lawmakers' views of enslaved African Americans: They "are of barbarous, wild, savage natures, and . . . constitutions, laws and orders, should in this Province be made and enacted, for the good regulating and ordering of them, as may restrain the disorders, rapines and inhumanity, to which they are naturally prone and inclined."[60] This language not only shows vigorously stereotyped views of black Americans as uncivilized, but also notions of them as dangerous and criminal, a distinctive legal and moral stereotyping in which whites were then, as now, viewed as having the superior "laws and orders." Undeniably, white views of black criminality accented over recent decades have not been newly created, but have come relatively easily to white leaders and others, including those in the criminal justice system, who have likely learned them in the age-old racist framing inherited from parents, other relatives, and peers.[61]

In the 1980s, accelerated by the Reagan administration, white officials at various government levels—police, prosecutors, judges, and members of Congress—sharply accented an authoritarian, get-tough, "law and order" approach to drug crime and other street crime by people of color and began a dramatic increase in the imprisonment of Americans of color, most especially black Americans. Facilitating this aggressive criminalizing and policing, a conservative Supreme Court majority has also over time allowed a move away from important constitutional protections, such as allowing police to do warrant-less searches in this war on drugs; they also have permitted racial-profiling discrimination in police stops of various kinds.[62] Significantly, however, there was no crime wave to generate the dramatic expansion of law enforcement in the Reagan 1980s; indeed, U.S. crime rates had actually been falling. Given too the reality that whites were using illegal drugs at least as often as blacks were, clearly black Americans were singled out by the criminal justice system in an extremely discriminatory way and intentionally criminalized in the increasing police and prosecutorial attacks of the war on drugs. Since this era most of those arrested in these drug policing efforts have not been held for major drug crimes, but for simple drug possession; most have not been involved in violent crimes or significant drug dealing. In this new prosecutorial world there have also been great increases in prison sentences, including for modest drug offenses.[63]

The impact on black America of this so-called war on drugs and other street crime has been highly discriminatory and extensive now for decades. This elite-led crusade unmistakably reveals the contemporary reality of systemic racism. Law professor Michelle Alexander has demonstrated how the U.S. policing/prison complex has become a legal system of Jim-Crow-like segregation in which a great many black Americans get arrested and imprisoned at highly disproportionate rates for crimes committed as often by whites. Once caught up in the judicial system and prison complex, they are very seriously handicapped when they are freed. Having a record, they often lose the right to vote, serve on juries, get decent-paying jobs, rent public housing, and secure normal loans of various kinds. As a result of these state-imposed difficulties, they frequently end up back in prison. Such extensive imprisonment and denial of post-prison citizens' rights, in their turn, have had a severe and lasting negative impact on many black families and all black communities.[64] Once again, these imposed barriers have definitely kept many black Americans and their families from real competition with whites for formerly all-white privileges and positions and thus from significant socioeconomic movement up in U.S. society. More-over, this discriminatory white-controlled policing and prosecution, which accelerated in the Reagan 1980s, has come to mirror much in the old southern segregation patterns, except that it is now legal and framed as "real black criminality" and not about whites' racist framing or fears of black Americans.

Resistance to Reagan's Arch-Conservatism

The Reagan administration's reactionary backtracking on major New Deal and Great Society civil rights programs and other socially progressive programs generated significant resistance from political leaders from communities of color and numerous union leaders, as well as their multitudinous constituents. For example, in the 1980s the multiracial Rainbow Coalition registered two million new voters, created multiracial organizations in many states, and won political power at the local level in a few states. Newly registered voters helped elect numerous liberal and moderate Democrats to Congress in 1984 and subsequent years, members of Congress who tried hard to keep the Reagan administration from making major changes in civil rights and other important social reform programs.[65]

The Reagan administration's sustained weakening of civil rights enforcement was met with recurring resistance from numerous Democrats in Congress and important civil rights groups such as the Leadership Conference on Civil Rights. Often fighting uphill battles on civil rights enforcement since at least the 1970s, the black and other liberal Democratic members of Congress have regularly pressed for expanded civil rights legislation and other antidiscrimination legislation. One reason for these recurring efforts is the significant increase in members of Congress from communities of color. For example, from the mid-1960s to the present black representation in the U.S. House grew from just five members to 42 members. The important Congressional Black Caucus (CBC) was formed in the 1970s, one major result of the ending of legal segregation. Since its founding, the CBC has kept pressure on Republican and Democratic presidents to support programs to positively improve the civil rights and socioeconomic conditions of Americans of color. In 1975, the CBC began the long effort to get a Dr. Martin Luther King, Jr., national holiday, which finally became law, in spite of President Reagan's resistance, in 1983. The CBC successfully pressed for extensions of the Voting Rights Act and its amendments, again against the strong resistance of the Reagan administration. And in 1985–1986 the CBC played an important role in efforts to prevent significant loans to and investments in the apartheid-centered, highly racist South Africa, including passage of some U.S. legislation. President Reagan's veto of this consequential legislation was overridden by Congress. Since the Reagan era, the CBC has continued to play a very major role in pressing for new civil rights legislation and related political legislation, such as that facilitating new voter registration across the country.[66]

The George H. W. Bush Era: More Pro-White Strategies

The 1980s Reagan administration played a central role in the large-scale conservative resurgence of recent decades and moved to implement many of the very conservative goals of the contemporary Republican Party. Quite clearly, the Reagan team utilized and inspired much far-right and authoritarian social and political thinking and led a major right turn in the contemporary political era. Moreover, much of the aggressive attack on the civil rights and other progressive domestic policies of earlier Democratic administrations has continued to be implemented in conservative Republican administrations and Republican-controlled congresses put in place since Reagan's terms as president. Thus, Reagan's vice president, the wealthy George H. W. Bush, successfully ran for office following Reagan and provided yet more major steps in this very-conservative direction, including on numerous important civil rights and equal opportunity issues.

In his legendary 1988 election campaign, Bush gave great emphasis to themes of law and order, and his campaign teams explicitly targeted black and urban criminality for much political gain. Bush and his Republican advisers continued the intensively pro-white strategy used successfully in the Reagan campaigns and administration. Party officials again built much of his presidential campaign using the white-oriented southern and suburban strategies to attract conservative white Democrats and independents into the Republican Party and to ensure an excellent turnout by Republican voters, the overwhelming majority of whom were now white.

One effective strategy involved the use of racialized campaign advertisements. As we have previously observed, since the 1970s the increased importance, especially in public settings, of less overtly racist language has pressured many white political operatives and officials, including Republican Party leaders and consultants, to send more implicit and coded racial messages to the white public, instead of the more explicit racial messages of earlier political eras. In this era, as now, the Republican Party officially supported racial integration in abstract terms. Nonetheless, Republican Party officials have effectively used, and often pioneered, implicitly racist appeals aimed at conservative white voters in various class groups. Indeed, in the contemporary era numerous influential advertising campaigns have been implicitly racist. That is, they are campaigns that most whites, and many others, may not "see" as racist and that appear at first glance to be silent on racial matters. Explicit appeals use specific racist words and language from a hard version of the old racial frame. As social scientist Tali Mendelberg notes, however, implicit racial appeals do not use overtly racist terminology, but make use of coded words, such as "law and order" and "urban crime," and visual images that are also effective in communicating coded racial appeals.[67]

During the 1988 Bush presidential campaign conservative Republicans made effective use of such implicit racial appeals, especially in the famous

"Willie" Horton ads. During the campaign a conservative Republican group linked to the Bush organization conducted an advertising campaign using a strong visual image of a disheveled black murderer and rapist (actually named *William* Horton), who had participated in a Massachusetts prison-release program during the years in which the Democratic candidate for president, Michael Dukakis, was governor of Massachusetts. This was obviously an attempt to recruit white voters to the Republican Party and away from Democratic candidate Dukakis. Without using explicit racist terminology, this political campaign still targeted white voters with an aggressive and visual message about threats of black "street crime," and thereby articulated a barely disguised, menacing racial message to white male and female voters. Noticeably, Republican strategists did not use prominent visual images of the more common rape threat to white women —white male rapists—in their 1988 campaign ads. This omission signaled that these prominently discussed ads were indeed a racial appeal; the intent was to make such an appeal without appearing to do so, at least in the eyes of a great many whites.[68]

We might note that a somewhat similar ad was used two years later by Democrat-turned-Republican Senator Jesse Helms in a difficult re-election campaign, one in which he used political consultants then working for President Bush. Senator Helms, the North Carolina Republican mentioned in a prior chapter, likewise played into the fears of racial change among many white voters, including white middle-class voters. In one major television advert he falsely attacked his Democratic opponent, a black candidate then ahead in the polls, as favoring racial quotas. Helms's effective advertisement operated with a strong photo and visual impact, this time showing white hands with a job rejection letter and a verbal caption saying: "You needed that job and you were the best qualified. But they had to give it to a minority because of a racial quota. Is that really fair?"[69] No openly racist language was used, just codewords like "racial quota." Not surprisingly, a substantial majority of North Carolina's white voters that year opted for Helms, and he was re-elected. Such campaign ads underscore the fact that perhaps the most negative impact of implicitly racist ads is often not on the political candidates involved or the voting process, but on the groups of color that are actually targeted by them. Thus, ads like these centered on a black prisoner and on white hands implicitly sustained the old racist frame's accent on the social and moral superiority of whites and the social and moral inferiority of people of color.

Over the four years of his presidency, George H. W. Bush and his Republican advisers and associates extended the Reagan rollbacks of certain government equal opportunity programs and other civil rights programs, opposed important new civil rights legislation, and attacked various strategies of moderate multiculturalism in public speeches. Bush's key advisers broke up negotiations over renewed civil rights legislation between civil rights officials and top corporate executives. Bush himself gave speeches attacking important courses on college campuses that teach about the forgotten histories of racism and sexism in U.S. society, picking up on the conservative cliché of "political correctness" to attack these usually data-based programs dealing with the history and contemporary reality of racial and gender oppression. Bush also placed great emphasis on the Reagan-initiated "drug war" and accented urban drug use, thereby racializing the "war" once again.[70]

Moreover, in a bold political move, Bush appointed the very conservative black judge, Clarence Thomas, to the Supreme Court, claiming at the time that he was one of the top legal minds in the country. As Jane Mayer and Jill Abramson note, "In Clarence Thomas, Bush found a nominee whose personal contradictions perfectly matched his own political ones. Thomas was a black conservative who could symbolize diversity while denouncing the very concept of affirmative action."[71] Thomas was well known as the former EEOC head who had often operated there out of a very individualistic, white-oriented framing in dealing with legal issues involving institutionalized racism.

According to unofficial biographical books dealing with his life, Thomas has suggested that the dream of equality articulated by the 1960s civil rights movement leaders was contaminated in the political shift to providing remedial programs, such as various types of affirmative action, to undo the harm done to Americans of color by legal segregation and continuing discrimination. Over the decades Justice Thomas appears to have long accepted, relatively uncritically, the common white perspective on numerous antidiscrimination and affirmative action programs as unfair preferential treatment significantly hurting whites, even though Thomas himself benefitted greatly from affirmative action programs earlier as a student and as a Republican administrator and judicial appointee. Thomas has been reported to be uncomfortable around most black activist leaders, and in a famous newspaper article he was quoted as saying that all civil rights leaders did was "bitch, bitch, bitch, moan and moan, whine and whine." Thomas has also been well known for attacking 1960s Great Society programs, with comments that such social programs were a "narcotic," supposedly seducing black Americans and others away from a conventional work ethic.[72] Evidently, Thomas has also adopted the very negative perspective on social welfare programs articulated by his mentor, President Ronald Reagan, including the latter's notions of black "welfare queens" dependent on undeserved welfare checks, and applied that view to his own sister.[73] In addition, Thomas, a rare black Republican, has often operated out of a variation of the old white racial frame when it comes to his public comments on racial matters and his legal analyses, as Supreme Court justice, of certain racial matters.

The Clinton Era and Republican Control of Congress

In 1992 the Democratic Party managed to win an election after three losses, and Bill Clinton became the new president. As soon as he was inaugurated in 1993, however, this first two-term Democratic president since the 1940s faced great pressure from the corporate elite and more conservative Democratic Party leaders to meet the corporate goals of reducing federal deficits and cutting back on existing social support and welfare programs. Beginning in the late 1970s, the greatly expanded political organization of corporate and small business communities increased pressure not just on Republican Party officials, but also on Democratic Party leaders. The latter also sought out more political and financial support from corporate lobbyists and various business groups.

One obvious effort in this regard was the creation in the 1980s of the Democratic Leadership Council (DLC). These more conservative Democratic leaders aggressively sought closer connections with major elements of the corporate community and pursued numerous policy goals of the corporate sector, including tax and deficit reduction and cutting back social support and welfare programs. These were efforts on the part of the more conservative wing of the Democratic Party, a party that had for decades been committed to major social support and welfare programs, as well as a Keynesian approach to government budget and deficit expansion when unemployment significantly increased. At one point, in apparent frustration, President Clinton even asserted loudly:

> Where are all the Democrats? I hope you're all aware we're all Eisenhower Republicans. We're Eisenhower Republicans here, and we are fighting the Reagan Republicans. We stand for lower deficits and free trade and the bond market. . . . I don't have a goddamn Democratic budget until 1996. None of the investments, none of the things I campaigned on. We must have something for the common man.[74]

He was correct, for this Democratic president and his Democratic Party had incorporated leading white corporate officials into the administration, and they were periodically meeting significant demands of the corporate sector, including demands in regard to the conservative goals of major welfare reform, deficit reduction, and financial deregulation.

Moreover, the sweet smell of the Democratic victory in 1992 did not last. By 1994, the mostly white Christian right voters and other conservative voters, especially in southern areas and in suburban areas in all regions, were yet more influential and successful. Organizing efforts from the 1970s to the 1990s were paying off as many millions of white Christian conservatives were now supporting the Republican Party, and their votes helped the Republican Party win a decisive 1994 mid-term electoral victory in which they captured both Houses of Congress for the first time in decades. This meant even greater conservative Republican control of the House of Representatives—now under southern suburban Republican Newt Gingrich as House Speaker—and Republican control of the Senate for the first time since 1954.[75] For the Democratic Party, this was a major political setback, for it took place not long after the Democrat Bill Clinton had become president. We should note, too, that subsequent congressional and presidential elections have periodically yielded yet more in the way of political benefits to the Republican Party from the extensive Christian right political organization since the 1990s.

Growing substantially in numbers, white suburban voters were clearly very important in these turbulent 1990s elections. One major sign of the demographic and political importance of southern and border states, and often of the mostly white suburban areas there, could be seen in the reality that after 1992 powerful white conservative Republican leaders in Congress mostly came from these areas. These included the very powerful Gingrich, from the Atlanta suburbs, Dick Armey, from the Dallas suburbs, and Tom DeLay, from the Houston suburbs. They also included the powerful southern and border state senators Trent Lott (Mississippi), Mitch McConnell (Kentucky), and Bill Frist (Tennessee). Eventually, they also included the yet more famous Republican Dallasite George W. Bush as president. Coupled with the rise in power of southern Republicans was a significant shift in the Republican percentage of members of the U.S. House who came from the South.[76]

Recall too the previous discussion of white suburbanization and privatization after the major desegregation efforts in various cities and states during the 1960s and 1970s. Since that era the southern, often suburban, Republicans have taken "the politics of white flight to the national stage."[77] Over the years since the 1990s, this politics of white flight and white suburbia has obviously been much more than just a southern phenomenon. Across the country the old conservative accent on free enterprise is now regularly joined with newer emphases on the privatization of existing public services and, unsurprisingly, on sharp reductions in government taxes and numerous domestic social programs that have been thought to be politically untouchable for decades.

After the major congressional victories in the mid-1990s, the Republican leaders in Congress aggressively asserted a very conservative congressional agenda on a variety of free enterprise and socio-racial issues, even more so than in previous decades. In regard to the free enterprise and privatization efforts, consider the powerful Republican senator Phil Gramm (Texas), a former economics professor and a Republican presidential candidate in 1996, who helped to lead the charge to extensively deregulate the U.S. economy. His and other Republican conservatives' efforts, together with those of conservative and moderate Democrats, succeeded in the major deregulation of banks and financial institutions in the 1999 Financial Services Modernization Act and later legislative action. A few years later this corporate-sought, large-scale deregulation would play a major role in the 2007–2008 crash of the U.S. economy and the subsequent major recession. In this period after that pivotal 1994 election, influential Republican leaders thus continued with their very conservative and often authoritarian agenda seeking to eliminate or reduce the scope of many 1930s New Deal and 1960s Great Society government programs. Their targets included corporate and environmental regulation, Medicare, corporate taxation, and civil rights enforcement. The desire was generally to return to an imagined past of traditional religion, free markets, and small government, much of which past was misrepresented or fictional.[78]

Relevant Republican Racial Perspectives and Actions

During and after this Clinton era, in regard to important racial matters, key Republican Party leaders and media commentators seem to have decided their party could become even more one that operated primarily in the interest of white Americans, with still mainly token appeals to Americans of color. As we already noted, from the 1970s onward most Republican leaders and political candidates have demonstrated a distinctive lack of concern for the political or economic interests of African Americans and most other Americans of color, including their interests in more socioeconomic mobility, reducing racial inequalities, and much more societal desegregation.

Since the 1990s, moreover, numerous prominent Republicans have signaled more openly their problematical racial views. Consider, for instance, assertions and arguments made by Senator Bob Dole in 1995 about the lack of white culpability in regard to racial discrimination. At that time Senator Dole, later the losing Republican presidential candidate in 1996, expressed in an interview substantial concern about the many "displaced" white men who had to compete "unfairly" with black workers supposedly favored because of affirmative action programs. He questioned if "people in America," by which he clearly meant white people, should be suffering for racial discrimination "before they were born." While acknowledging "we did discriminate," Dole questioned whether substantial compensation for such racial discrimination and its damage was now due. Evidently, Dole's main concern was with the racial and economic interests of white Americans, and operating out of a white frame he completely ignored the perspectives of Americans of color on past racial oppression and also showed no recognition of the continuing costs of the large-scale discrimination still targeting Americans of color.[79]

In addition, in several speeches and commentaries Patrick Buchanan—a senior adviser to Republican presidents Nixon, Ford, and Reagan and candidate for the Republican presidential nomination in 1992 and 1996—made arguments against multiculturalism and immigration such as this:

"Our Judeo-Christian values are going to be preserved and our Western heritage is going to be handed down to future generations and not dumped on some landfill called multiculturalism."[80] Here we see the old white concern accenting the superior virtue of Judeo-Christian religion and a strong sense of the supremacy of European civilization. We observe fear about the proper reproduction of a white-dominated society from the current generation to future generations. In the early 1990s Buchanan also told an interviewer that:

> If we had to take a million immigrants in, say, Zulus next year or Englishmen, and put them in Virginia, what group would be easier to assimilate and would cause less problems for the people of Virginia? There is nothing wrong with us sitting down and arguing that issue that we are a European country, English-speaking country.[81]

Here, the Zulus, who are black and African, seem to represent the specter of uncivilized immigrants who would not assimilate well with what he regards as the superior white European civilization. Yet, taking note of the character of the state population, Virginia then probably had an African-ancestry population at least as large as its English-ancestry population. In addition, Buchanan gave numerous speeches and commentaries accenting the cultural issues like abortion and homosexuality noted previously. In 1992, he gave a famous speech at the Republican National Convention celebrating the Ronald Reagan and George H. W. Bush years and accenting explicitly the importance of the conservative side in the society's "culture wars."[82]

Significant racial desegregation and other changes in the direction of a more racially egalitarian and diverse society frequently challenge or anger those who operate out of the old white frame and an associated strong traditionalist or authoritarian frame, including prominent white leaders and commentators like Dole and Buchanan. By the 1980s and 1990s even a few conservative intellectuals who had ties to the Democratic Party were negatively targeting affirmative action programs and increases in immigrants of color, especially those from Latin America. For example, Samuel Huntington, prominent political scientist and co-founder of the elite policy journal, *Foreign Affairs*, argued in a 1997 issue of that influential journal that the U.S. situation is one where immigrant "groups feel discriminated against if they are not allowed to remain apart from the mainstream. The ideologies of multiculturalism and diversity reinforce and legitimate these trends. They deny the existence of a common culture in the United States, denounce assimilation, and promote the primacy of racial, ethnic, and other subnational cultural identities and groupings."[83] Huntington made clear that he was very concerned that the immigrants were "overwhelmingly from Latin America and Asia." Like Buchanan, he suggested with little evidence that, if multiculturalism ever becomes central, the United States will join the former

Soviet Union "on the ash heap of history."[84] In his various 1990s and early 2000s writings, Huntington, whose Harvard institute and research received significant support from far-right Republican funding agencies like the Olin Foundation, wrote influentially about a "clash of civilizations" and argued there is growing conflict between a superior Western civilization and inferior world cultures, including Middle Eastern (Muslim) and Latin American cultures.[85] Huntington's arch-conservative views on immigration have been widely cited and significantly influential, especially in numerous conservative white political circles. Among those he influenced have been nativistic Republican House members working aggressively to limit U.S. immigration.

Also in the 1990s, a leading conservative Republican activist and former executive director of the Christian Coalition, Ralph Reed, admitted that in recent decades "the way the Republican Party has made its stand in the South has been through the subtext of being a white conservative party opposing a shrinking Democratic Party dominated by minorities, labor unions and the left." That is, they used a conscious racist appeal to white voters of all classes. Reed continued by describing the future of the Republican Party from the mid-1990s forward in a similarly revealing manner: "You're going to see a new Republican party that is still primarily white and that is fiscally and morally conservative, but that also is attempting to project an image of racial tolerance and moderation."[86] In this candid commentary Reed signals that he and many of his conservative Republican colleagues still envisioned a Republican Party that was primarily white, but that looked good on the surface and projected an "image of racial tolerance." Public image, not significant desegregated reality, seemed to be a central concern. Reed and the Christian Coalition played a very significant role in the Republican political resurgence during the 1990s.

Over the years since the 1960s, as we have seen over the last two chapters, almost all major leaders in this resurgent Republican Party have been white, and mostly male, and they have brought about the party's resurgence from that time to the present by frequently using a national politics that has directed barely disguised or subtle appeals to versions of the white racial frame, and especially its antiblack subframe, in the minds of a great many white voters and officials. These Republican leaders generally deliver to working-class and middle-class whites a strong racial framing, one that implicitly or explicitly accents white interests and white-run governments. Much previous evidence reveals that over recent decades the Republican Party has generally been an omnipresent guardian of white societal interests while frequently using a certain imagery and tokenism to appear non-racist. For example, a deceptive façade has been partially created by token appointments of a few black Republicans like Clarence Thomas and General Colin Powell to visible political positions in Washington, D.C.

Some of this rather deceptive construction of a party "image of tolerance" can be seen in conservative-generated, race-related ballot initiatives in California and some other states during this political era. Social scientist Daniel HoSang has shown that numerous anti-civil-rights, anti-immigrant, anti-bilingualism, and anti-affirmative-action initiatives voted on, and often passed, by voters in California in the 1990s and previous decades were frequently cast by their mostly white, usually conservative strongest advocates in terms of the language of "rights," "tolerance," "freedom," and "opportunity." These California ballot initiatives were regularly described by their advocates as recovering "our rights" and about saving "our jobs, schools, homes" or "the English language." The mostly white leaders of most of these California proposition campaigns rejected a public language of the old overt racism, yet their "rights" language barely hid the reality that these political initiatives were designed to protect whites' substantially privileged status, major material advantages, and actual racist framing of society. As HoSang has underscored, various whites could embrace this "rights" and colorblindness language even as they went out to vote down antidiscrimination and remedial government programs like affirmative action and bilingual education that might bring some significant changes in the still extensive patterns of racial discrimination and the still massive racial inequalities. Most revealing was the fact that attempts by civil rights and other anti-racism advocates to demonstrate the ways in which individual and systemic racism persisted—and thus to demonstrate the need for antidiscrimination programs—were ignored by a great many conservative whites, including many in the local elite groups of politicians, realtors, school board members, city council members, and educators.[87]

Significantly, this often heralded colorblindness perspective and its "rights" rhetoric have in fact been just a contemporary, somewhat "softer," version of an old white racial framing of this country, a framing that has long viewed whites as virtuous even if they are still racist in their views of society or if they still perpetuate or allow significant discrimination against Americans of color.[88]

Racial and Related Issues in the Democratic Party

During the 1970s–1990s era the conservative turn in U.S. society could also periodically be seen among leading white Democratic Party officials in their orientations and actions (or lack of actions) on issues of great interest to African Americans and other Americans of color. Recall that during the critical 1960s era numerous white Democratic leaders' support for civil rights efforts had been shaped in part by an important convergence between their strong concern about the U.S. image overseas during the Cold War and the Vietnam War and the black civil rights movement's pressures for desegregation and greater political freedom.

However, some of the white Democratic leadership's support for some desegregation goals of the civil rights movement alienated many other elite and ordinary whites, especially in the southern and border states. Fearing that what many whites viewed as "black issues"—public efforts in regard to residential segregation, affirmative action, social programs for poor Americans, and justice reform—were alienating many white voters, important white Democratic leaders had gradually backed off on strongly supporting important civil rights goals, just as Republican leaders had done earlier. Many white Democratic Party leaders and activists had reduced their support for new civil rights programs and for aggressive enforcement of existing civil rights laws in the years after the major election defeat of the Democratic Party by Nixon in 1972. From then to the 1990s there was a gradual shift in a more conservative direction among numerous white leaders at the top of the Democratic Party on important civil rights issues.

Evidence for this shift can be seen in the moderate racial positions and antidiscrimination policies of the 1970s Jimmy Carter administration and the 1990s Bill Clinton administration, although they were certainly more substantial than under Republican administrations. For example, Clinton did appoint more blacks to important government positions, including judgeships, than former presidents Reagan and Bush, and some of his appointees put more emphasis on the enforcement of existing civil rights laws. Nonetheless, both Carter's and Clinton's public positions on civil rights enforcement and expansion were generally quite insufficient by the standards of most black voters and leaders in the Democratic Party. Most ironically, Clinton, whom some humorously called the "first black president" because of his interest in certain aspects of black culture, made very clear as president his concern for or acceptance of many white voters' racial views. A major sign of Clinton's dramatic weakness in this regard could be seen in how he treated the case of Lani Guinier, a distinguished African American law professor and civil rights attorney who advocated more effective enforcement of the voting rights laws and regulations, as well as other civil rights laws. Soon after Clinton became president, and to his credit, he nominated her for an Assistant Attorney General post. Very soon, however, the white right wing started attacking her as a "Quota Queen," yet another racial codeword calling up in many minds the racist term "welfare queen" often used for poor black women in the old white frame; this attack included a *Wall Street Journal* lead story. Faced with hostile racist attacks by many conservative elite and ordinary whites on Guinier, a white-oriented Clinton did not defend her extensive professional qualifications nor her very reasonable views on enforcing civil rights, and her nomination was soon withdrawn.[89]

Moreover, in his first presidential campaign in 1992 Clinton had played the racial moderate by periodically asserting he had a good civil rights record as Arkansas governor and by generally, if vaguely, condemning discrimination. Yet he more than counterbalanced this moderate stance for white voters by intentionally distorting and publicly and aggressively attacking the views expressed by the young black rapper Sister Souljah, a college-educated former community activist. In summer 1992, after another major riot by black Americans (and Latinos) in Los Angeles, the talented young rapper was asked if the actions of blacks rioting there were "wise."[90]

Sister Souljah tried to explain why young blacks had rioted by using the hypothetical voice of a local gang member: "If the social and economic system has neglected your development and you have become a casual killer who will kill even your own brother, in your mindset, why not kill a white person?" Souljah was by no means personally advocating violence, just trying to explain to a white audience that violence directed by blacks against nonblacks during the riot was unsurprising given the commonplace black-on-black killings and oppressive, often white-controlled socioeconomic realities that ultimately generated much urban violence. In her representation of this black perspective most elite and ordinary whites are viewed as not caring about the oppressive underlying conditions that generated riotous protests.[91] On a CNN show after Clinton had made his strongly white-framed comments, Souljah offered a political interpretation of Clinton's attack on her: "America needs Sister Souljah to be the black monster, to scare all of the white people to the polls because they were disinterested in a very boring, very sloppy political campaign that's been put forth by not only Clinton, but George Bush himself."[92] On another television show she reiterated strongly that it was "absurd" to conclude that she advocated killing whites, as Clinton had suggested. She further noted the hypocrisy of many white politicians, including many supposedly more liberal Democrats: "Bill Clinton is like a lot of white politicians. They eat soul food, they party with black women, they play the saxophone, but when it comes to domestic and foreign policy, they make the same decisions that are destructive to African people in this country and throughout the world."[93]

Virtually no influential whites in politics or the media tried to publicly understand Souljah's black point of view, and there was extensive support for Clinton's viewpoint. Former president Jimmy Carter asserted that Souljah was wrong and that he admired Clinton "for being brave enough to say it in that particular forum."[94] On the other hand, many black commentators explained clearly what Souljah had meant. Thus, Jesse Jackson noted that Clinton's attack was just another attempt by numerous white Democratic leaders to ignore the views on many issues of the more liberal wing of the party: "This was a move by the right wing of the party to pull away from the DNC [Democratic National Committee] because the DNC was too multiracial for them and too democratic . . . The further attempt to isolate the Rainbow [coalition in the party] is just another dimension of their strategy."[95]

In his political campaigns and over much of his presidency, an often moderate Clinton and key associates did play into the dominant white frame and frequently distanced themselves from more liberal racial views, liberal black leaders, and the aggressive civil rights enforcement desired by many Democrats of color. Indeed, in this 1990s era many white Democratic leaders and activists, like their Republican counterparts, worked hard at attracting white voters, and often by implicitly or explicitly asserting white interests or views and neglecting black voters and other voters of color and their social justice interests. One key example of this distancing of black voters could be seen in the relatively weak Democratic get-out-the-vote efforts for black voters in numerous important elections.[96] This is one of the political contradictions that periodically surfaces in Democratic Party campaign efforts and other actions. Since the 1960s black voters have been critical to Democratic victories and usually the most loyal part of the party base. After the 1960s civil rights movement, with the right to vote legally guaranteed, black voters in southern and border states began actively participating in local, state, and national politics, and principally in the Democratic Party. As a result, over recent decades the Democratic Party has become increasingly diverse, with a large percentage of its membership being African Americans and other Americans of color who generally buttress the more liberal party wing to which Jesse Jackson referred.

During the 1990s the Democratic Party continued to have a liberal public image, albeit one that was often exaggerated by the mass media. Certainly, in the 1980s–1990s era various important liberal groups did emerge under the Democratic Party umbrella, but many of them focused on rather specific social or political issues. In this era these liberal groups often did not replace the high level of campaign legwork done previously by the labor unions (now declining in number) that were once a key part of the Democratic base. These liberal groups also did not, for the most part, focus on ordinary American workers' employment and housing issues, but rather on other important but specialized issues like women's issues, pro-choice issues, and the environment.[97] Since the 1980s and 1990s these liberal interest groups and remaining labor unions, have been very significant in getting Democratic candidates elected, but they have not really controlled the Democratic Party, in contrast to the strong control that conservative corporate and business interests have over the Republican Party. Moreover, the Democratic Party has regularly found itself faced with major internal conflicts between the interests of groups representing the generally more liberal Democratic base and some powerful party officials more oriented to certain corporate interests that seek to greatly influence the party's policies by means of funding, lobbying, and networking. Indeed, in recent decades the liberal Democratic groups often found themselves somewhat down the ladder of influence in regard to actual decision-making power on major public policies, especially on those related to the capitalistic economy, once numerous Democratic candidates became important elected officials.

Conclusion

For the most part, the political era of the 1970s to the 1990s was one of increasing, if sometimes oscillating, conservative political resurgence and power. In rather pointed language, Allan Lichtman has summed up the numerous victories over time of the expanding and successful right-wing and authoritarian political efforts from the 1940s through the 1990s. As he summarizes, over this significant era the far right had "turned back the tide of union organizing. They had slashed taxes, deregulated business, and rewritten the welfare laws and America's criminal statues." In addition, he adds, they "blocked the Equal Rights Amendment, turned civil rights measures into quota laws, and sounded the alarm against deviance and decay."[98] In this process, moreover, the far-right resurgence has united many white religious conservatives from various Christian groups and has made the white South into a major long-term stronghold of arch-conservative Republicanism.

This was a political party era that, like previous eras, constantly revealed numerous aspects of systemic racism, including versions of the old rationalizing white frame. This racist reality could be seen repeatedly in an array of political activities, party events, party organizations, and government policies. Much in this racist array was accentuated in the efforts of Republican Party leaders and voters, but it could also be seen in the efforts of some Democratic leaders and officials. These racially revealing endeavors included electoral campaigns pervaded or undergirded by racist strategies, presidential candidates intentionally appealing to white voters' racist framing, and racialized governing strategies that sought to weaken civil rights laws or enforcement. Although the most recent years in this political era brought us some new racial terminology such as the "end of racism" and "post-racial America"—terminology that first began to appear among white media commentators, experts, and politicians—the actual political realities examined in this chapter, as well as those we assess in the next few chapters, directly contradict such transparent attempts at obscuring or defending the continuing and substantial reality of white racial power and privilege.

6

The George W. Bush Era
Racial and Class Dimensions

The potent political efforts of the Christian right came to a significant realization with the election and re-election in the 2000s of George W. Bush, a president who viewed himself as a born-again Christian conservative and one who made frequent and strong religious references. The labors of Christian right groups to influence elections could be seen in the forceful political activism and related "values voting" efforts that their members continued to put into the George W. Bush era elections, as they had since the heady years of Ronald Reagan.

Recall from Chapter 5 that, in making sense of contemporary political authoritarianism, one can distinguish between authoritarian leaders and followers. In this society some people greatly desire to dominate other people, and periodically succeed. A great many others are willing to more or less be the followers of powerful leaders. As we noted previously, some research data on U.S. political leaders indicate that many operate out of a strong authoritarian framing of society. Bush frequently exuded a type of authoritarian perspective with its desire for strong leadership and a certain either/or thinking, often wrapped up in a Christian right religious perspective. Not surprisingly, many conservative Republican voters and members of Congress were ready to follow such a strong political leader. In this period, there was a trend for those who identified as Republicans to accent a more authoritarian framing of society, while those who were self-identified Democrats were frequently oriented to a less authoritarian framing.[1] A certain type of authoritarian submission was clear in the expressed political views of many conservative Republicans. For example, many such conservatives were quoted as saying something to the effect that "God had sent" conservative Republican candidates like George W. Bush and Ronald Reagan to lead the country out of its many difficulties and troubles.

Moreover, when the World Trade Center attack took place in 2001, even those citizens who usually do not operate out of a strong authoritarian framing came to accent certain aspects of it—such as accepting a "get tough," more militaristic leadership and by allowing significant new restrictions on civil liberties in the so-called Patriot Act. Social science research indicates that the level of societal threat can make a difference in the activation of strongly authoritarian views. Major external threats to society can shift people who are relatively non-authoritarian or moderately authoritarian in their socio-political framing in the direction of a more authoritarian framing, at least for a time. Under certain circumstances, thus, major political leaders can play on these fears in order to shift the general population in the direction of less open and even more elitist government actions, including those people who are ordinarily not as susceptible to such strong authoritarian appeals. This is what the Bush administration and its conservative allies inside and outside Washington, D.C. did in the years following the dramatic events of late 2001.[2]

Party Polarization and the Era of George W. Bush

During the decades from Richard Nixon to George W. Bush, some political scientists and other political analysts argued that U.S. political parties were not very ideological, especially in comparison with European political parties. Actually, however, both major U.S. political parties have been significantly committed to spreading strong political ideologies and, most especially, the very conservative Republican Party since the 1970s. The latter party's top leadership has been relatively clear about what the society's economic and political inequalities should be like and about the business-oriented values and conservative goals of their governing strategies. Some political analysts also speak of the "disappearing center" in U.S. politics, but the disappearing center has been much more characteristic of the Republican Party, where Republican leaders and operatives working for Republican candidates like George W. Bush have sought to move the party solidly to the right, in the process often frustrating or marginalizing more moderate and centrist Republicans.[3] The Democratic Party has also been politically ideological in this era, but its substantial group and demographic diversity has made it likewise more diverse in political ideologies, with significant numbers of political moderates and political liberals both being important in the party.

While recognizing that there has always been significant partisanship in U.S. party contests and elections, several authors have argued that there is much more political partisanship today. Writing on this partisan shift, Matthew Levendusky, like some other analysts, has shown how much has changed in voting and party ties. Over the last few decades political liberals and conservatives have been much more likely to stick with the Democratic Party and the Republican Party, respectively, in state and national elections. Similarly, describing the contemporary situation as much like a "second Civil War," Ronald Brownstein argues that there was less partisanship from the late 1930s to the mid-1960s, an era followed by a long transitional period to much more partisanship during the 1990s, which was signaled by such political examples as the highly polarized party vote to impeach Bill Clinton in 1998. Since the early 1990s, the ideological divide between the two major political parties has been at least as large as in any previous era.[4]

One major explanation for this polarization is that the major political leaders, including top elected politicians, of the two parties have themselves become more politically polarized. In recent years, top leaders in the Democratic Party have mostly been politically liberal or moderate, while top leaders in the Republican Party have mostly been conservative or arch-conservative.[5] In addition, this political polarization has been greatly shaped by the rise in right-wing think tanks and other very conservative political organizations, most of them well funded by conservative individual and corporate interests. This aggressive organization has pressed both parties in the conservative corporate direction, but has had the most consistent and profound impacts on Republican officials. Moreover, since the late 1960s the increasing political and ideological polarization of the major parties in Congress has been the result of party caucuses becoming less politically diverse as white southern Democrats have been replaced by numerous white Republicans and some Democrats of color, and white northern Republicans have mostly become more conservative. With this significant party repositioning, as Sean Theriault shows, has come more power in the hands of the leadership of each party. Party leaders, and most especially in the Republican Party in recent decades, no longer have to do as much negotiation between strong contending factions in their party as they once did.[6] As a result, polarized voting has also become more characteristic of the U.S. House and Senate, especially since the 1990s. In congressional voting, the tendency of most House and Senate members to go along with the majority in their party on contested legislative votes increased to 82–90 percent of votes in the Bill Clinton and George W. Bush years, up significantly from the 1950s.[7]

The significant rightward shift and the polarization in the party leadership has had significant impacts on many ordinary voters who now view each party as having a clearer political ideology. While voters as a group may not have polarized ideologically as much as their party leadership, they can usually, at least roughly, relate their political views to one or the other set of party leaders. Contemporary poll data indicate many voters tend to shift their own ideologies somewhat to fit in with their leadership rather than to actually shift from one party to the other. The polarization in political leadership ideologies, Levendusky and other scholars have suggested, has shaped public opinion on certain current political issues substantially because most ordinary Americans do not have the interest or time to keep up with numerous shifting political-economic issues like their party leaderships do. Typically communicated by an elite-run mainstream media, thus, the party leaderships' ideologies help party members to come to some common understandings, however inadequate or mythical, of the socio-political world.[8]

This impact is perhaps most obvious among each party's political activists. This can be seen in their greater monetary contributions, party participation, and strong sense that their party stands for a distinctive point of view. The ideological orientations of these most active party members frequently shape in part the character or views of party candidates in primary elections, who in turn also often shape the views and actions of the party activists. In addition, in recent decades the party polarization has tended to accelerate many voters' participation and engagement in party and election activities, further dividing party members into the more and less politically engaged, with the former typically most affected by their party leadership's political orientations.[9]

Nonetheless, one needs to be cautious in extending the argument about party polarization, party leaders, and party activists to the views of the general voting population on all important political, social, and economic issues, because that voting population includes many who are not politically active or who are only occasionally interested in politics. According to national opinion surveys, and depending on the question phrasing, there is less opinion polarization on certain important political and economic issues in the general public, as can be seen in some voters who show up in the political middle, than there often is between the two main parties' leaderships and activists.[10]

Why have party leaders and activists become more differentiated and polarized than in the past? Numerous important explanations have been offered, and we have already noted a number of key factors. On the Republican side, these have included the significant increase in organized and aggressive political action by Christian right groups and, as previously noted, the aggressive funding of an array of conservative political organizations and reputed experts by wealthy capitalists and corporate executives now heavily involved in politics. We have also noted the research that shows that continuing and often dramatic white opposition to antidiscrimination programs and desegregation efforts such as in public schools and residential housing, together with other racial concerns remained central in the concerns of a great many white voters in this era. Their conventional racial framing and/or authoritarian framing have since then shaped or become associated with other important social issues, and with conservative solutions such as various privatization schemes. Thus, in the late 1990s and early 2000s very conservative approaches to several important societal issues— including racial issues, women's and gay rights issues, and military intervention in the Middle East—were often clustered together in the frequently substantially authoritarian political worldview of a great many white voters.[11]

Interestingly, too, an array of political analysts in the media, politics, and academia have failed to examine fully the significant diversification of actual

U.S. voters since the 1960s. One major reason for the greater party ideological polarization is the significant change in who participates and votes in political actions and elections since the 1960s. Up until the 1960s almost all voters in many geographical areas were white. This began to change dramatically in the late 1960s and 1970s. Over time, the end of legal segregation and Jim Crow restrictions on voting brought a very significant increase in the political role of black voters and other voters of color, and an increase in their civic and political organizations involved in elections. (In addition, the feminist movement accelerated the role of women of various backgrounds, and women's political groups, in U.S. politics.) Over the last few decades the substantial growth from immigration and other factors in the numbers of Americans of color has further changed this voting and general political picture. In numerous elections, voters of color have been a very substantial and growing proportion of all voters, and a majority of the voters of color have shown in numerous elections that they are opposed to the white-oriented candidates and certain positions of the contemporary Republican Party. Since the 1970s, thus, the Democratic Party has been much more racially diverse than the Republican Party, with white liberal leaders and voters, leaders and voters of color, and a business-oriented faction of mostly white political moderates. The current Democratic Party is less homogeneous at the leadership and rank-and-file levels than the Republican Party. In contrast, as we have seen, the Republican Party has in effect become the "white party" in terms of its activists, membership, and numerous party positions greatly favoring (especially better-off) white voters' political-economic interests.

This substantial growth in and activism of voters of color, when coupled with the continuing high levels of racial separation and segregation in housing, has had a major impact on political polarization across geographical areas. For example, in recent presidential elections some significant geographical polarization has been documented. Consider briefly the 2008 presidential election, which we will consider in detail in the next chapter. About half of all presidential votes in 2008 were in polarized counties where either Obama or McCain won by at least 20 percent. Over the last few decades, the percentage of voters residing in these polarized "landslide" counties has grown substantially, from 27 percent of all U.S. voters in 1976 to 48 percent of voters in 2008. One key reason for this 21st-century reality is that geographical segregation along racial lines is closely linked to political polarization. Those U.S. counties where the Republican candidate McCain won with a landslide margin of 20 percent or more were also overwhelmingly white, with the black and Latino voting-age population being a rather modest proportion of those counties' populations. Where candidate Obama won a county, in great contrast, the black and Latino population averaged about 43 percent of the voting-age population.[12] For at least a century the

United States has been very segregated residentially, especially in racial terms, and racial (and ethnic) segregation has commonly meant political segregation and polarization. This has particularly been true in recent decades once large numbers of black and Latino Americans (and some other groups) finally secured meaningful access to the ballot box and to political party organizations and activism.

We should note too that in the contemporary United States economic class position often links to political orientation and voting. Corporate executives and, more generally, those in upper-income groups generally identify and vote Republican more than lower-income groups. Frequently for time and work reasons, and frequently too because of imposed voting barriers, low- and modest-income Americans are not as politically active on the average as middle- and upper-income Americans, especially in non-presidential elections. Upper-middle-income and upper-income Americans, who are disproportionately white and face fewer socioeconomic and political barriers, are more likely to be politically active and to vote than lower-income Americans, and this frequently gives them much more power in determining many political elections and who are the officials at local, state, and federal government levels.

The Bush Era and Later: Capitalistic Restructuring and Control

As we have seen previously, important to a full understanding of the conservative resurgence of recent decades is the centrality and power of corporate executives and other allied business officials. Major blocs of business leaders have shifted from one party to another over the generations of U.S. politics, but in these recent decades the mounting political organization and influence of particularly conservative U.S. capitalists on the Republican Party has in several ways been a striking political development. George W. Bush himself arose from their capitalistic ranks. He was a business entrepreneur, although he failed at several business efforts before he became governor of Texas, and later on president.

Let us consider briefly some capitalistic developments that had major economic and political impacts on U.S. society before and during Bush's presidential years. United States capitalism is of course a very profit-oriented system, and profit-making has generally taken precedence over more humanistic values in a great many decisions made by corporate and other business executives. Top corporate executives frequently have little commitment to providing U.S. jobs for U.S. workers if that means significantly reduced profits. In recent decades, and dramatically since the election of George W. Bush in 2000, the U.S. economy has changed considerably, as many blue-collar and white-collar jobs have been exported overseas by U.S.-based corporate executives seeking less environmental or other regulation and lower wage costs in Asian and other countries, which in many cases have significantly increased their numbers of well-trained and educated workers. Indeed, one-fifth of U.S. factory jobs disappeared just over Bush's two presidential terms. Many remaining blue-collar and white-collar jobs have been weakened in terms of their wages, benefits, or working conditions. Increasing numbers of large companies have even developed a two-tier wage structure, with lower wages replacing formerly better wages for their newly hired workers.[13]

Thus, contemporary U.S. capitalism relies more and more on armies of relatively low-wage U.S. workers, armies often disproportionately workers of color, and these can be found in many economic sectors. This often unnoticed low-wage workforce has long been central to the economy and has suffered increasingly impoverished conditions. Trying to maintain their standard of living, many families at lower- and middle-income levels have taken on substantial debt, taken out second mortgages, or seen mothers with young children go to work.[14] Given increasingly difficult economic circumstances for many workers, the reality of government inaction on their behalf was particularly striking in the long Bush era of Republican control. Among those in need, a declining percentage—by the last year of the Bush administration (2008) only a third—got government unemployment compensation, and federal job training programs had been significantly reduced. Responding to corporate goals, government investigations of unsafe workplaces had become less frequent as the number of workers grew, and major officials like Bush's Secretary of Labor made comments supporting federal inaction on workplace regulation. The Bush administration cut deals with major firms, including major donors to the Republican Party, to give them notice of federal workplace inspections. In addition, the minimum wage was kept at a low $5.15 an hour until significantly changed by a newly elected more liberal Democratic Congress in 2007.[15] Moreover, for most of the Bush era corporate profits were generally up significantly, and many top executives of larger firms continued to pull down huge salaries and bonuses—even as the U.S. economy they led went into serious economic decline toward the end of the Bush administration.

Given the Bush administration's actions, or lack of necessary action, one is not surprised to learn that President Bush's most valued political base was, as he occasionally noted explicitly, disproportionately very affluent and mostly white. Certainly, in recent years the upper-income groups have voted Republican more than lower-income groups and have also shown less support for government social programs and more support for tax cuts for well-off Americans than other American income groups. In recent years, numerous scholarly and journalistic analyses have shown the dramatic impact of the Reagan and Bush administrations' efforts to reduce taxes on very affluent and rich Americans. Several research studies have shown that the top 1 percent of U.S. families has seen significant increases in average incomes in real terms in recent decades, and especially in the Bush years, while average incomes in lower-income brackets have declined or stagnated. In terms of shares of income, the top 1 percent increased its share by more than 120 percent between 1979 and the 2000s, with sharp increases in the later years of the Clinton administration and in the long Bush administration. The top 20 percent of families saw their share increase by nearly 30 percent in this period, while the income shares of the *other four fifths* of Americans declined. In addition, the average income of corporate CEOs increased significantly to *185 times* the average income of workers over this era.[16]

In addition, since the election of Bush in 2000, top Republican Party leaders have pressed hard for continuing, or increasing, major tax cuts for corporations and rich Americans, even when this strategy means very large and continuing federal budget deficits. Bush inherited from Clinton a federal budget that was reasonably balanced, but his large tax cuts especially benefitting well-off and rich Americans, together with his extremely costly military invasions of Iraq and Afghanistan, soon created massive federal budget deficits. Together with weak government regulation of the finance industry, the massive Bush deficits helped to create the "great recession" that affected a great many Americans at the end of the second Bush term and persisted in its impact into his successor's term as president. Such ill-advised budget deficits, then as now, have often brought a serious reduction in congressional interest in creating or greatly expanding much-needed federal social support programs, including unemployment assistance, health care assistance, and retraining and educational programs for ordinary workers and their families who have faced hard economic times.

Recall too that one of the major ironies of the frequent Republican control of the presidency or the Congress from the Reagan years to the second Bush's years was that conservative Republican politicians and much of their conservative base sought an expansion of certain federal programs, funding, or contracts, even as they rhetorically condemned big govern-ment.[17] Indeed, expansion of the federal government has taken place during these conservative Republican administrations, and especially during this Bush administration; and many older Republicans have long depended on major federal programs like Medicare and Social Security. In addition, Republican cutbacks in other federal programs and the weakening of federal agencies under earlier conservative Republican administrations created serious operational problems for the Bush administration, as when it faced national crises like the major Gulf Coast hurricane Katrina with quite insufficient federal disaster-response capabilities and administrators.[18]

The Bush Era and Later: Finance Capitalists and Systemic Racism

Consider too that at the center of contemporary capitalism are the influ-ential finance capitalists, who have in recent years dominated something like

40 percent of the U.S. economy in terms of their business profits. Indeed, various finance capitalists have often been more important in the contemporary U.S. economy than the more celebrated high-tech capitalists. Before and during the Bush era, and continuing more recently, finance capitalists at investment banks, private-equity firms, and hedge fund firms have gained much power to pressure even top executives at manufacturing and service firms to squeeze their workers even more in the name of yet more profits.[19] In making their profits these finance capitalists generally make use of financial paper products such as various kinds of securities and of extensive trading in several different securities markets, in contrast to entrepreneurial capitalists who seek profits by creating goods and services to trade in more conventional markets. Recall that blocs of major political investors periodically coalesce to advance candidates for Congress and the presidency who will move forward their economic goals and interests. In recent decades the finance capital sector has been a very powerful political-economic bloc shaping both political parties and important elections.

Like other major corporate executives, these finance capitalists have vied for much assistance from the federal government—both supportive economic programs and less government regulation. Recall the successful efforts of Republican senator Phil Gramm and other conservatives and moderates in Congress who, with assistance from the moderate business-oriented Democratic president Bill Clinton, deregulated several corporate sectors in the U.S. economy. These efforts included deregulation of major banks and financial institutions, many of which eventually played an important role in crashing the U.S. economy in 2007–2008. The economy in turn soon required a huge bailout of these and other "too big to fail" corporations by the federal government. During the late 1990s Clinton era and the 2000s Bush era numerous poorly regulated finance capitalists had moved into risky derivatives investments, including credit default swaps and packaged mortgage securities. Many of these were packaged securities that were grounded in home mortgages made by banking firms without examining carefully, as such firms had typically done in the past, how credit-worthy the designated loan recipients actually were.

Many of these securities were linked to subprime (high interest) loans that were often aggressively sold by loan officers and other banking agents working for mostly white-run banking firms to homeowners of color. One story in *The New York Times* reported on white loan officers at a major bank who aggressively sought out working-class African Americans, and apparently other working-class people of color, to get them to take out these questionable subprime loans. As part of a special markets unit at the bank, one loan officer reported that her colleagues sometimes referred to these as "ghetto loans" and to African American borrowers as "mud people." In what was a type of racial profiling, black church leaders were especially pressured to get out the information about these very risky loans to black homeowners.[20] After aggressive selling to these potential borrowers, who were encouraged to seek the loaned cash for an array of uses (including home remodeling and the like), many working-class and lower-middle-class homeowners refinanced and took out subprime loans, with their estimated house value frequently based on a then-inflated housing market value. These frequently overvalued homes, when the housing and job markets crashed dramatically during and after the Bush era, left many borrowers with large subprime loan debts they could not repay, and often with houses now dropping sharply in value. As a result, many people defaulted on these highly risky loans, leading in turn to many foreclosures and vacant homes, very disproportionately in residential areas populated by black residents and other residents of color. This weakly regulated capitalistic activity contributed greatly to the financial crisis and larger recession beginning in Bush's second term.[21]

In reality, there has been much profit-generated inducement to fraud and other questionable investment activities in recent years in the heavily white-run finance capital companies and markets. Americans of various backgrounds, and disproportionately Americans of color in many areas, have paid a very heavy price for such highly problematical activities ultimately generated or controlled by the ruling elite. Once again, we observe how systemic racism shaped and undergirded the ways in which many of these risky, if not fraudulent, capitalistic investment and loan activities temporarily succeeded, but then failed dramatically in ways that seriously damaged the present and future socioeconomic mobility chances of many families of color and their communities.

The Best Government Money Can Buy: The Bush Years

In the United States we have long had a kind of political "poll tax" that legally discriminates against less well-off Americans, and especially Americans of color. Most substantial contributions to major political campaigns come from very affluent or wealthy donors, the individual and corporate political investors who are mostly white. One mid-2000s study by Public Campaign and others, titled *Color of Money*, reported that in the 2004 presidential campaign some 90 percent of those who contributed more than $200 for federal political campaigns lived in predominantly white zip codes, with more than half in well-off or wealthy areas. These substantial political investors, representing less than 0.33 percent of the U.S. population, contributed two-thirds of all the money from individuals to the presidential campaigns. For the George Bush and John Kerry campaigns in 2004, the top contributing zip code area was Manhattan's wealthy and heavily white Upper East Side. That area led in what has been termed the "wealth primary," one that a top presidential candidate must ordinarily try to win in our undemocratic electoral system. These researchers also found similar wealth-biased patterns for previous presidential campaigns.[22] Not surprisingly, in their political goals expressed in political backstage or frontstage areas, presidential candidates often reflect the political and economic interests of those who provide the most money to fund their campaigns for the presidency and Congress.

After well-funded presidential and congressional elections are over, yet more well-heeled Americans, especially the lobbyists, make a major difference in shaping the creation and maintenance of federal policies. One important 1999–2002 research study, at the end of the Clinton administration and the beginning of the Bush administration, conducted interviews with more than 300 lobbyists and government officials in regard to nearly 100 diverse public policy issues of various degrees of magnitude that were raised at the federal government level. Among the many such advocates working on these issues, about six in 10 were lobbyists for various organizations, and the rest were government officials, most often members of Congress. Among the outside lobbyists, 46 percent represented trade associations, business organizations, professional associations, or specific businesses. Just 26 percent represented citizens' groups, and only 6 percent represented unions. Think tanks and foundations accounted for 6 percent, with the rest being miscellaneous groups such as religious groups.[23]

Clearly, in the day-to-day lobbying process of this era, unions were far outnumbered by business organizations and other business lobbyists. The study also found that, while citizens' groups, many of them progressive, were involved in numerous public policy issues, they were often relatively weak in lobbying resources and spread so thinly that they could not compete with the frequently huge resources—such as numerous major lobbyists and much money—that business and trade groups could bring to lobbying for policy issues that the latter were most interested in. Such data indicate just how disproportionately powerful big business groups are, over against unions and progressive citizens' groups, and it is these powerful groups that have frequently set federal policy agendas and the range of policy options around which other groups must compete.[24]

In addition, as we will see from more recent data in Chapter 8, among the many thousands of registered lobbyists who pressure Congress and many federal government agencies the overwhelming majority are white, with the most powerful lobbyists being almost all white men. Only about 4 percent are currently African American, with much smaller percentages of lobbyists being other Americans of color. Indeed, most major lobbying firms have historically had few or no lobbyists of color. Like the rest of the top political structure in the United States most important lobbying arenas are as a rule heavily white and very disproportionately male.

Bush's White Perspective: Racially Segregated Settings

As president, George W. Bush was not only an evangelical Christian with backing from the Christian right, but also evangelistic in his white-enclave framing of U.S. society. Born in 1946, baby-boomer Bush spent his early years in Midland, Texas, an oil town that was highly segregated along racial lines and whose white population no doubt had segregationist and other white-enclave values similar to those of the booming suburbs around many Sunbelt cities. As one journalist has noted, "Black children went to their own school rather than to Sam Houston Elementary with George Bush. The bus station and train station had separate waiting rooms for blacks and whites, and there were separate, dilapidated drinking fountains marked 'colored' at the stations and at the courthouse."[25] After Midland, Bush lived for a time in an upscale white suburban enclave in southwestern Houston, and then spent high school years at private, heavily white Phillips Academy (Andover) in New England. Later on, after some years at mostly white Ivy League universities, he lived in a super-elite Dallas suburb with rich, mostly white neighbors before becoming governor of Texas—and lived there again after stepping down from the presidency. Bush was a Texas politician, yet atypical in that he had numerous very elite East Coast ties.

Bush's white-enclave perspective was likely shaped significantly by his experiences growing up in Midland and Houston, but he was also significantly influenced by being around many Mexican American workers there. Biographical accounts indicate that he had seen large numbers of Mexicans come to work in Texas oilfields and gotten to know Mexican and Mexican American businesspeople while doing business before and after his stint as governor of Texas. Bush came out of this southwestern experience evidently recognizing the need of numerous southwestern farmers and other businesspeople for low-wage Mexican and Mexican American labor. Indeed, during his terms as governor and as president, Bush periodically opposed the views of anti-immigrant Republican nativists like Pat Buchanan. He also brought a few people of color into the Republican sphere so long as they held to a patriotically conservative, white-framed viewpoint like his. As governor, he worked to get some conservative Mexican American voters into the Republican Party, had close ties to some Mexican American businesspeople who were Republicans in Texas, and sought closer market-oriented economic ties to Mexico.[26]

Nonetheless, Bush generally came to the U.S. presidency and major policy issues with a substantial white-enclave perspective, doubtless the result of his years being a resident of and socialized in the mostly white and elite schools and suburban residential areas. (Not surprisingly, thus, in both his 2000 and 2004 presidential elections, voters in substantially white suburban areas helped Bush very significantly in securing major electoral victories.) As we saw previously, numerous powerful Republican leaders have come from white suburban areas or other predominantly white residential areas, and this was especially true during the Bush era. This lived reality of leading Republicans probably accounts, at least in part, for their very conservative perspective, one often shaped to a degree by some years of white resistance in these geographical areas to desegregation of public schools and residential areas. Recall too that the white-enclave perspective of well-off whites often carries a religious-like faith in the superiority of the free market and a denigration of important concerns of central city residents who are not affluent or white. It has also typically involved a negative view of numerous New Deal and Great Society social programs seen as encroaching on the prerogatives of affluent and rich whites. This neoliberal perspective aggressively asserts a preference for private markets and often for the privatization or ending of numerous government social programs. This orientation could frequently be seen in Bush's aggressive pressing for privatization of various public services and programs, including some public schools (for example, with voucher programs) and social security accounts.[27]

Race and Republican Electoral Strategies

In his Texas political days, Bush had made some effort to bring some black conservative leaders into the Republican Party, but his party's efforts in approaching black voters from 2000 to 2008 were often problematical or discriminatory. During the Bush presidential years, a few Republican political leaders like Charles Colson, who had earlier worked on Richard Nixon's so-called southern strategy, occasionally tried to identify the Republican Party with the positive aura around civil rights legends like Dr. Martin Luther King, Jr. For example, in one 2006 radio statement Colson asserted that King was "a great conservative. Were he alive today, I believe he would be in the vanguard of the pro-life movement and would be supporting [conservative Supreme Court] Judge Alito."[28] One apparent goal was to attract some conservative black voters into the party, yet under false pretenses, for King was by no means such a political and social conservative. As they had in the Reagan era, some Republican operatives also tried to create a few groups that appeared to be shaped or organized by conservative voters of color. For example, one group called Project 21 has been portrayed by Republicans as "a leading voice in the black community," but was in fact created by a white Republican, who even appeared on one television program as a key spokesperson for that "black group."[29]

Over recent decades Republican Party electoral attempts at the local, state, and national levels have included a range of very questionable or discriminatory voter limitation activities. During the Bush presidential elections, as well as in previous and subsequent presidential (and state) elections, numerous Republican activists and operatives have engaged in voter restriction activities aimed at Democratic voters, sometimes even insisting that such voter suppression is as important as actually getting out Republican voters. Some of these are the so-called ballot security programs. They typically target voting precincts where a large percentage of likely voters are Democratic voters of color, usually with weak or no evidence of a claimed voter fraud to justify such intrusive actions. Over the last few decades such problematical ballot security programs have involved, according to a major 2004 research report, the use of "intimidating Republican poll watchers or challengers who may slow down voting lines and embarrass potential voters by asking them humiliating questions," "people in official-looking uniforms with badges and side arms who question voters about their citizenship or their registration," "warning signs . . . posted near the polls," and "radio ads . . . targeted to minority listeners containing dire threats of prison terms for people who are not properly registered—messages that seem designed to put minority voters on the defensive."[30] Most of the recent serious voter limitation efforts have involved Republican political operatives, not Democratic political operatives.

Other knowledgeable reports have revealed how Republican and other conservative political operatives have encouraged Green Party candidates to run so as to siphon off likely Democratic voters from the main Democratic candidates, have arranged to have Democratic Party phone banks jammed so they could not reach voters, and have gotten actors with fake "ghetto" or Spanish accents to make calls for Democratic candidates to white voters whom the Republicans feel might be scared off by such accents.[31]

Race and Diversity Issues in the Bush Era

In his terms as Texas governor and his run for president, Bush occasionally made statements about the value of a diverse "New America," such as in an important August 2000 speech as candidate for the presidency. As president, he generally avoided the overtly racist language of prior Republican presidents, and his administration mostly did not seek the open racial confrontations sometimes seen in the earlier Reagan and Bush administrations discussed previously. Moreover, as president, Bush appointed a few conservative people of color to important government positions. Like many white evangelicals in the last decade or so, he seemed to be comfortable with some racial inclusion on an individual level.[32] His important cabinet appointments included the first two African American secretaries of state, former top general Colin Powell and his friend and academic Condoleezza Rice, and the first Latino Attorney General, Alberto Gonzales. We should note, however, that such men and women of color are typically allowed into the higher political-economic reaches controlled by the white political elite, especially that of the Republican Party, only if they substantially conform to certain white perspectives and expectations. Some years ago, one of the country's most talented journalists, Leanita McClain, became the first

African American to serve on the Republican *Chicago Tribune's* editorial board. After her early death by suicide, one friend noted the great conformity to white ways faced by black professionals like McClain in such high-level workplaces. They must "consciously choose their speech, their laughter, their walk, their mode of dress and car" to fit in with white expectations.[33]

Black Republicans like Powell, Rice, and Clarence Thomas have typically become very strong advocates for the conservative elite's policies and perspectives. Thus, at the important 2000 Republican convention that nominated Bush for president, Colin Powell spoke on his behalf, asserting that Bush had been "successful in bringing more and more minorities into the tent by responding to their deepest needs . . . I know he can help bridge our racial divide—I know that."[34] Yet, over the years Bush helped greatly to increase the racial divide between the two parties and more generally in the country's politics.

Both Powell and Condoleezza Rice seem to have played a much different role in the Bush administration than had black Republicans within pre-1960 Republican administrations; for in their positions Powell and Rice never made external criticisms of the administration's important actions, even when they related to issues of great concern to the black community. Both apparently played important roles in discussing foreign policy internally, but publicly were in line with the often imperialistic foreign policy positions articulated by Bush and his conservative white advisers. Like other contemporary black Republicans, according to the analysis of researcher Clarence Lusane, both Powell and Rice distanced themselves from numerous major concerns of the larger black community, especially on issues such as recognizing the severity of current racial discrimination and the need for expansion of civil rights laws and enforcement. While white Democratic leaders have occasionally chosen black Democrats for important positions because they were black, these black Democrats have been much more likely than most black Republicans to be very representative of their communities, have close ties to those black communities, and hold views overlapping substantially with the views of the country's black majority on major public policy issues. Over the last two decades these black Democrats have also been much more likely to openly articulate the black majority's views on civil rights and institutional racism, and indeed to gain some significant political power within the Democratic Party.[35]

There have been inside reports of a negative racial climate in at least some parts of the Bush White House's administrative operations, reports similar to those that arose about the Reagan White House. In a book on his experiences there, Ron Christie, the black deputy assistant on domestic policy for Bush's vice president, Dick Cheney, reported on some racist framing that he encountered. One day a senior member of the Cheney staff commented that Christie's office area was "starting to look like a ghetto down here." Christie's reflections indicate much disconcertion and pain at the time and later: "The ghetto? I was crushed. I wasn't sure what to think or how to react. I was angry, sad, and confused. I wanted to lash out, but I felt [too] paralyzed to move."[36] Moreover, inside and outside the Bush White House, there was periodic criminalization and related stereotyping of black Americans by some conservative Republicans. For example, in public and backstage discussions of the 2005 Katrina hurricane disaster in New Orleans, some Republican politicians and media commentators periodically spoke of the displaced black residents there, who were mostly poor and working-class people, as "criminals," "thugs," "hoodlums," or "looters." Such language, yet again, linked ordinary black Americans in great distress with whites' racially stereotyped images of urban criminals.[37]

As president, George Bush did seek to assist impoverished Americans with the supportive but individualistic educational program called the No Child Left Behind Act (NCLB) and with private religion-based social programs. The positive goal of the NCLB was to facilitate poor individuals' achievements, yet without the substantial government programs needed to bring much-needed *structural* changes in the often seriously deteriorating and underfunded urban school systems in which the underachieving students frequently had to operate. Many of the schools in which the students needed this special government NCLB attention were those attended by students of color, whose racial groups have long been targets of various types of white discrimination and government policy neglect. In addition, the goal of the Bush administration's religious thrust in various poverty policy areas was again privatization—that is, to reduce government anti-poverty programs and to get private groups into more extensive efforts at taking care of the poor.[38] In addition, Bush's support for these educational and other social programs was more than offset by his desire, and that of his elite supporters and funders, to sharply reduce federal taxes on the corporations and the rich. Together with his huge increases in federal expenditures for the Middle East invasions and wars, these tax reductions made certain that there would quite inadequate funding for educational efforts like the NCLB and for faith-based social programs that were supposed to help offset declines in government social support programs.

Likely influenced by his previous economic efforts as Texas governor, Bush also developed significant international policy efforts in regard to Latin America. As Gary Gerstle has explained, one broad goal was to build more economic ties between the United States and Latin America so that there would be a fully open capitalistic market in the Western hemisphere, a market with yet more areas for U.S. corporations' recruitment and exploitation of low-wage Hispanic labor. In addition, to accomplish these policy goals Bush and some of his advisers reportedly saw that it was necessary to try to bring more Hispanic voters into the ranks of the Republican Party; that is, some in the Bush administration sought to use a "soft diversity" approach in the "service of corporate expansion and enrichment."[39]

Retreat on Civil Rights: The Bush Administration

Once he became president, Bush's white-enclave and individualistic orientation could also be observed in his administration's approach to reducing or eviscerating much federal civil rights enforcement aimed at patterns of discrimination. While he had good relationships with a few conservatives of color like Rice and Gonzales, like many white evangelicals and other whites his individualistic view of racial relationships clearly made it difficult for him to see the realities of systemic racism and acknowledge the institutionalized barriers experienced by many people of color.[40] Thus, a draft report of the then relatively moderate U.S. Commission on Civil Rights described the Bush administration's civil rights efforts as mainly designed just "to carry out official duties, not to promote initiatives or plans for improving opportunity" and to implement conservative federal "policies that have retreated from long-established civil rights promises in each of these areas."[41] Such administrative actions appeared to be part of the long-term Republican strategy that since the Reagan administration had sought to end efforts at significantly desegregating major institutions along racial lines. These actions were mostly carried out by conservative high-level presidential appointees in various federal agencies, periodically with the support of a conservative Supreme Court majority. To take one major example, Bush's first Attorney General, John Ashcroft (2001–2005), showed little interest in aggressively enforcing or expanding U.S. civil rights laws.

From 2001 to 2009, numerous federal judges and other federal officials worked with local and state officials to end even voluntary school desegregation and other antidiscrimination and remedial programs. Bush's two Supreme Court appointments tipped the high court in more of a conservative direction on these racial matters. With the three other conservatives on the court, they often operated as right-wing activists in deciding some important decisions, including important civil rights and desegregation decisions. For instance, in a pivotal 2007 decision Bush and other court conservatives intentionally and greatly weakened the classic 1954 *Brown* decision by deciding that public school systems could *not* make use of racial markers along with other factors to try to increase the desegregation of otherwise de facto segregated high schools on a local and voluntary basis. Moderately liberal justice Stephen Breyer made the case for the local school plans in his dissenting decision representing the losing side of four Supreme Court justices: "The school board plans before us resemble many others adopted in the last 50 years by primary and secondary schools throughout the Nation. All of those plans represent local efforts to bring about the kind of racially integrated education that *Brown* v. *Board of Education* . . . long ago promised."[42] After describing how U.S. progress in school desegregation had stalled at still high levels of de facto racial segregation, he underscored how local white school and other government officials, together with discriminatory housing patterns, had played a significant role in school segregation, and then later added this:

> If one examines the context more specifically, one finds that the districts' plans reflect efforts to overcome a history of segregation, embody the results of broad experience and community consultation, seek to expand student choice while reducing the need for mandatory busing, and use race-conscious criteria in highly limited ways that diminish the use of race compared to preceding integration efforts.[43]

Breyer argued that these local plans were constitutional and fully in line with the goals of *Brown*, and then he concluded with this sharp judicial commentary: "The last half-century has witnessed great strides toward racial equality, but we have not yet realized the promise of *Brown*. To invalidate the plans under review is to threaten the promise of *Brown*. The plurality's position, I fear, would break that promise."[44]

Significantly, the one black justice on the court, the very conservative Clarence Thomas who had been appointed by Bush's father, asserted in his opinion on this case that "Simply putting students together under the same roof does not necessarily mean that the students will learn together or even interact. Furthermore, it is unclear whether increased interracial contact improves racial attitudes and relations."[45] In his controversial opinion Thomas played the social scientist, contending that his largely unsupported reading of the social science research is best, yet he and his legal assistants were misinformed about, if not intentionally distorting, the social science data on interracial interaction. As the leading social scientist working in this particular area of research, Thomas Pettigrew, aptly put it: "Apparently, Thomas found inconclusive the findings of my meta-analysis with Linda Tropp that demonstrated that intergroup contact typically and significantly reduces prejudice with 515 studies involving more than 250,000 subjects from 38 nations around the globe."[46] The social science data were clear that equal-status, interracial interaction usually contributed to the improvement of racial attitudes and views of those involved in such interactions.

This racially backtracking decision by Republican-appointed justices demonstrated just how radical numerous Supreme Court decisions have become with the Court's very conservative Republican majority, a result unmistakably desired by the last few Republican presidents. This process of moving backward on the racial integration of major U.S. institutions has largely been intentional and oriented to the interests of many elite and ordinary whites. Recent research and analysis like that of Pettigrew has shown that the Supreme Court has, in several ways, gone back to the old 1896 *Plessy* v. *Ferguson* decision that sustained Jim Crow by actually upholding the legality of racial segregation in public school systems even though it has been created or facilitated by the intentional actions of local government officials or real-estate firms.[47]

This Bush era backtracking on societal integration took place as it was becoming clear that the *Brown* decision had had numerous positive effects on U.S. society. Several important court cases dealing with other serious societal inequalities, such as those stemming from gender discrimination and from physical disabilities, have drawn well on important insights and arguments of the *Brown* case. In addition, qualitative and quantitative research on the impact of school desegregation typically shows significant positive effects for children. Research on both attenders and graduates of desegregated high schools—especially that carried out in the 1970s before the Reagan administration's open retreat from racial desegregation in numerous public institutions—has shown that a substantial majority of students benefit from such desegregated educational experiences. These school settings tend to increase student interactions with youth from a diversity of other groups, not just other racial groups, and they tend to reduce racial and other prejudices for white and other students. However, other social science research shows that successful school desegregation has led to only modest collateral desegregation of society, in large part because school desegregation efforts have mostly not been accompanied by sustained private or government efforts at effectively desegregating other major institutions such as residential subdivisions. Indeed, since the 1960s white conservatives' efforts to counter serious attempts to fully desegregate numerous institutions of the larger society have been quite successful. As Pettigrew has put it, much conservative "political force has consistently led the fight against *Brown* and virtually all other efforts" to dramatically end educational segregation and other U.S. racism. "It is not coincidental that the five Supreme Court justices currently undercutting *Brown* are all Republican appointments. *Brown* did not fail America; rather, America failed *Brown*."[48] Or, more exactly, conservative white American leadership has failed in regard to the social justice goals of *Brown*.

In the George W. Bush era, periodically, the white-racist framing and orientations of some key Republicans became quite visible. Recall that Bush appointed John Ashcroft as Attorney General, a leading Republican who had been interviewed and praised by the white supremacist, neo-Confederate magazine, *Southern Partisan*. In his interview, Ashcroft had called for respect for, and a positive defense of Robert E. Lee and other pro-slavery Confederate leaders.[49] Moreover, at a December 2002 birthday party for Senator Strom Thurmond, then Senate majority leader Trent Lott (R-Miss.) openly praised Thurmond with the comment that when Thurmond ran for president as the 1948 candidate for the white supremacist and segregationist States' Rights (Dixiecrat) party, "We voted for him. We're proud of it. And if the rest of the country had followed our lead, we wouldn't have had all these problems over all these years, either."[50] A key Dixiecrat Party theme had, not surprisingly, been racial "Segregation Forever."

Conspicuously, there was no negative response from Lott's audience at the party, and the mainstream media ignored his commentary until an important online blogger noted its racist content. Slowly the public discussion spread throughout the mainstream media, and a few weeks later Lott had to resign his position as Senate majority leader. Still, Lott's price for his nostalgia for a racially segregated past did not cost him his job as a senator, and he remained chair of the Senate Rules Committee and of the inauguration ceremony for Bush's second term. Clearly, the White House and Republican leadership had found Lott's individualistic apology acceptable. In addition, very little of the mainstream media commentary noted that this was a racist remark or interpreted it as part of a possibly racist backstage political climate. Lott himself described it as just a "mistake of the head, not of the heart."[51] Anthropologist Jane Hill has noted that Lott's racialized commentary was mostly interpreted by the mainstream media as just an unfortunate gaffe or light-hearted comment that should not be taken seriously. Thus, this clear revelation of the racist framing of major white politicians could be generally ignored. Hill has also noted that mainstream reporters and editors gave no attention to the harm that such racist comments by white leaders do to African Americans, and most especially those who lived through the near-slavery of Jim Crow.[52]

Conclusion

Among the elite and among ordinary Americans, the doctrine of U.S. exceptionalism has long been very important in much thinking about this society and the global scene. In this perspective the United States has a God-ordained role to spread its values and conception of democracy and liberty across the globe. Many examples in this book show that such American exceptionalism has been a common religious, political, and economic doctrine from the first centuries of European colonization. In this and previous chapters, we have discussed recent U.S. presidents, such as Ronald Reagan and George W. Bush, who regularly and openly viewed important national and global issues from a rigid either/or, good-versus-evil Manichaean perspective in which the United States represents political virtue. Dramatic terms like Bush's "axis of evil" for the countries of Iran, Iraq, and North Korea have been applied to countries that refuse or resist U.S. goals on the international scene. Earlier, in the 1980s, Reagan had spoken in similarly grand and exceptionalist terms of the "evil empire" for the Soviet Union. Such perspectives represent a type of naively dualistic thinking that has provided much support for U.S. overseas imperialism, both in the past and in the present.[53]

From the beginning of U.S. expansion as a country, the framing of the world by the elite has often been both exceptionalist and white-expansionist, a more or less racialized perspective accenting the manifest destiny of U.S. corporate and government interests to expand across the continent and the globe, by military means if necessary. Over recent decades, this exceptionalist destiny of the United States continues to be central to the political-economic framing of the globe by many in the U.S. elite and the general public. No nation state that tries to develop with socialistic or nationalistic political institutions and that also directly counters or limits U.S. political or capitalistic interests there will likely be allowed to do so without some U.S. or associated Western intervention. From the perspective of many in the elite virtually all areas of the globe must be made safe for U.S. government or corporate intervention and corporate exploitation. In part about corporate exploitation of Middle Eastern resources, George W. Bush's invasion of Iraq under the ideological argument of bringing democracy to a country with a political dictator is clearly an example of contemporary U.S. imperialism. This and other recent Middle East intervention has periodically been legitimated with an exceptionalist rationale and an implicit or explicit racial framing accenting U.S. superiority over people whose racial or ethnic characteristics, cultural institutions, or socio-political systems are supposedly inferior to their European and North American counterparts.[54]

7
The Barack Obama Presidential Campaign

The 2008 election was distinctive in several ways, the most important of which was the election of the first U.S. president who was a man of color. Initially, few thought Senator Barack Obama would have a chance to become president because of the long tradition of whites' racist framing of African Americans, his relative lack of political experience, or the strong competition within the Democratic primaries and in the general election. When the electoral process began heating up in the winter of 2007/08 and spring of 2008, Hillary Clinton, an influential senator and former first lady, was the front runner for the Democratic Party nomination. Over a series of primary contests, she won some important primaries, as did her rival Obama.

Over time, Obama won out, but his journey to the nomination in August 2008 and to the presidency in November 2008, although historic, did not come easily. Many aspects of blatant, covert, and subtle racism crashed into his political journey, so much so that it soon became apparent that the United States was anything but the "post-racial" paradise that many whites have claimed it to be over recent decades. We will now examine selected critical moments and events that illustrate the continuing significance of systemic racism throughout the pathbreaking primary and general election campaigns of the watershed U.S. election year of 2008.

A Fabricated Media Crisis: Dr. Wright's Prophetic Sermons

During the 2008 primary campaign, perhaps the most critical moment for Senator Barack Obama involved the mainstream media's picking up on a few older sermons of Obama's African American minister, Dr. Jeremiah Wright, one of the country's most distinguished Christian clergy and celebrated religious authors. Dr. Wright had been awarded numerous honorary degrees from U.S. colleges and universities and had notable military service, and he served as the long-term minister of Chicago's large Trinity United Church of Christ.

This rather contrived media event was centrally about the racialization of Obama and his political messages. In a prophetic sermon cited in the media, Dr. Wright called for God to "damn America" for its societal sins, including its long history of racial oppression and imperialism, which he reviewed in this long sermon in detail. The mostly white-controlled mainstream media regarded his well-crafted sermons, with their prophetic preacher-like language, as reflecting Dr. Wright's supposedly radical views of U.S. society. Often behaving like a wing of the Republican presidential campaign, the mainstream media may have initially picked up this highly distorted story about Wright's old sermons from racist websites on the internet.[1] Significantly, the mainstream media and conservative commentators inside and outside the media mostly focused on small snippets taken out of context from these sermons. Only a few minutes out of hundreds of thousands of minutes of Wright's recorded sermons were selected and repeated many times by these commentators.

In this manner the mainstream media reporters and analysts colluded in a concerted, distorted, and highly politicized imaging of Dr. Wright's serious in-church sermons. Both the mainstream media and various white suprema-cist websites on the internet periodically focused on these sermons over the months of the primaries and general election, and some continued to focus on them long after the general election. Both the mainstream and extremist media sectors took Wright's mostly accurate sermon comments about U.S. history and systemic racism out of their sermonic contexts, thereby creating significant political problems for Senator Obama, and especially with a great many white voters. In their commentaries, the mainstream media com-mentators and numerous politicians generally operated out of some version of a well-institutionalized white framing of society.[2]

Not only did Dr. Wright himself criticize the often crude and defamatory mainstream media commentary, but several knowledgeable observers of Dr. Wright's church career and prophetic sermons made clear how distorted the media and politicians' attacks on him were. After the mainstream media regularly took Wright's sermon snippets out of their sermonic and church context, Rev. John Thomas, the white head of the United Church of Christ denomination spoke out forthrightly and accurately. As the distinguished president of this mostly white and mainstream Protestant denomination— begun long ago in part by the famous Pilgrims—Thomas condemned the distorted, inflammatory, and racist news coverage of Wright and of Chicago's Trinity United Church of Christ. In an important statement, Thomas first noted that Dr. Wright had been the pastor of this church for nearly four decades, half of that time for the Obama family, and then added that the short sermon clips and associated news reports were "served up with frenzied and heated commentary by media personalities expressing shock that such language and sentiments could be uttered from the pulpit." Accenting media illiteracy about U.S. religious history, Thomas then suggested that the media commentators had little or no knowledge about the long "history of preaching in the United States from the unrelentingly grim language of New England election-day sermons to the fiery rhetoric of the Black church prophetic tradition. Maybe they prefer the false prophets with their happy homilies." He then accented how generally poor the mainstream news analyses were in taking little phrases out of many hours of sermons and thereby pulling out just "a few lurid phrases" and also how "those who have aired them repeatedly have only one intention. It is to wound a presidential candidate."[3] Rev. Thomas thus emphasized the real intent of much media and politicians' commentary on Wright's damning of America for its history of racism—to hurt or derail Senator Obama's nomination.

Rev. Thomas continued by calling out the contrast between Wright's being criticized harshly for "using a mild 'obscenity' in reference to the United States" and the unnecessary war in Iraq that was started with deception and then put into place with "foolish arrogance." For him, the thousands of Americans and Iraqis slaughtered in an unnecessary war marked the true national obscenity. Next, Thomas moves to what may be a deeper problem for much of the white-controlled mainstream media. In the poverty-stricken area of Chicago where Wright's church is "race continues to play favorites in failing urban school systems, unresponsive health care systems, crumbling infrastructure, and meager economic development. . . . Is it racist to name the racial divides that continue to afflict our nation, and to do so loudly?"[4]

Interestingly, Rev. Thomas was not the only national religious figure to call out the racist attacks on Dr. Wright and, by implication, on Obama. In an important commentary on the media-generated controversy, Frank Schaeffer, a former Christian right activist and conservative Republican—and son of an influential evangelical theologian—argued that the mainstream media and broader political framing of Wright was in fact discriminatory. While Obama suffered much "smear-by-association" from his minister's sermon snippets, the same did not take place for white politicians: "But when my late father—Religious Right leader Francis Schaeffer—denounced America and even called for the violent overthrow of the U.S. government, he was invited to lunch with presidents Ford, Reagan, and Bush, Sr." Schaeffer added that across the country on Sundays a great many white religious-right ministers preach very aggressively against this country's "sins from tens of thousands of pulpits," condemn America as "evil," and "warn of immanent destruction." In comparison, thus, "Obama's minister's shouted 'controversial' comments were mild."[5]

In Schaeffer's insider's view, the religiously-cast, often highly political language was, and still is, much stronger coming from many conservative white ministers—including those associated with recent Republican presidents—yet no extensive and lasting media and political uproar had arisen over these prominent white religious commentators. In this instance, as in many others involving Obama's years as senator and president, the deeper realities of systemic racism regularly made themselves evident in the differential treatment of him and other important African Americans in the public commentaries and other public actions of many influential white Americans.

Reacting to a Political Crisis: Obama's "A More Perfect Union" Speech

Both Thomas and Schaeffer were much bolder in their critical responses to the mainstream media commentators' and several Republican politicians' distortions of Dr. Wright's sermons than was candidate Obama when he finally responded to these events during this racially heated primary season. On March 18, 2008, Senator Obama gave what is likely the most important public speech ever given by a leading presidential candidate on U.S. racism issues, one that was both praised and condemned across the mainstream media, including major internet blogs.

Let us look closely at some important points Obama made in this "A More Perfect Union" speech.[6] In this attention-getting speech, the then candidate Obama's opening statement was strong and expected, given that he was in Philadelphia's constitution center: "Two hundred and twenty one years ago, in a hall that still stands across the street, a group of men gathered and, with these simple words, launched America's improbable experiment in democracy." A bit later he made some accurate critical observations on the long struggle of people's movements for racial change in this country:

> And yet words on a parchment would not be enough to deliver slaves from bondage, or provide men and women of every color and creed their full rights and obligations as citizens of the United States. What would be needed were Americans in successive generations who were willing to do their part—through protests and struggle, on the streets and in the courts, through a civil war and civil disobedience and always at great risk—to narrow that gap between the promise of our ideals and the reality of their time.

In the speech he thus connected current efforts to bring social change and unite Americans across racial lines to the long years of past protest aimed at bringing the mostly rhetorical ideals (for whites) of the old liberty-and-justice framing of the United States to full societal reality.

As might be expected, Senator Obama then worked in some of his own dramatic biography, and followed with commentary on Dr. Jeremiah Wright, whose brief phrases as put out in the media Obama condemned:

> I have already condemned, in unequivocal terms, the statements of Reverend Wright that have caused such controversy . . . the remarks that have caused this recent firestorm weren't simply controversial. They weren't simply a religious leader's effort to speak out against

perceived injustice. Instead, they expressed a profoundly distorted view of this country—a view that sees white racism as endemic, and that elevates what is wrong with America above all that we know is right with America.

Obama's speech adopted the essentially white-framed position that Dr. Wright's critical assessments of major negative features of U.S. society, such as large-scale discrimination within its borders that destroys black and other lives every day, were false and wrongheaded. Yet, in contrast, a majority of African Americans, and many other Americans, would probably at this time have agreed with Wright's critical points about persisting racial discrimination, as well as his barbed points about U.S. imperialism overseas.[7]

After examining briefly the impact of the racial past of slavery and Jim Crow segregation on the present, Obama added:

A lack of economic opportunity among black men, and the shame and frustration that came from not being able to provide for one's family, contributed to the erosion of black families—a problem that welfare policies for many years may have worsened. And the lack of basic services in so many urban black neighborhoods—parks for kids to play in, police walking the beat, regular garbage pick-up, and building code enforcement—all helped create a cycle of violence, blight, and neglect that continue to haunt us.

Here and in his larger speech the contemporary anger of African Americans about racial oppression seemed to be more a matter of recoiling from past discrimination than a reaction to continuing present-day discrimination.

A bit later, Senator Obama made his one tough assessment of current racial matters:

In the white community, the path to a more perfect union means acknowledging that what ails the African-American community does not just exist in the minds of black people; that the legacy of discrimination—and current incidents of discrimination, while less overt than in the past—are real and must be addressed. Not just with words, but with deeds—by investing in our schools and our communities; by enforcing our civil rights laws and ensuring fairness in our criminal justice system; by providing this generation with ladders of opportunity that were unavailable for previous generations.

Though Obama did here mention contemporary discrimination, he downplayed it by suggesting it was not as blatant as in the past, and did not analyze this crucial issue further; but in the next segment of the speech he moved away from this continuing reality of individual and institutional racism to reject change advocates like Wright as "breeding division." Then, before telling a final poignant campaign story, Obama accented the unity for which he is famous: "I would not be running for President if I didn't believe with all my heart that this is what the vast majority of Americans want for this country. This union may never be perfect, but generation after generation has shown that it can always be perfected."[8]

Senator Obama thus presented a bold speech dealing centrally with issues of race and racism, the first of this kind by any major U.S. presidential candidate. Yet its principal weakness lay in his failure to address more fully and frontally the contemporary realities of racial hostility and oppression that still pervade most major U.S. institutions, realities that had been forthrightly dealt with in the many sermons of Dr. Wright. Indeed, Obama decided to focus on serious racism as substantially something of the U.S. past, and beyond two brief phrases he did not analyze or suggest major solutions for the extensive individual and institutional racism of the present day. In this way Obama himself played into the perspective of many whites who view the United States as substantially post-racial and rather different today from its racist past, and as having mostly ridden itself of its patterns of institutional racism. In effect, as Adia Harvey Wingfield and I have argued at book length, Obama himself was here publicly using several elements of a colorblind ("soft") version of the still-dominant white racial frame.[9] This political strategy was not at this time, or indeed later, atypical because Obama consistently used elements of this softer colorblind version of the contemporary white frame throughout his primary and general election campaigns; and he continued to use this perspective throughout his first years as president. We will explore further some of the reasons why he may have adopted this approach in a later section of this chapter.

Corroboration for this point about his moderate but substantially white-oriented framing could be seen in much of the public reaction to his unprecedented anti-Wright speech. After the speech, the majority of the white public seemed relatively satisfied with what was called the "honesty" of his speech, and the majority of white political and media commentators expressed the view that the speech was a successful political gamble. A short while later in the election cycle, when Dr. Wright made additional comments about the political character of Obama's speech that were critical of him, and after some other controversial comments were made by Wright and others associated with Trinity United Church of Christ, Obama resigned his membership in the church.

Democratic Activists and Primaries: More White Framing

Republican officials and mainstream media commentators were not the only ones making use of the Dr. Wright story. Among the politicians whose political advisers wanted them to consider attacking Obama for his minister's sermons was Senator Hillary Clinton, Obama's main opponent in the Democratic Party primaries, In late spring, according to an *Atlantic Monthly* article, Mark Penn, a top campaign strategist, wanted Clinton to be much harder on Obama, and in a memo he made this suggestion: "Does anyone believe that it is possible to win the nomination without, over these next two months, raising all these issues on him? . . . Won't a single tape of Wright going off on America with Obama sitting there be a game ender?". Apparently, Penn and other white Democratic operatives did not understand that African American ministers like Dr. Jeremiah Wright and their parishioners might be disturbed about persisting racial discrimination in the United States. In addition, Penn seemed to link his view of Obama to other racially stereotyped imagery, writing to Clinton that "I cannot imagine America electing a president during a time of war who is not at his center fundamentally American in his thinking and in his values."[10] Here we have the persisting framing of Senator Obama as somehow foreign, not fundamentally American, and possessing certain weak values. These are recurring images in whites' racial framing of black Americans that have been used for centuries to rationalize slavery, Jim Crow, and contemporary discrimination.

Also during this primary campaign, another strong Democratic supporter of Senator Clinton, former vice-presidential candidate Geraldine Ferraro, accented her also white-framed perspective in assessing other aspects of the Obama campaign: "[N]either the Barack Obama campaign nor the media seem to understand what is at the heart of the anger on the part of women who feel that Senator Clinton was treated unfairly because she is a woman or what is fueling the concern of Reagan Democrats for whom sexism isn't an issue, but reverse racism is."[11] Senator Clinton did face significant sexism, although more outside the Democratic Party than inside. Yet, in this *Boston Globe* opinion piece, Ferraro seemed to be at least as much concerned with "Reagan Democrats," a codeword that has typically meant white Democrats of working-class and lower-middle-class backgrounds, especially those somewhat conservative or living in southern areas. She used the white-coined conservative term "reverse racism," a term suggesting, erroneously of course, that there was a societal reality of blacks discriminating against whites on a large scale. Most importantly, given the recurring and systemic racism Senator Obama was facing in his campaign (see below), Ferraro at no point called out whites for this antiblack racism or white men for their gendered racism in attacks on his actively campaigning wife Michelle Obama.

In her opinion piece Ferraro later returns to her white-framed concern with the feelings of "Reagan Democrats." She adds that:

> [W]hen I was accused of being racist for a statement I made about the influence of blacks on Obama's historic campaign, [white] people have been stopping me to express a common sentiment: If you're white you

can't open your mouth without being accused of being racist. They see Obama's playing the race card . . .[12]

Here too are common clichés out of the contemporary white frame. The phrase, "If you're white you can't open your mouth without being accused of being racist" is an extreme exaggeration many whites have repeatedly used to take the focus off actual discrimination against people of color and, often, to defend their openly racist comments or views. Ferraro also used another conservative racial code-phrase, "playing the race card," which racist whites have frequently utilized to put down African Americans fighting against racial discrimination. Indeed, it is significant that this racialized phrase about a "race card" appears to have increased significantly in use among whites in numerous areas of the country since Obama's primary campaign, again likely indicating the importance of racial framing in many white minds.

Clearly operating from an unreflective and rather aggressive white framing that was often used by many whites in both parties during the primary and general election campaigns, Democratic Party leader Ferraro was here taking whites off the hook for their individual and collective racism and blaming black Americans for creating much-deserved "racial resentment." Her racialized commentary illustrates the way in which even many well-educated whites have difficulty accurately and critically assessing the hard evidence about systemic racism. Indeed, her prominent opinion piece provided a conspicuous example of just how normalized the white racial frame has been in recent politics and media commentary.

Obama's Nomination: A Watershed Moment

In August 2008, at the Democratic Party convention in Denver, Senator Barack Obama's selection as the first person of color, and first African American, ever nominated for president by a major political party was a moment underscoring an array of important political and racial realities. Significantly, Obama's acceptance of the nomination was a watershed moment that took place some 45 years after Dr. Martin Luther King, Jr.'s famous 1963 "I Have a Dream" speech, which had marked an acceleration of civil rights protests against Jim Crow segregation. Central to Obama's great political achievement had been the hard work of many Americans of all backgrounds who had sought that moment. Among these were the many African Americans who had struggled for nearly four centuries to break free of slavery, Jim Crow, and contemporary racial discrimination. At several progressive racial steps in U.S. history—the abolitionist movement of the 1840s–1860s, the civil rights movement of the 1950s–1960s, and the continuing rights movements of the present—African Americans and their allies have pressed for major racial changes, and have quite likely made this country a more just and democratic one than it otherwise might have been.

As prominent black writer and activist Amiri Baraka has noted, many Americans do not "understand that the logic and strength of Obama's candidacy is the 21st century manifestation of the Civil Rights and Black Liberation Movements, impossible without it. Jesse Jackson's two impressive [candidacies] were also part of that motion, [and] not to accept both these phenomena as positive aspects and results of our collective struggle is to lack 'True Self Consciousness.'"[13]

This was indeed an era of "firsts." Ironically, just a few weeks before Senator Barack Obama was nominated as the first major black presidential candidate in U.S. history, the U.S. House had very belatedly passed an historic resolution apologizing for slavery and Jim Crow segregation. Some 120 members of Congress—revealingly, only two of them Republicans—co-sponsored the very important resolution that "acknowledges the fundamental injustice, cruelty, brutality, and inhumanity of slavery and Jim Crow" and "apologizes to African-Americans on behalf of the people of the United States, for the wrongs committed against them and their ancestors who suffered under slavery and Jim Crow." The resolution further expressed the U.S. House's "commitment to rectify the lingering consequences of the misdeeds committed against African-Americans under slavery and Jim Crow and to stop the occurrence of human rights violations in the future." However, the non-binding resolution explicitly denied with a white-oriented disclaimer at its end the possibility of reparations for the government's role in the extreme oppression of slavery and Jim Crow: "Nothing in this resolution (a) authorizes or supports any claim against the United States; or (b) serves as a settlement of any claim against the United States."[14] Once again, U.S. political leaders demonstrated the great ability of government officials to engage in liberty and justice rhetoric, but without a major material implementation of that important liberty and justice perspective.

In addition, the important symbolism of the government apology evaporated rather quickly. The mainstream media gave brief and cursory attention to the unprecedented apology resolution, and most especially to its call for remedies for the "lingering consequences" of slavery and Jim Crow. In addition, so far as I can find, no powerful white politicians have paid any significant and direct attention to the apology since it was issued. Indeed, it seems probable that most Americans today do not know that such a congressional apology for the country's long history of systemic racism was ever issued.

The General Election: Political Symbolism and Racial Framing

Political symbolism is central in most election campaigns, yet often remains under-analyzed or sometimes unremarked. In the middle of the 2008 general election, prominent linguistics scholar George Lakoff assessed the quite divergent ways that major political issues were being assessed and framed by important Democratic and Republican Party candidates and their political advisers. In his evaluation, the Republicans understand much better than Democrats that major elections are often more about patriotism, nationalism, "family values," and other feel-good general symbolism than about data-based arguments targeting specific societal problems and major policy issues. The Democratic leaders' orientation in major elections is too often one assuming that most voters are politically rational and evaluative in assessing their own interests and are thus seeking considered data-grounded answers to serious government policy issues.[15]

Thus, during the 2008 election numerous Republican Party political decisions, such as choosing Alaska governor Sarah Palin for the Republican ticket, were not so much about systematic evaluations of serious public policy issues, as about the "symbolic mechanisms of the political mind."[16] Lakoff listed other important symbols used historically in Republican campaigns, such as those of Ronald Reagan and George W. Bush we have noted in prior chapters. In Lakoff's view they got elected in substantial part by "running on character: values, communication, (apparent) authenticity, trust, and identity—not issues and policies." In recent decades, conservative Republican candidates have accented strict family values, which are taken beyond individual families to "apply via metaphorical thought to the nation: good vs. evil, authority, the use of force, toughness and discipline, individual (versus social) responsibility, and tough love." Given this strict family morality and metaphor, thus, government "social programs are immoral because they violate discipline and individual responsibility." The Republicans' relatively authoritarian emphasis on strict family values, guns, the military, and free market forces are asserted to "show force and discipline."[17] As we have seen over recent decades, Republican presidential and vice-presidential candidates such as Reagan, the Bushes, McCain, and Palin have indeed made much use of this strict-discipline, get-tough, good-versus-evil, "cultural values" symbolism in their various political campaigns.

However, like many election analysts at the time, Lakoff left out what was perhaps the most important political symbolism for a great many voters in the 2008 election and other recent elections—the racial symbolism, which is often intertwined with other potent political symbols. Thus, John McCain and Sarah Palin evidently came to symbolize in many white voters' minds a certain prized whiteness, as political examples of the virtuous white Americans that have been at the heart of the white framing of this society since the 17th century. Such racial symbolism, as we observe throughout this chapter, was important in the 2008 presidential election. Not only did most Republicans, then as now, stand for toughness, conservative family, and certain good-versus-evil values, but these asserted cultural values were often racialized and whitened in their political exhibition or interpretation. Candidates McCain and Palin were regularly portrayed and seen by many white voters, and some others, as those truly representative of the "real Americans."

Evaluating the 2008 general election, Mark Schmitt, a fellow at the New America Foundation, noted well the explicit and implicit focus of the Republican campaign on just such a "who is American" identity politics. In Senator McCain's first general election advertisement, a key slogan proclaimed that he was the "American President Americans Are Waiting For." Strongly implied here was that candidate McCain was the real American in the campaign, a view buttressed by the numerous Republicans who repeatedly attacked Obama for not wearing a flag pin and for supposedly not saluting the flag. While nothing was explicitly said in this McCain advertising about Obama's racial identity and international background, there was a clear implication of his foreignness in this and other early Republican political efforts.[18] Such a perspective on the foreignness or marginality of many Democratic Party politicians and their supporters has been common in the Republican Party. For example, one very influential Republican commentator, David Frum, argued in a 2007 book that the Republican Party was the party of real "American democratic nationhood," in contrast to a Democratic Party that attracted "marginal" people like "intellectuals, Catholics, Jews, blacks, feminists, gays." Frum further suggested that, "As the nation weakens, Democrats grow stronger."[19] From this elite conservative and straight-white-male perspective, the country's increasingly diverse majority has greatly weakened its important social fabric.

Like Frum, many white (and some other) commentators, politicians, and ordinary citizens commonly use distinctive words like "American" and "Americans" to mean "white Americans." One can pick up major newspapers and news magazines and find "American" or "Americans" used in ways that undoubtedly mean *white* Americans. Consider this sentence from a Florida newspaper: "The American Public isn't giving government or police officers the blind trust it once did."[20] Here "American" unreflectively means "white American," for a great many black Americans and other Americans of color have never blindly trusted the police. In addition, recent conservative candidates in numerous local and state elections have also used phrases like "traditional American values" in ways that suggest they have in mind white Americans. In recent psychological studies, major researchers like Thierry Devos and Mahzarin Banaji have examined how strongly certain racial groups are implicitly associated with the category "American." Their numerous respondents saw African Americans, Native Americans, and Asian Americans as *less* associated with the category "American" than were whites. For their white subjects, they found that the association of "American" with whites was positively correlated with the strength of these white subjects' own national identification. They conclude that their research strongly indicates that "American is implicitly synonymous with being white."[21]

Given this substantial research, constant references to McCain being a "real American" and to the Republican Party as the party of "real American" patriotism appear as barely disguised appeals to the old white racist framing of society and its often negative framing of Americans who are not white. Thus, once Senator Obama became the Democratic candidate, the Republican campaign cranked up a recurring political attack on him as somehow not being a real American. Sometimes this attack was explicitly racist, and sometimes it was more implicitly racist. For example, there was the strong sustained attack of Steve King (R-Iowa), who told an Iowa radio station that:

> I don't want to disparage anyone because of their race, their ethnicity, their name—whatever their religion their father might have been. . . . When you think about the optics of a Barack Obama potentially getting elected . . . if he is elected president, then the radical Islamists, the al-Qaida, the radical Islamists and their supporters, will be dancing in the streets.[22]

Obama's religiously diverse and mixed racial background is linked by this important representative of the Republican attack cohort to his negatively viewed physical appearance (his "optics")—a traditional white-racist framing of a black man since at least the 17th century. King here called out Obama's Muslim African father, yet did not mention that Senator Obama himself was a Christian or that Obama had regularly denounced political terrorists of all types. It is significant how often religious issues came up during the election campaigns, usually signaling that Christianity was the appropriate religion for national political candidates.

Other Republican politicians and activists linked various other stereotypes to this "othering" and "foreignization" of Senator Obama, actions often buttressed by a substantial level of white-hot emotion. Many raised questions about whether he was actually born on U.S. soil, an issue that persisted so long into his presidency that in 2011 he finally had the long form of his birth certificate released. During the campaign, moreover, one emotional email sent by a volunteer activist at one county Republican office in Florida was passed along by a top political official in that office, who told recipients to also pass it along and help "us to win this election." This was part of that intentionally capitalized email sent out just before the November 2008 election:

THE THREAT: HERE IN TEMPLE TERRACE, FL OUR REPUBLICAN HQ IS ONE BLOCK AWAY FROM OUR LIBRARY, WHICH IS AN EARLY VOTING SITE. I SEE CARLOADS OF BLACK OBAMA SUPPORTERS COMING FROM THE INNER CITY TO CAST THEIR VOTES FOR OBAMA ... THIS IS THEIR CHANCE TO GET A

BLACK PRESIDENT AND THEY SEEM TO CARE LITTLE THAT HE IS AT MINIMUM, SOCIALIST, AND PROBABLY MARXIST IN HIS CORE BELIEFS. AFTER ALL, HE IS BLACK.[23]

This rather emotional email about "the threat" of black voters was sent around in bold capital letters. Some of the message suggests the old racial framing of scary black folks "coming from the inner city." One can feel the emotions, the palpable fears. One also senses the fear of a foreign political influence in the form of an alleged "socialist," a theme used by many Republicans in later political commentaries about Obama as president. Again, thus, we see the belief that somehow Obama is foreign and not a real American. Illustrating just how powerful the contemporary white racial framing can be, this central theme would persist throughout the 2008 campaign and into the years of the Obama presidency.

Moreover, during the 2008 campaigns several outspoken Republican officials ran for higher political office adopting openly racist views and aggressively white-framed political orientations. One was Indiana lawyer and prosecutor, Tony Zirkle, who has a Georgetown University degree. He ran in the Indiana Republican Party primary as a candidate for a major congressional district. According to one news report, Zirkle openly asserted that "whites are victims of a 'genocide,' that the races should be segregated into different states." The report also noted that Zirkle had addressed some U.S. Nazi Party members who were commemorating Adolf Hitler's birthday. This news account reported further that Zirkle "doesn't think he is too far out of the Republican mainstream . . . He believes the solution to STDs and out-of-wedlock births is to separate blacks and whites into segregated states, but he says that's fully in the tradition of the party."[24] Local Republican officials did view Zirkle as outside the mainstream, endorsed another Republican candidate, and disavowed his more openly racist views. Zirkle finished third in the primary, but still garnered thousands of Indiana votes. During the 2008 campaign the more openly racist campaign efforts by numerous Republican officials, activists, and voters seem to have marked a shift away from the campaign strategies in the George W. Bush campaigns in 2000 and 2004. Many Republicans were moving back to certain overtly racialized campaign strategies more like those of the Reagan and George H. W. Bush years.

During the first decade of the 2000s several southern Republicans had periodically revealed their own racist views and/or links to white nationalist groups. One reportedly nationalist group is the Council of Conservative Citizens (CCC), with links to the old White Citizens' Council. This group has had as speakers or participants former Republican representative Bob Barr (Georgia), former Senate majority leader Trent Lott (Mississippi), and former Republican National Committee chair, governor, and onetime

Republican presidential hopeful, Haley Barbour (Mississippi). At one local meeting, Lott praised the CCC for holding to the "right principles," and in 2003 Barbour attended the Council's fundraising event for the segregated white private academies.[25] Occasionally, too, an active member of an openly white supremacist group has become a member of an important southern Republican organization, as happened in the 2008 case of an elected member of the Republican Executive Committee in Palm Beach County, Florida.[26]

According to political analyst Cliff Schecter, for many years Senator McCain himself had openly adopted a strong white-racist framing of society and politics. He had opposed the Dr. Martin Luther King, Jr. holiday and had also gone back and forth in his public view of the use of the Confederate battle flag in an earlier 2000 political campaign. In addition, in 2000, McCain had for a time hired a political adviser with a white supremacist past. The man was known for "openly praising David Duke (he called him a 'maverick'), selling t-shirts praising the assassination of Abraham Lincoln and writing/editing for a magazine (*Southern Partisan*) that reminded us that slave masters just really weren't all that bad."[27]

A Cascade of Racist Attacks on Senator Obama

During the general election campaign, many racist attacks were made on Obama and his candidacy by those participating in various capacities in the Republican political campaign, including Senator McCain's many supporters and participants at campaign events. Thus, at a rally in Des Moines, Iowa, one white woman yelled "He's a nigger!" at the mention of Obama. She was not an isolated individual. At numerous other rallies, white participants called out or put on their signs an array of blatantly racist comments. For example, at some McCain–Palin rallies one saw racist signs with revealing political messages like "Vote Right, Vote White." Racist dolls and effigies of Obama were also popular in a diverse array of geographical areas during the general election campaign. At one campaign rally whites had monkey dolls with Obama's name or Obama-mocking notes on them. One company had made monkey puppets to look like Obama, which were distributed nationally. Occasionally, effigies of Obama were displayed or hung from trees and other objects by his political opponents, such as one Obama effigy at the University of Kentucky with a noose placed around its neck.[28]

Antiblack stereotyping and imagery were commonplace. White activists at one conservative political forum, sponsored by Focus on the Family Action, bought many boxes of waffle mix that racially caricatured and mocked Obama, who was shown on the box with a stereotypically Arab headdress and in stereotypically Mexican dress and with mocking slogans like "Open Border Fiesta Waffles." Other McCain–Palin supporters printed up mock food stamps portraying a mule with Obama's face on it and presenting items many whites stereotypically associate with black Americans, such as watermelons and barbecue ribs.[29]

In Snohomish County, Washington, a Republican Party official had to apologize for his group's selling at a state fair "$3 bills" showing Senator Obama in Arab dress with a camel and mocking "black speech." The official blamed a volunteer and said the bills were removed when she heard about them. These $3 bills were being sold nationally by an arch-conservative website that sold other racist paraphernalia. A Democratic Party supporter complained at the fair's Republican booth, but was given a hard time: "The bills offended some passers-by at the fair, including . . . a Monroe woman who said Republicans at the booth threatened to call security on her after she complained . . . a volunteer at the nearby Democratic Party booth at the fair, also saw the bills, which were present at the booth for at least two days this week."[30] During the campaign other Republican groups also passed out or circulated by email similarly mocking "Obama bucks." Another Republican group in California sent out 200 newsletters with the picture of a $10 "food stamp" that had a chicken, a watermelon, and Obama's picture on it. The group's president said of this joking imagery that she "doesn't think in racist terms." Like many whites, she claimed to be colorblind and actually to not see racist imagery in the chicken and watermelon pictures with Obama on the fake food stamp: "It was just food to me."[31] Yet the supposed joke in this food-stamp imagery clearly requires that the readers know antiblack stereotypes from the old white racial frame.

During the presidential campaign these racist attacks sometimes spread dramatically at Republican candidates' rallies across the country. Only occasionally did McCain or his campaign staff publicly condemn the openly racist activities of white supporters at particular campaign rallies. The often numerous racialized signs, dolls, effigies, bucks, and other items helped to create a white-oriented racial climate in much of the national Republican campaign, one that evidently appealed to many white Republican activists and Republican-leaning voters.

Significantly, a supporter of Obama's candidacy and former conservative activist, Frank Schaeffer, was at the time critical of what he described as the hate-filled character of much of the McCain–Palin campaign. Late in the general campaign he called on McCain to change his campaign's significant negativity: "If you do not stand up for all that is good in America and declare that Senator Obama is a patriot, fit for office, and denounce your hate-filled supporters when they scream out 'Terrorist' or 'Kill Him,' history will hold you responsible for all that follows . . . You are unleashing the monster of American hatred and prejudice. . . ."[32] Later on, after Obama's inauguration as president, Schaeffer commented that in his view the Republican Party was so negative nowadays that earlier figures in the development of contemporary conservatism would not likely recognize it.[33]

We should note too that nothing like these aggressive and recurring racial attacks on Senator Obama were directed by Senator Obama's supporters against Republican John McCain. Unmistakably, during this 2008 election season there was much evidence of the pervasiveness of contemporary white racism, now often seen in its more overt frontstage forms such as in political campaign rallies.

Democrats Racially Framing Obama

The 2008 general election campaign revealed that many whites in both major parties looked at the political world from some version of the white racial frame. This included many of Obama's supporters who periodically used a version of the white racial frame in interpreting Senator Obama's background or campaign issues, albeit usually a less harsh version of that white frame than was adopted by many white Republicans. Thus, various white volunteers for the Obama campaign downplayed in one way or another his being black. One Alabama volunteer reportedly spoke to local whites about how Obama "doesn't come from the African-American perspective—he's not of that tradition . . . He's not a product of any ghetto."[34] In a western state another volunteer spoke with a white voter who said that she was worried that black people were "nice to your face but then when they get around their own people you just have to worry about what they're going to do to you." The white Obama volunteer replied that "One thing you have to remember is that Obama, he's half white and he was raised by his white mother. So his views are more white than black really."[35] Later, this volunteer said that, if she had had more time, she would have explained that "Obama is the best candidate to run for President since I have been voting."[36] Clearly, numerous comments made by Democratic volunteers and campaign officials about Obama's persona and candidacy seemed to fall back upon an old feature of the white racial frame—the view that makes a few black Americans "an exception to their race," that is, an exception to certain common stereotypes of black Americans.

The often harsh and more openly white-racist framing of many Republican officials and activists, together with the somewhat softer framing of some white Democrats like those just noted, made quite clear just how racially framed the entire general election was in 2008. It was conducted very substantially within, and against the background of, this old and deep white racialized framing of U.S. society.

The November Election Results: More Racial Dimensions

The political wisdom of Democratic Party officials, including Senator Obama, in running the general campaign by drawing on elements from a colorblind version of the white frame and mostly ignoring issues of racism could be seen in the significant proportion of white voters, some 43 percent, who turned out and voted for Obama in the 2008 election. Without this significant minority of white voters, Obama clearly would not have become president. Yet there was much more to the racial dimensions of the Obama–McCain electoral results than that particular electoral fact.

Well before the general election, political analyst Roger Simon reported in spring 2008 that he had talked with an influential Republican who had asked him about McCain's strongest issues for the presidential campaign: "Lower taxes and the argument he will be better able to protect America from its enemies, I said . . . The Republican shook his head. 'You're missing the most important one,' he said. 'Race. McCain runs against Barack Obama and the race vote is worth maybe 15 percent to McCain.'"[37] In the actual election McCain did win 12 percent more of the white vote than did Obama. Opinion polls had long suggested this would be a factor. One national AP-Yahoo poll in April 2008 found that 8 percent of white voters openly admitted they would be "uncomfortable voting for a black for president," with more likely not willing to talk about their views.[38]

CNN exit polls for the 2008 election revealed very significant variation in who voted for senators Obama and McCain. Overall, whites made up about 75 percent of voters in this election, compared to 12 percent who were black voters, 9 percent who were Latino voters, and the rest who were from other racial groups (mainly Asian). Yet only 43 percent of white voters went for Senator Obama, including just 41 percent of male voters and 46 percent of female voters. There was also a little class division within the white group. Less affluent whites, those making under $50,000 a year, were somewhat more likely to vote for Obama than those making more than that, although neither group gave him a majority. As expected from the interest that many younger whites had shown in the Obama campaign, those white voters aged 18–29 were more likely than older whites to vote for Obama (54 percent versus about 41 percent).[39]

Perhaps the most dramatic aspect of the voting patterns revealed in exit polls concerned the fact that voters of color cast ballots in very large majorities for Senator Obama. Some 95 percent of black voters went for Obama, and so did 67 percent of Latino voters and 62 percent of Asian American voters. In addition, one evaluation of counties with numerous Native Americans in the Dakotas, Nebraska, Montana, Nevada, New Mexico, and Colorado estimated that roughly 62 to 87 percent voted for Obama.[40] Most of these voters were doubtless very aware of the pathbreaking character of having the first major party candidate of color running for the presidency, and their significant turnout for Obama was indeed critical. If the election had only been up to white voters in the pivotal states that Obama actually won—Florida, Indiana, North Carolina, Ohio, Pennsylvania, and Virginia—McCain would also have won these states, and the national election.[41] Voters of color were thus essential to Obama's win in these states. Of course, the minority of white voters who did vote for Obama in these and other states were also important in the coalition that put him into office. Fortunately for Obama, a significant minority of whites did gravitate to the point of being willing, in the middle of a very severe economic recession, to vote for a black man, with many perhaps viewing him as an "exception to his race."

We should note, too, the innovative and effective campaign that Senator Obama and his advisers ran. Since the 1930s, presidential campaigns have often been more candidate-centered than party-centered, and as a result both major parties have reshaped their campaign strategies over time. Public opinion polls, an array of political and media consultants, and internet technologies have become very important in recent presidential campaigns. Television, emailings, and internet media—including the all-important and recently developed online social media—were very heavily used by the Obama campaign. The Obama operation raised more than $750 million for its campaign, much of it from aggressive internet fundraising, and the heavy and savvy internet use also brought in many younger and tech-oriented voters who might otherwise have been unenthusiastic about this presidential election.

More Dramatic Party Differences: Beyond the 2008 Election

There are numerous social and political lessons to be learned from the 2008 Obama–McCain election. This election again revealed rather sharply just how different the country's major political parties have become in voter composition and voting patterns. The character of Democratic and Republican voters in national elections has changed significantly over the decades since the New Deal era. Between the 1952–1960 presidential elections and the 2000–2008 presidential elections the proportion of Republican voters who were southern whites increased dramatically from 8 percent to 32 percent. During this time the proportion of Democratic voters who were black and Latino also increased dramatically from 7 percent to 33 percent.[42] Moreover, in elections between 1992 and 2008 the Republican Party pulled in a remarkably small percentage (about 4–12 percent) of black voters; and in 2008 pulled in only a minority of other voters of color. Over recent decades Democratic Party voters have become significantly more racially diverse; typically, large percentages of black, Latino, and Asian American voters opt for Democratic candidates in presidential elections. Note too that shifts in congressional representation have paralleled the regional shifts in party voters. The percentage of Republican seats in the U.S. House from southern areas increased dramatically from 5 percent in 1954 to 45 percent in 2009, while over this same period the percentage of Democratic seats from those areas decreased significantly by about half, from 47 percent to 24 percent.[43]

Contemporary political parties are, of course, much broader than just being voter turnout machines in an array of local, state, and federal elections.

Their leaders, including their national committees, select candidates for elections, lay out party platforms, and plan party conventions. In all of its major party features—including as we have seen its voters—the Republican Party remains very white or white-oriented. In the last several presidential election years, delegates at Republican Party presidential conventions have been overwhelmingly white. The percentage of black delegates at national Republican conventions has oscillated but remained in low figures, between 1.0 percent and 6.7 percent, since 1964. In contrast, Democratic Party percentages have ranged around 20 percent. At the 2008 Democratic convention some 23 percent of the delegates were black, and 11 percent were Latino. More than one-third of the delegates were delegates of color. That year the figures for the Republican Party convention were only 1.5 percent black and 5 percent Latino. Ninety-three percent of Republican convention delegates were white, compared to just 65 percent of Democratic delegates.[44]

Moreover, in recent years the Republican National Committee has had very few black members. In 2004 there was only one African American from the 50 U.S. states among the 165 members of the Republican National Committee. This compared to the 97 black members on the Democratic National Committee, more than one-fifth of the total membership at about the same time. By 2011, the number of black members on the Republican National Committee was still just *two* from the 50 states out of a total of 168 members. In addition, most black Americans in positions with the numerous state Republican Party organizations have been involved in minority-oriented political programs, in contrast to the far more numerous black members of state Democratic Party organizations who have mostly been active outside such minority programs. Moreover, we should note that in 2011, for the first time since 2003, there were (two) black Republicans in the U.S. House, among the 40 black Democrats there, but not one black Republican or Democrat in the U.S. Senate.[45]

At one time centered significantly in the states of the East and upper Midwest, today the Republican Party is, as a result of its political remaking since the 1960s, increasingly centered in the South, some parts of the Midwest, and many Rocky Mountain areas. Numerous southern states increasingly have become politically divided between a Republican Party that is almost entirely white and centered in predominantly white residential areas and a Democratic Party that is much more diverse and multiracial and more oriented to residential areas substantially populated by people of color. (Florida is an exception because Cuban American voters still vote substantially Republican.) Consider too that over half of all black voters are today in southern and border states where they are often effectively disempowerment when it comes to state and presidential elections because they are consistently outvoted by the huge white majorities that vote for the usually conservative Republican Party candidates and against any political candidates seeking to further desegregate racially the major institutions in those areas, or indeed nationally, in significant ways.

Obama's Election: Moving to a Post-Racial America?

In August 2008 *The New York Times* published a major cover story, "Is Obama the End of Black Politics?" In that article white political journalist Matt Bai argued that older African Americans, the civil rights generation, had failed to take seriously enough the "success of their own struggle— to embrace the idea that black politics might now be disappearing into American politics in the same way that the Irish and Italian machines long ago joined the political mainstream." Older black leaders still saw themselves, inaccurately in his view, "as speaking for black Americans" and "as confronting an inherently racist white establishment." Bai further argued that younger black politicians have now assimilated into mainstream politics and can now just be themselves. That is, they can mostly just govern without considering race. Bai suggested too that younger black leaders have tried to reform the CBC and NAACP, which they have allegedly viewed as outdated and too oriented to the past.[46] Bai's white-framed contention was that the U.S. has become post-racial and fully integrated at the political level, and thus probably no longer needed the old "black politics."

Over recent years this post-racial notion has become commonplace outside black America, yet it has been strongly criticized as whitewashed by many black leaders and activists. For example, on a 2008 black-and-progressives website for the then candidate Obama, the influential writer–activist Amiri Baraka provided a strong critique of this *Times* story. In his analysis Baraka pointed out that black politics "will only disappear when the Black majority disappears" and that the "foundation of Obama's successful candidacy is the 90% support by the Afro-American people."[47] This is a critical point about the 2008 election, the full implications of which were missed by numerous mainstream media analysts. Black voters and campaign workers were critical to Obama's election victory. On this same website, the distinguished professor and political activist Maulana Karenga added important points about the white-racist perspective in the *Times*'s weak analysis. Karenga pointed out that, while the article seemed favorable to younger black politicians, it still accented a whitewashed view of "a deficient, divided and self-destructive community. It is an old racialist ploy of singling out and praising the few in order to better condemn the many." He further critiqued the *Times* journalist for arguing that the Obama campaign signaled a post-racial era where older black politicians and civil rights strategies had become irrelevant. Operating from a clear white racial framing, the journalist sought to "dismiss the older generation of leaders and at the same time the legitimacy and relevance of their social justice claims, their rootedness in community, and their recognition of the centrality of multiform struggle around issues of wealth, power and status." [48]

Soon after Obama's dramatic election, the post-racial politics suggestions of this story in *The New York Times* were emphasized across the country. Many political leaders and mainstream media commentators accented the white-framed mantra that Senator Obama's election had accelerated the development of a truly "post-racial America." Interestingly, this theme of national virtue had a heritage going back to at least the 1970s, when phrases like a "colorblind society," "reverse racism," and "the end of racism" were coined and utilized by whites and others attempting to paper over the still harsh realities of continuing individual and systemic racism. Especially since the 1980s Reagan era, as we have seen previously, such extensive terminology and framing of a post-racial, colorblind society have become part of an aggressive white defense against yet more racial desegregation and substantial societal change in the direction of real equality and social justice.

A very important and revealing example of this post-racial rhetoric could be seen in the country's most influential business newspaper, the conservative and Republican-oriented *Wall Street Journal*. A prominent article after the election insisted that the U.S. was now decidedly post-racial: "A man of mixed race has now reached the pinnacle of U.S. power only two generations since the end of Jim Crow. This is a tribute to American opportunity, and it is something that has never happened in another Western democracy." This strongly white-framed *Journal* editorial continued by lecturing the new president. The editorial further argued that Obama did well with the country's voters because he "muted any politics of racial grievance" and then continued by insisting that this significant achievement now should put to "rest the myth of racism as a barrier to achievement in this splendid country. Mr. Obama has a special obligation to help do so."[49]

After noting how Obama himself had ignored or played down some racism issues, strikingly enough, this aggressive editorial then gave the new president the specific obligation of ending what it termed the "myth of racism." This is not a new white-framed perspective, for black Americans who do well are frequently given such "obligations" by whites—that is, to help whitewash or obscure the society's continuing racist realities. Note too here, as in many other places, that white power and privilege generally provide the ability even to define these racial and related political realities of the society. We have previously assessed the still substantial mythology around this country's founders and founding. Today, these older white-framed myths are regularly joined by new myths about this society, including notions of "reverse racism" and a "post-racial society."

Conclusion

Unmistakably, the 2008 election should be remembered as a watershed moment for the United States, but not necessarily for the reasons the *Wall Street Journal* emphasized. This country's gradual expansion of civil and human rights is substantially the result of more than a century of pressures and organization for change coming from its black population. Thus, since the 1870s Reconstruction era and the securing of voting rights for black men in the 15th amendment (1870) to the U.S. Constitution, many black voters, activists, and politicians have pressed for significant expansions of political and other freedoms in the United States. The pathbreaking 15th amendment, together with its sister amendments (the 13th amendment in 1865 ending slavery and the 14th amendment in 1868 adding "due process" rights), were put into the U.S. Constitution by liberal white Republicans who were responding to their consciences and the growing pressures and demands of many black Americans, including the hundreds of thousands of formerly enslaved black southerners and free black northerners who had served in the Union armies. For a brief Reconstruction era, significant numbers of liberal Republican legislators successfully fought to expand the rights and political-economic opportunities for black Americans. However, by the late 1870s and 1880s black Americans and these liberal Republican legislators were losing out to a resurgent, all-white Democratic party, substantially in the South, and to conservative business-oriented white Republicans in the North and South. Much of the progressive civil rights legislation, as well as the 14th and 15th amendments, were weakened or eviscerated by the business-oriented white Republicans on the U.S. Supreme Court beginning in 1873 or thereabouts. Soon this resurgence brought the near-slavery of Jim Crow segregation.

One has to wonder what the United States would be like today if this freedom-expansion agenda of these liberal white Republicans and the newly freed black Americans had been allowed to continue after the decade of the 1870s. Undoubtedly, if it were not for the long African American struggle for liberation from systemic racism—from before the Civil War, to Reconstruction, to the civil rights movement, to the present day—the United States would almost certainly not have made as much progress on civil rights and human rights matters as it has so far. African Americans have long been perhaps the most consistent and insistent carriers of the liberty and justice frame in this country, a liberty and justice frame that has too often been mostly rhetoric for the country's white majority, both in the past and the present.

Unquestionably, Barack Obama and his successful presidential campaign clearly stood on the shoulders of those African Americans and other Americans who had previously sacrificed and engaged in extensive political and civil rights efforts to increase freedom, equality, and social justice in the

United States. Black voters, activists, and politicians should be greatly credited with playing a critical part in the pathbreaking election of President Barack Obama. Without the black voters and other voters of color, who voted lopsidedly for him, Obama would not have been elected the 44th President of the United States. This central role for voters of color is one of the most important stories about the historic 2008 election. Yet, since the 2008 election I have seen very few substantial scholarly or mainstream media analyses that have adequately assessed the statistical and social significance of the demographic shift in U.S. voters or what these voters may mean for the future expansion of multiracial democracy in the United States.

8

Barack Obama's Presidency
Racial and Class Dimensions

The Barack Obama presidential campaign was successful substantially because of the past efforts of millions of African Americans and others engaging in many decades of abolitionist, desegregation, and civil rights efforts, as well as by those recently playing a critical part in his election. Yet in his presidential inauguration address President Obama did not cite those on whose shoulders he stood. Only the benediction by Dr. Joseph Lowery, former president of the Southern Christian Leadership Conference (SCLC), and the poem of Elizabeth Alexander, the African American poet chosen for the inauguration, cited the long history of black workers and civil rights pioneers. Alexander's words included these: "Sing the names of the dead who brought us here, who laid the train tracks, raised the bridges, picked the cotton and the lettuce, built brick by brick the glittering edifices they would then keep clean and work inside of."[1]

The past and recent efforts of African Americans and other Americans of color do indeed help to explain how President Obama got elected when a majority of white voters were apparently opposed to his election. Nonetheless, Obama spent almost all of his campaign, as noted in the last chapter, keeping a low profile on racial discrimination issues of great concern to African Americans, doubtless in part on the advice of his mostly white advisers, in order not to alienate too many white voters. He continued this approach well into his presidency.

Racist Attacks: Leading White Conservatives

Still, the new president's attempted low profile on racial matters did not protect him from the recurring impact of the country's pervasive and systemic racism. Repeatedly, many conservative whites at various political and economic levels did not let him forget that he was black, foreign, unwanted, and someone who would regularly be targeted with racist commentary, racist mocking, and other racist actions—and often by people who did so with impunity. As we have noted, since the time Senator Obama became a viable presidential candidate in 2007, numerous whites, including many important Republican officials and commentators, have engaged in significant and recurring racial stereotyping and other racist framing directed at Obama and his political positions and actions. Let us consider some significant examples.

Soon after his election, and continuing to the present, many white conservatives have attacked and mocked President Obama racially, such as with various sarcastic terms like "the magic Negro." Recently, I searched the internet for the phrase "magic Negro" in connection with Obama's name and got the huge number of 369,000 hits. This racially mocking phrase really took off in public and private use after a journalist wrote a 2007 article titled "Obama the 'Magic Negro,'" in which he assessed the phrase in regard to the then Senator Obama.[2] The phrase later apparently inspired Paul Shanklin, a conservative speaker, to write a song called "Barack the Magic Negro." The song was taken up by a prominent Republican radio commentator and became popular among many white conservatives. After the 2008 election, moreover, a white candidate for the chair of the Republican National Committee (RNC) even circulated a CD to that committee that had the song and mocking lyrics, the latter presenting a negative racialized parody of black leaders supposedly critiquing Obama.[3] The involvement of Republican commentators and officials made it evident that such overtly racist framing was not just a political fringe activity in President Obama's first years.

Media commentators like Rush Limbaugh, often called "Mr. Republican," have frequently made hostile comments about Obama out of their strong white racist framing of society. Because he is a shaper of the opinions of millions, particularly of conservative whites, Limbaugh's commentaries are influential in perpetuating the centuries-old negative framing of black Americans. Limbaugh has said that he believes Obama is an "angry black guy" and has periodically mocked Obama with phrases like an "affirmative action candidate" and "halfrican American." He described a new Oreo cookie as "Or-Bam-eo."[4] Limbaugh also accused Obama of destroying the U.S. economy and polity with comments such as these: "Who is Obama? . . . I think we face something we've never faced before in the country—and that is, we're now governed by people who do not like the country, who do not have the same reverence for it that we do." Later, Limbaugh went on to argue that President Obama viewed African Americans as not being treated fairly in the United States, and for that reason, Obama and his adminis-tration were actually seeking significant "payback" (a word he used at least twice) and were thus "presiding over the decline of the United States of America."[5] In this far-right media commentator's white-framed view, Obama was getting even with whites for discrimination. Conspicuous in such harsh examples is that conformity by leading whites to past racist imaging and framing is still quite important in the maintenance of contem-porary racist imaging and framing in many spheres of U.S. society.

At local and state levels, a significant number of white Republican officials have been documented engaging in a mocking racist framing of President

Obama. As we observed in the last chapter, such mocking has frequently made use of old white stereotyping of black Americans as supposedly having a strong craving for such food items as watermelons and chicken. In another recent search of the internet I came up with nearly 11 million hits on the joint words "watermelon" and "Obama." Some of these web accounts were about the Republican mayor of Los Alamitos, California, who in spring 2009 sent out an email to his network showing the White House lawn planted with watermelons and captioned "No Easter egg hunt this year." Later, the mayor apologized for his joke, claiming he did not know the stereotype of blacks and watermelons.[6] However, as we noted previously, this common white defense is extraordinarily weak and unlikely, since the so-called joke requires knowing old racist stereotypes about black people. Note, thus, that no white political commentators were posting images of the White House lawn planted with such items as potatoes or corn.

To cite yet another example of contemporary racist actions mimicking older racist actions, in June 2009 a staff assistant of a Republican legislator in Tennessee distributed by email a set of photos of all U.S. presidents with the caption "Historical Keepsake Photo," but in the last photo area where President Obama should have been there was just a dark area with two big eyes peering out. Such big-eye mocking imagery is much like that of the many caricatured cartoons of black Americans that have been produced by whites since at least the 19th century.[7]

The racialized attacks on President Obama by leading Republican politicians persisted at the national level as well. In summer 2011, prominent Republican senator Tom Coburn of Oklahoma made some hostile, racially stereotyped comments about Obama's educational background. In one speech Coburn asserted that Obama's legislative "intent is to create dependency because it worked so well for him . . . As an African-American male . . . [he got] tremendous advantage from a lot of these programs."[8] Such unsubstantiated assertions about Obama's special "dependency" reflect many whites' framing of black Americans as especially and unfairly benefitting from federal assistance programs, even as politicians like Coburn know well that white Americans—such as the white beneficiaries of massive agricultural subsidies in his area—benefit the most from many large-scale government programs. Moreover, contrary to common white assumptions, recent research shows that white students, not students of color, are disproportionately the beneficiaries of college student aid and scholarship programs.[9]

Simianizing the Obama Family

From 2007 to the present, many of the major stereotypes and associated racist narratives from the old white framing of black Americans have periodically appeared in the political commentaries and messages of conservative white politicians and other white conservatives, including influential media commentators. Many racist images and messages have involved the framing of black Americans as being somehow ape-like, and thus as supposedly primitive and inferior to whites. For example, in spring 2011 a Republican official in southern California circulated by email a photo of a chimpanzee family with Obama's picture on one ape and the caption "Now you know why—No birth certificate!" When some local people called on this official to resign her position, including some other Republicans, she declined and asserted the common white defenses: "I am not a racist. It was a joke. I have friends who are black."[10] Such animalized stereotyping of black Americans goes back at least four centuries in the development of systemic racism in North America, and it has often been important in the commonplace white framing of black people as racially inferior.

In other parts of the United States influential conservatives have recently passed along similar simianized images. In Nashville, a racist message was sent out by a Tennessee hospitality organization official. His email had a photo of the chimp Cheeta (from racist Tarzan movies) next to one of First Lady Michelle Obama, with this message, "I was at the store yesterday, and I ran into Tarzan! . . . I asked about Cheeta, he beamed and said she was doing good, had married a Lawyer and now lived in the White House!!"[11] This racist message had been sent to him by someone else, and he forwarded it to other prominent Nashvillians. Once outed, the official said it was just good "political humor," that he was not racist, and that he meant it to be private. Yet again, conventional white defenses are offered. Here, as was likely true for the southern California case, we may have a type of backstage racism where a white person seems to have felt safe circulating racist messaging to presumably white acquaintances. Note too that whites caught in such racist actions typically claim they are somehow "not racist."[12]

Similar animalizing imagery directed at Obama has been propagated in some major media outlets. For instance, early in 2009 the conservative Republican-leaning newspaper, Rupert Murdoch's *New York Post,* published a cartoon showing police officers who had shot an ape with the caption "They'll have to find someone else to write the next stimulus bill." This widely circulated cartoon referenced President Obama's crafting of a stimulus bill aiming to revive the declining U.S. economy. Once again, the whites who published the cartoon claimed they did not mean it to be racially offensive.[13]

The widespread character and intensity of much racial mocking directed at President Obama and his family, and its acceleration quickly after the inauguration, seem unique for presidents in recent memory. Significantly, many of these racialized attacks have been set in a supposedly joking framework. In assessing this type of attack, my colleagues and I have elsewhere argued that such joking frequently allows whites to downplay the significance of blatantly racist performances by themselves or others. Blatantly racist ideas, images, and gestures are regularly exchanged in a joking manner in the white backstage, and indeed often in the public frontstage, yet they can be excused, if challenged, as not meant to be taken seriously. What's more, much contemporary racialized political activity, and defenses of it as "not racist" or "only joking," once again demonstrate many whites' assumptions about their societal superiority and collective or individual virtue.[14]

Violent Racial Imagery: Creating a Toxic Climate

White expressions of a racist framing of President Obama and his policies or administration have often progressed well beyond such racist "joking." They have periodically become intensely emotional and violence-oriented. For instance, some months after President Obama's inauguration, Matthew Rothschild, savvy editor of *The Progressive* magazine, noted the significant amount of racist mail he was getting, one piece of which spoke of a "Third World chimp as President. So who can be surprised now that Barack Hussein Obama is spending our money like a drunken nigger on Saturday night." Such mail is more vicious than the previously cited cases, but similar in its animalizing. Rothschild suggested such widespread venomous attacks had created a toxic racial atmosphere leading some to consider violence against Obama or his associates. At the time, indeed, the U.S. Secret Service was reporting about 30 death threats against Obama daily, four times the number made against the previous president.[15] The threats had become so numerous even before Obama's actual election that the Secret Service started protecting him long before they had for previous presidential candidates.

Concrete signs of the significant dangers of this toxic atmosphere have been obvious over the Obama presidential years. In the year after his inauguration, at rallies against his legislative program, some whites carried signs with captions like "Death to Obama." In summer 2009, one white supremacist attacked the Washington, D.C. Holocaust Memorial Museum with a rifle, and murdered a black guard there. Operating out of an antiblack and anti-Semitic framing, the attacker asserted that President Obama "was created by Jews." Other white supremacists have been monitored or arrested for posting death threats against Obama on their websites.[16]

Hostile racialized language against President Obama spread like wildfire on some internet sites and talk show programs, and sometimes on conservative media programs on certain television networks. A *Boston Globe* story reported that early in his presidency, the Secret Service had investigated a vicious Facebook poll about killing the president and also had interviewed the host of a conservative radio show about someone who called in and talked about target practice and President Obama. In addition, the *Globe* report noted, "federal officials have raised concerns about several instances in which protesters carrying weapons showed up at Obama events, including a man at an August town hall [meeting] in New Hampshire."[17] As a result of these possible threats, the Secret Service budget was increased significantly.

Lynching imagery was chronic in the Obama campaign period and persisted after his election. For example, another Facebook group posted an image of President Obama hanging by a rope because they did not like the U.S. government aid provided to Haitian relief after a severe 2010 earthquake.[18] Among other things, the viciousness of these lynching-type images and death messages suggests a deep racist framing of Obama as a "dangerous black man." During the Obama presidency the internet has become a major place for extensive racist attacks, often because of its anonymity. In addition to these aforementioned racist attacks, there have been numerous additions to the internet of new or enhanced white supremacist websites since Obama's primary campaign, some with hundreds of thousands of members or monthly viewers. Such sites regularly engage in harsh and blatantly racist attacks on Obama's image, policies, and family.

Note, too, that much intensely hostile racial imagery has appeared outside media and internet settings. In spring 2010, whites at a bar in West Allis, Wisconsin, burned an effigy of Obama. Recently, in Colorado, an anonymous individual or group put up a hostile billboard attacking Obama with aggressively caricatured images of him as a terrorist, a gay man, a criminal, and an undocumented immigrant.[19] This billboard provided an example of the extreme anti-Obama commentary that has been commonplace in some areas of the United States, in this case with highly negative and racialized images of Muslims, Latinos, and African Americans. While other presidents have certainly been politically mocked, the early intensity, extensiveness, and often highly racialized character of these various attacks on President Obama seem distinctive and revealing of their likely roots in an old white framing of black Americans, and especially of black men.

Moreover, in mid-2011, one white activist leader associated with the conservative group Americans for Legal Immigration spoke with a Christian talk radio host about how, in his view, the Obama administration was "putting out videos and propaganda telegraphing what I believe to be a conflict with White America they're preparing for." He called for impeachment or greater action against Obama for being a "dictator" and added that some people were talking "about the military coming in or somebody just coming in taking this guy into some form of arrest." Later, he backtracked on his statements, insisting he was not talking about a violent overthrow of the Obama administration. Nonetheless, many whites online and elsewhere have voiced similar sentiments, and in this case, the Christian talk show host reportedly did not take offense at his very provocative comments.[20]

Prominent Republican Officials' Overt Racism

Over the Obama campaign and presidency the overtness of much racist framing by important white conservatives, including several prominent Republican officials, has been striking. We have noted some of this framing in the chapter on the 2008 election. We should note that much of this revealing white framing and associated actions have accented issues besides President Obama and his administration. For example, during his controversial 2010 senatorial campaign, Senator Rand Paul (R-KY) fired a white campaign spokesperson because the latter had put on his Myspace page a photo of a lynching with a "Happy Nigger Day" caption.[21] It seems only a small step from this type of general racist framing to the racist attacks on the Obamas noted previously. In addition, Rand himself took a public position, like 1960s presidential candidate Barry Goldwater, actually opposing a major section of the 1964 Civil Rights Act prohibiting racial discrimination in public accommodations.[22]

Additionally, recall from Chapter 7 the early 2000s involvement of Mississippi governor and onetime presidential possibility, Republican Haley Barbour, with the contemporary white-oriented Council of Conservative Citizens (CCC). Later on, in a 2010 interview with the *Weekly Standard* during Obama's presidency, Barbour favorably reviewed the efforts of white segregationist groups called the Citizens' Councils during the early desegregation era in Mississippi. These white business-led groups typically operated to forestall or slow racial desegregation, such as in public schools, although they sometimes worked against violence once desegregation was inevitable. Referring to the era of Jim Crow segregation, Barbour also said, "I just don't remember it as being that bad."[23]

These leading conservative politicians have demonstrated that they too are elite men holding to racial positions that reveal the strong white-group interest in preserving existing racial privilege and power. They also show how little they want to understand or remember the extreme oppression of the Jim Crow segregation. There seems to be little or no interest in the local or regional black perspective on, or memory of, this painful racist history. Their whitewashed comments and actions reveal much that is significant about the contemporary racial framing of U.S. history for a great many whites—a powerful framing that includes a sanitized collective memory of what was in fact a highly undemocratic United States with very extensive, totalitarian-like Jim Crow segregation in numerous states for nearly a century.[24]

The Tea Party and White Nationalist Views

For decades the U.S. has seen the organizing of hundreds of anti-government "patriot" and "militia" groups. Some have had a significant white supremacist connection or orientation, while others have mostly been just strongly anti-government. Many have mixed the two perspectives. The Southern Poverty Law Center has issued regular reports indicating growth over the last few decades in these extremist groups, with an especially significant increase in membership since Obama became a presidential candidate.[25] White supremacist leaders have even argued that the 2008 election of a black man is useful in recruiting whites to supremacist organizations. David Duke, onetime Klan leader and Louisiana politician, reportedly said Obama's election was "a real shock to me and it should be a shock to the community that European Americans now have to fight for our rights, in I guess Obama's 'New America' . . . do whites have rights? . . . I don't see him as our President."[26] Quite significantly in the minds of such white supremacists, the federal government that they have traditionally feared and hated is now governed at the top by a feared black man.

One can observe much blending of anti-government and racial framing in sectors of the contemporary Tea Party, a major political movement that arose shortly after Barack Obama's election and has actively opposed his presidency and many of his policies. In addition to the many Tea Party members who have visible links to white nationalist groups, most other members are conservatives who are Republicans or leaning Republican, but are not openly supremacist. Some of the latter are Republican political activists and officials. Interestingly, in spite of the impression one has often gotten from the mainstream media, the Tea Party movement has not been representative of the general population. One national poll found that just under a fifth of all respondents could even be considered Tea Party sympathizers. Three-quarters of sympathizers were older (over the age of 44), and a substantial majority were male. Sixty percent reported they often or always voted Republican; only 5 percent reported being Democrats. Very few were black. Significantly, too, most sympathizers were not active members of a Tea Party organization. Most reported they had not attended a Tea Party rally, accessed a Tea Party website, or contributed money to a Tea Party group. In this poll the racial views of these Tea Party sympathizers were also distinctive. They were much less likely than the general population to believe whites have more opportunities to get ahead in society, and much more likely to believe that too much was being made of the problems facing black Americans. They were also more likely than the general population to openly assert the view that the Barack Obama administration favored blacks over whites.[27]

One major research study by the Institute for Research & Education on Human Rights examined six national Tea Party groups. Assessing public statements by these groups, the researchers found the groups had created several political myths about themselves, such as that they were mainly concerned with federal deficits and "big government" issues. Yet, in actual operation the groups revealed a heavy emphasis on racial and national identity issues, including such topics as President Obama's birth certificate and national origin, alleged socialism and terrorist sympathies, and supposedly African foreignness. One Tea Party group was substantially composed of nativistic whites who had been active in an anti-immigrant organization. The two largest included many white supremacists and anti-immigrant activists. Five had some "birthers" questioning Obama's birthplace as their leaders. The researchers found that, in spite of occasional participants of color, almost all Tea Party activists have been white. Most have also been middle class. In addition, like other conservative activists noted previously, the members of several Tea Party groups frequently express their white-framed views with racist images of Obama, as well as with Confederate battle flags or signs about the U.S. being "a Christian nation." Some Tea Party rally participants have held signs like "Don't tax me, bro" and portraying Obama as a "thug" or "witch doctor." Interestingly, a few conservative analysts generally supportive of the Tea Party have even noted publicly that there is an important racial dynamic to the movement, a dynamic that again demonstrates the lasting power of many whites' racial framing of society.[28]

The Tea Party groups' anti-government framing has taken various forms. In 2011, one Iowa Tea Party group put up a billboard with Obama's photo and photos of Adolf Hitler and Vladimir Lenin, with captions like "Democrat Socialism" and "Marxist Socialism."[29] Much of this anti-Obama, anti-government framing also seems, explicitly or implicitly, linked to a strong racial framing. Many Tea Party activists have frequently asserted that Obama or his administration has taken over "their country" and that they want to "take our country back." Much Tea Party and other conservative discussion over the course of Obama's presidency has also argued that he is somehow "out of touch with the American majority," with what some call "middle class working people."[30] However, such language ignores, among other things, the reality of a large percentage of the country's working people and middle-class families not being white—a substantial majority of whom have supported President Obama. In addition, the common Tea Party and Republican theme of President Obama being too "professor-ish," an elite intellectual, or "out of touch" with ordinary Americans not only has ignored his modest middle-class beginnings, but also plays off the problematical anti-intellectualism one finds among many religious conservatives and other conservative Americans. Even more importantly, this view of Obama ignores the reality of the elite and upper-middle-class backgrounds of a great many Republican Party members, as well as the numerous elite Republican leaders such as the two George Bushes, John McCain, and Mitt Romney.[31]

Many Tea Party members and leaders have also asserted that "their country" is being taken over by growing numbers of people of color, including immigrants from Latin America, and thus most have actual or rhetorical links to anti-immigrant organizations. For instance, in one March 2011 "Tea Party Nation" email message, an article written by a member bemoaned the end of the "White Anglo-Saxon Protestant" race because of the declining white birth rate in the United States.[32] This fear appears as one reason that many Tea Party members and other white conservatives seek to roll back amendments to the U.S. Constitution that have made it more democratic. Some thus want to reinterpret or revise the 14th amendment so there is no birth-right citizenship for (especially undocumented) immigrant children.[33]

Protesting Tea Party Racism and Republican Pushback

In summer 2010, some 2,000 delegates at a national NAACP convention unanimously approved a reasonable resolution calling out the "explicitly racist behavior" in some Tea Party groups and calling on them to repudiate such behavior. The NAACP president insisted Tea Party members should "be responsible members of this democracy and make sure they don't tolerate bigots or bigotry among their members."[34] As a result, local and national NAACP offices got numerous hostile, often racist comments on their websites and some death-threat messages. Few white officials, even in moderate and liberal political groups, spoke out and backed the NAACP resolution. Both the racist reactions to the NAACP and its accurate resolution, and the lack of outside white political support for the resolution, suggested again just how strong and normalized the reality of overt racism remains for this society.

The important NAACP resolution got a strong pushback from a few major conservative Republicans. Former governor and vice-presidential candidate Sarah Palin, ignoring the unanimous views of African Americans in the country's oldest civil rights organization, strongly condemned the NAACP resolution, saying "the Tea Party movement is a beautiful movement, full of diverse people, diverse backgrounds. Folks of all walks of life who, for the most part, happen to oppose President Obama's policies. Not the color of his skin."[35] Other leading Republicans have also had close links to Tea Party groups. For example, in 2010 the very conservative Representative Michele Bachmann (R-Minn.), later a candidate for president, organized a U.S. House Tea Party caucus, with more than 50 Republican representatives but no Democratic members. Although Tea Party leaders and members have periodically asserted the notion that they are in strong opposition to elites in both political parties, such close connections to leading Republicans reveal that this is not in fact the case.

Indeed, several "grass-roots" Tea Party groups originated or expanded with substantial organizational help provided by conservative Republicans in the country's elite. Several were funded or otherwise assisted in organization by leading Republican Dick Armey's FreedomWorks organization in

Washington, D.C. and by other well-funded conservative organizations or individuals seeking to counter the Obama presidency. Even the Tea Party groups that grew up initially as grass-roots organizations have periodically relied on their links to other elite-funded groups or to conservative elite funders. The Institute for Research & Education on Human Rights report summarized the reality of the Tea Party movement as "a multi-million dollar complex that includes for-profit corporations, non-party non-profit organizations, and political action committees."[36] This organizational complex is very much linked to the conservative sector of the mostly white elite. Plainly, too, it is not just chance that accounts for the fact that the Tea Party movement arose within a few weeks of President Barack Obama's inauguration.

Elite Domination of Political and Economic Institutions Today

President Barack Obama, like all presidents before him, has also had strong ties to and the backing of certain supportive segments of the country's elite. Without the backing of at least a key segment of that mostly white elite, he could not have become president. As noted previously, the U.S. economy and politics have long been controlled at the top by an oligarchical elite that has three general factions: a small liberal segment; a significant moderate segment; and a major conservative segment. The conservative camp has been unsympathetic to liberal and expanding-democracy ideas and the liberal camp has been more receptive to some liberal and expanding-democracy ideas. The moderate camp has generally taken a centrist position in between. In recent decades the growing conservative segment has positioned itself almost entirely in the Republican Party and the liberal segment has located itself substantially in the Democratic Party, with some in the moderate segment moving into the former and some into the latter depending on political circumstances. Nonetheless, today both the Republican and Democratic Parties are rooted in and greatly shaped by the elite propertied class and its major political-economic interests, as major political parties have been since their beginnings.

Let us consider briefly the character of the mostly white elite that still rules U.S. society with a relatively firm hand. The top of the U.S. economic system today is a white male club and economic paradise. Thus, among *Forbes* magazine's 400 wealthiest Americans, those worth at least a billion dollars, 86 percent are white men. Only one person is black (Oprah Winfrey); there is not even one black man in this highest economic group. There are just 42 women, all of them white except for Winfrey. Judging from their names and profiles, there appear to be two Latino men and 12 Asian American men. Thus, white men make up the overwhelming majority of the very richest 400 Americans, even though white men currently make up only about 36 percent of the adult population.[37]

Broadening the economic elite somewhat, we can consider top corporate executives. More than 93 percent of CEOs of Fortune 500 firms are still white men. Only six black CEOs and seven Latino CEOs are currently among the top executives heading these major companies, and few of them have *ever* had a black or Latino CEO. There are just 14 white women heading up these major companies. Studies of Fortune 500 boards reveal that white men likewise constitute about 95 percent of the chair positions on corporate boards. Not surprisingly, too, the few CEOs who are not white men are very socialized into white-male-generated corporate values and in the conventional racial-class framing, so that they generally behave in their corporate decision making much like the dominant white male executives.[38]

Today, white men remain very central to major U.S. political institutions. For example, the 112th Congress, like previous congresses, is very disproportionately white male. In this 2011–2013 Congress, the Senate is 96 percent white in composition, with just two Latino, two Asian American (both from Hawaii), and no black senators. Some *81 percent* are thus white men. The House is 83 percent white in composition, with *72 percent* of members being white men. In addition, the very top political leadership of the U.S. Congress and the White House has for centuries been white male—with only two rather recent exceptions since the country's founding (Barack Obama and House Speaker Nancy Pelosi, both in the 2000s). As in the economy, whites, and mainly white men, have dominated the major political institutions to the present day.[39]

We should also note the class characteristics of those with major political power. In addition to its significant racial and gender unrepresentativeness, the U.S. Congress is highly unrepresentative in terms of income and wealth. For example, the median net worth of members of Congress in 2009 was a substantial $912,000, compared to the median net worth of all U.S. families two years earlier in 2007 of just $120,000. Nearly half of the members of Congress were millionaires in terms of net worth.[40] Clearly, most members of Congress have had a personal or family interest in government decisions about such things as income taxation. In terms of education, 95 percent of the members of the 111th Congress (2009–2011) had some type of college degree.[41] In contrast, only a quarter of the general population over age 24 had a college degree. Interestingly, this pattern of college education for a substantial majority in Congress has held true now for many decades.

White men not only dominate major corporations and Congress, but they also dominate the groups connecting these very important institutional sectors. For example, in recent years the annual number of active registered lobbyists who lobby Congress and federal agencies has been estimated to be in the 11,000–14,000 range. Most lobbyists are white, with an estimated 4 percent being African American and much smaller percentages being other Americans of color.[42] Most major lobbying firms have few lobbyists of color, and some of these work only on "minority issues." Not surprisingly, too, most of the more powerful lobbyists are white men. During the most recent decade, lobbyists and their firms or agencies spent an estimated 1.6–3.5 billion dollars each year lobbying. These were only the officially recorded dollars, for much more was spent in unrecorded ways. According to the Center for Responsive Politics, the powerful groups and companies spending the most on significant lobbying from 1998 to 2010 were, with but one exception (AARP, formerly the American Association of Retired Persons), major corporations or groups representing various corporations.[43] Note, too, that many members of Congress or congressional staff or other top federal employees go to work with lobbying firms once they leave the federal government. For example, in 2009–2010, financial services companies alone secured some 1,447 former federal employees to influence Congress and government agencies.[44] One reason that lobbyists of color are rare among powerful lobbyists is that relatively few of the most powerful members of Congress or the senior staff members working for key members of Congress have been people of color.

The elite or upper-middle-class positions of most members of Congress, of their senior staff members, and of most powerful lobbyists generally mean that they are very oriented to the political-economic interests of the country's mostly white elite. Consider that recent surveys have shown that 72 percent of ordinary Americans favor significantly raising taxes on the rich as a good way to deal with the country's large and persisting budget deficits.[45] Yet such critical views of the general public usually do not have much impact on the political leaders in Congress, for the well-off, mostly white upper 1 to 5 percent of Americans have *greatly* disproportionate influence on major decision making in Congress. In his recent research, for example, Larry Bartels has examined the voting record of U.S. senators as they relate to the important policy preferences of low-income, middle-class, and wealthy Americans. Generally these senators are "considerably more responsive to the opinions of affluent constituents than to the opinions of middle-class constituents, while the opinions of constituents in the bottom third of the income distribution have no apparent statistical effect on their senators' roll call votes."[46] In addition, this pattern of voting for the preferences of the affluent and wealthy was found to be much more pronounced for Republican senators than for their Democratic colleagues.

Persisting Undemocratic and Antidemocratic Barriers

A principal reason for the continuing and overwhelming influence of the elite and its assisting upper-middle-class executives over the country's political system is that they are, on the whole, much better organized and more effective in lobbying and otherwise shaping Congress and other major political institutions than other Americans. Indeed, most members of the ruling elite are well interconnected socially through prestigious clubs, other elite organizations, corporate boards and retreats, and family and marital connections. One recent interview study examined members of elite country clubs, which continue to be important places where the still mostly white, male, and wealthy upper echelon of the elite socializes, exchanges ideas, and makes important political and economic decisions. The token numbers of people of color and white women who were actually members of these elite clubs were cited by the elite white men as showing that their clubs were not segregated any more, yet the presence of just token numbers of members who were not white or male actually revealed how exclusive this powerful elite and its social clubs have actually remained to the present day.[47]

Not surprisingly, these wealthy white male Americans exert great influence in spite of a political system that appears to be democratic in some ways, such as in its voting opportunities. This is because they control much of the rest of the political decision-making process, such as major party funding and nominations, much influential lobbying of Congress and government agencies, and the mainstream media's shaping of public opinion on major political-economic and public policy issues. As researchers Winters and Page have put it, the political power generated by wealthy Americans is mostly not based on heavy expenditure of their time, because they often link to or "control large organizations, such as business corporations, that can act for them." These armies of assistants are frequently located in an array of "foundations, think tanks, politically connected law firms, consultancies, and lobbying organizations" and include "politicians or officials recruited and funded by the wealthy . . . to advance the basic material interests of the wealthy."[48] Wealth and power, that is, translate into control of major social, economic, and political organizations, which in turn easily control much of the political system most of the time.

The extraordinarily well-organized and powerful influence of wealthy white men in our undemocratic political system helps to explain why President Barack Obama has been unable to get certain of his more progressive policy goals passed into law. The U.S. constitutional system continues to aid the well-off elite in maintaining much political control. For example, our two-house Congress contrasts greatly with numerous European parliamentary political systems that have just one legislative house. In his first years, more of Obama's proposed, moderately progressive legislation probably would have become law if there had been just the U.S. House involved. Instead, the Democratic Party majority then in the Senate was insufficient in size to overcome the conservative Republican minority's opposition and the supermajority requirement (60 votes to overcome a filibuster) long imposed by undemocratic U.S. Senate rules. This congressional system has long kept many relatively progressive economic and social policies supported by a majority of the population from ever becoming law.

In traditional political theory, the major purpose for a U.S. political party is to present a serious platform representing the perspective of the relevant voting population and to try to implement that platform once elected. However, with our numerous undemocratic and antidemocratic constitutional and other political barriers, the implementation of a fully progressive economic program representing popular-majority views by a party that wins a major election has usually been impossible, except in scattered pieces or times of major societal crisis. Yet, when political parties are impotent in implementing needed progressive platforms, many party members become discouraged and do not participate in parties or elections. This further allows a party to be run by a small group of leaders more oriented to corporate and other elite interests than the goals of ordinary party members.

The dominant elite also controls major sources of information for the general population, most especially the mainstream media. These media include not only radio, movies, and newspapers, but also television, satellite and cable transmission, and the internet. Yet all but the last of these have been mostly under elite control. What some call a contemporary "infosphere," our large and enveloping informational environment, is for the most part controlled at the top U.S.- and global-impact level by powerful men operating out of corporate centers of power. As of the late 2000s just six huge media companies controlled most major U.S. news and entertainment media, a number that has declined over recent decades. A few dozen large corporations control most of the world's media operations.[49]

The power and control of these mostly U.S. and European multinational corporations—plus the power of other major corporations over media content through their advertising funding—mean that most news presentations in these mainstream media have been screened if not censored. Big companies control not only most news content but also which societal voices get effectively heard. One study of nightly news programs on the ABC, CBS, and NBC networks found that whites, mostly men, made up the overwhelming majority of significant news sources. Republicans made up a much larger proportion of these sources than did Democrats. Again whites, especially men, are the main experts in much of the mainstream media; and in spite of contentions that the media are "too liberal," conservative views are disproportionately dominant in many important media arenas. Likewise, the overwhelming majority of full-time news reporters, supervisors, and editors at the major mainstream newspapers and magazines are affluent whites; and on major television networks and cable channels whites are usually very overrepresented in managerial jobs and as on-air reporters.[50]

The dominant white elite has routinely manufactured much public consent for its political-economic policies and goals by using these mainstream media. Edward Herman and Noam Chomsky have argued that corporate control of mainstream media does not mean there is an organized conspiracy, but rather that these media are all shaped by a capitalistic system where corporate ownership is concentrated in a few hands, by intense focus on advertising and profits, and by dependence on relatively few sources, which include mainly a few wire services and many public relations releases.[51]

For decades, the ruling elite has depended heavily on the general voting population not having adequate access to the accurate economic and political information and data-oriented debate necessary to make truly informed political decisions. Today, this continues to be true, and most especially for a conservative Republican Party's political fortunes. Potential and actual voters cannot make informed political decisions without having full access to such societal information and to fully critical analyses of such important information. Some research shows that U.S. residents are, on average, the most poorly educated residents of the various European and North American industrialized countries. This is true for general educational achievement, as well as important civic knowledge. For example, *The Washington Post* published results of a 1990s survey of political knowledge in the United States. Less than a quarter of these respondents even knew the names of their U.S. senators, and four in ten could not name the U.S. vice president.[52] In more recent surveys most Americans have indicated that they do not know important information about our political system, such as that U.S. House members have a two-year term and U.S. senators have a six-year term. Over recent decades, large proportions of those surveyed also revealed that they do not know which party controls the U.S. House or Senate. Yet, as the social scientists Jacob Hacker and Paul Pierson suggest, this age-old pervasive public ignorance has not been widely discussed in public forums or the social sciences, and public explanations for the ignorance are typically weak.[53]

In addition to this lack of civic and international knowledge, there is a high level of ignorance in the general population, including the voting population, about a range of very important issues on which they periodically vote in some form. Consider, for example, today's growing wealth and income inequality. Most people today seriously underestimate how great that economic inequality really is. Researchers recently asked a large sample of Americans what they thought the U.S. wealth distribution was, and most described it as *much* more equal than it actually was. Interestingly, almost all respondents also wanted the U.S. wealth inequality to be significantly *less* than what they thought it was. Even more striking was the huge distance between their ideal, more egalitarian society and the extremely unequal society that exists in reality, but of which a great many respondents were quite unaware.[54] Conceivably, thus, if U.S. voters were better informed on issues like actual wealth and income inequality, they might be much more supportive of substantial increases in redistributive taxation and in new social support programs.

From the beginning of this country to the present day, elite whites have greatly dominated the societal construction and transmission through various media of the most important social, economic, and political frames designed to buttress the dominant system. Using older local and national media, and now much of the internet, this mostly white elite has the capability to periodically mobilize a majority political consensus on elite-shaped conservative or arch-conservative views. Given this great media control, the elite's conservative segment can frequently create a variety of barriers for a moderately progressive Democratic president like Barack Obama. Since his election Obama has faced a reinvigorated, extensive, and often racialized conservative propaganda effort, one well funded by the elite's right wing. Over his presidential years Obama has frequently been treated very negatively by conservative media commentators and conservative-leaning "news" networks. Some networks have cut to commercials when he was speaking at political summits, criticized him for calling members of Congress by first names like his predecessors, bashed his national security credentials, or caricatured him as "too professorish."[55] In addition, the mainstream media have often offered more conservative than liberal analysis of his important decisions. For example, on the Sunday in May 2011 after Obama decided on a successful raid in Pakistan that killed terrorist leader Osama bin Laden, the mainstream media talk and interview shows scheduled mostly conservative Republican commentators to talk about that very significant presidential action.

As we have already seen, conservative attacks on Obama's policies have regularly made aggressive use of the internet and other new mass media. For instance, one December 2009 YouTube video by an anonymous conservative group attacked the Obama health care plan, asserting that one does not have to be "a racist" to oppose it. Media sociologist, Jessie Daniels, has noted how conservative and racialized political messages like this have often gotten extensive publicity:

> The unknown political group releases a video on YouTube exclusively, and the video quickly goes viral and becomes one of the most viewed videos on YouTube. They do not buy air time on television to get their message out . . . because the video gets picked up by [a television] show . . . Then, the meme travels to Twitter . . . The political battle over race, and the meaning of racism, has moved into the digital era.[56]

Well funded by a wealthy conservative segment of the elite, numerous arch-conservative operatives have established various websites and organizations not only attacking President Obama but also groups allied with the Democratic Party that work for social justice causes such as the poor people's group ACORN (Association of Community Organizations for Reform Now). These arch-conservative operatives have even made use of deceptive internet websites that appear at first glance to be politically moderate or neutral, what Jessie Daniels calls "cloaked sites," in order to disguise their actual right-wing arguments and propaganda.[57] Note, too, that even when they are not in full control of Congress or the presidency, the mostly white conservatives' political strategies and perspectives in recent decades have still greatly shaped the course of U.S. politics, to a substantial degree because they have so much mainstream and other media power.

Obama's Cautious Approach to Racial Matters

In Obama's first years in office crucial questions about societal fairness, economic equality, and racial matters kept arising, and especially from leaders and voters in communities of color. Very persistent were questions such as "What has Obama done for black Americans and other Americans of color?" In a late 2009 interview, April Ryan, one of the few black reporters in the White House press corps, asked the president about his view of criticism from African Americans who had expected him to take action in regard to the particular issues faced by black Americans. Obama replied rather cautiously to Ryan: ". . . I am passing laws that help all people, particularly those who are most vulnerable and most in need. That, in turn, is going to help lift up the African American community." That is, his governing strategy was a broad one that did not address specifically African Americans' economic needs. Obama later added that "[N]ever has there been more opportunity for African Americans who have received a good education and are in a position then to walk through the doors that are opened." He then acknowledged that it was a very difficult period for the many Americans who were currently unemployed, especially in certain cities, and he added that he was pressing federal government agencies to take action to deal with those Americans in the "hard to reach places," implying again that African Americans would benefit as the overall U.S. economy improved significantly.[58]

In this eloquent but cautious reply President Obama accented the conventional white moderate and liberal framing of available education and equal opportunity for people of color. At no point in this major interview explicitly asking about racial issues did Obama note, much less discuss, the widespread discrimination facing Americans of color in areas of education, employment, housing, and policing. He did not touch on the critical need for the federal agencies he mentioned to aggressively enforce the often weakly enforced civil rights laws, or to expand them. Here, as elsewhere, Obama made public use of typical language from a soft individualistic version of the white racial frame, with language about education and opportunities that would not likely disturb many whites. Over his electoral campaign and first years as president, Obama, by intent or felt obligation, regularly used "great opportunity" and other language from this soft racial frame and thus never discussed structural discrimination or other structural oppression facing many Americans. Why did he do this? Was this a savvy political strategy, given white dominance of the society, or was he conforming for other reasons? As Latino scholar Richard Delgado has sharply phrased this issue, the rewards of conforming to the norms and folkways of whiteness, "which include acceptance, validation, power, and influence, can plant a seed of doubt in the mind of any but the most dedicated insurgent of color."[59]

Whatever his personal thinking and strategizing on these racial matters may be, Obama's recurring public use of elements from the individualistic and equal opportunity versions of the white racial frame is similar to the optimistic racial narrative he accented strongly in his famous speech during the Dr. Wright controversy (see Chapter 7). This widespread narrative assumes or implies, erroneously, that the U.S. has changed so much from its highly racialized past that it is now a country where white racism, whether blatant or covert, is no longer extensive or substantial. Obama has not been alone in making use of a too optimistic narrative about white America. A great many media analysts and some social scientists have embraced such imagery for the contemporary United States. In contrast, however, very substantial data in this book, as well as other social science research, show well that a great many whites continue to operate out of a strong racist framing in both frontstage and backstage settings, and thus often act in discriminatory ways out of that white framing.[60]

Closely associated with the equal opportunity and other versions of the dominant white racial frame are yet other major interpretative frames and narratives such as those involving individualistic values, notions of legitimate authority, free market norms, and omnipresent American exceptionalism. Significantly, thus, in April 2009, a newly elected President Barack Obama commented to a journalist in France that "I believe in American exceptionalism."[61] Clarifying, he asserted that "We have a core set of values that are enshrined in our Constitution, in our body of law, in our democratic practices, in our belief in free speech and equality, that, though imperfect, are exceptional." After accenting these conventional U.S. ideals, he did add later that the U.S. government had an obligation to partner with other nations "because we can't solve these problems alone."[62] He toned down his American exceptionalism somewhat in making this spontaneous response to his European audience.

Not surprisingly, most Democratic leaders and voters in Obama's political base, including many Americans of color, initially viewed him as a relatively liberal politician who would take large-scale economic action on behalf of ordinary Americans. An example of this strong expectation could be seen in some black Democrats' reactions to Obama's late 2010 agreement to a one-sided compromise with congressional Republicans extending huge tax cuts for wealthy Americans. Representing the Democratic base, a majority of the Congressional Black Caucus voted against Obama's compromise tax bill, including House Majority Whip Jim Clyburn, who said: "I hope that as we move forward and our economy continues to recover, we will restore some fairness to the tax code and reduce the burden we are putting on future generations."[63]

However, as more aggressive action on such progressive economic goals did not emerge, yet other African American leaders made stronger criticisms of the Obama administration. In a prominent 2011 interview the Princeton University professor, Cornel West, a leading black intellectual who had campaigned for Obama, made a harsh assessment of Obama as "a black mascot of Wall Street oligarchs and a black puppet of corporate plutocrats. And now he has become head of the American killing machine and is proud of it." West said he had expected Obama to be constrained by the capitalist elite, but had also expected him to bring in "some voices concerned about working people, dealing with issues of jobs and downsizing and banks, some semblance of democratic accountability for Wall Street oligarchs and corporate plutocrats who are just running amuck."[64] Yet, with a few exceptions, Obama did not do that, but instead initially appointed moderate and liberal members of the established elite to most top positions in his administration. A number had served in previous Democratic and Republican administrations, and a substantial majority of the traditional cabinet positions were filled by whites. Bill Domhoff has shown that the members of Obama's traditional cabinet, and a few other officials added to it, have mostly been elite Americans who previously served in major government positions or alternated between a government career and working in corporate America. As with other presidential cabinets, most of Obama's officials came from wealthy or very affluent backgrounds, and attended elite colleges and universities.[65] In his interview, Dr. West further insisted that to please this elite Obama has used an "intermittent progressive populist language" as a cover for a "centrist, neoliberalist policy" on critical economic matters.[66] Finally, West concluded that President Obama was passing up the country's last chance to aggressively counter the main economic interests of the powerful corporate sector and bring real democracy to the United States.

West had raised the central point about how individual black successes in U.S. politics have mostly not brought significant political advances for black Americans as a group. One thing that was missing from West's analysis in this interview was the issue of why Obama often conformed to the interests of the dominant white elite and/or of the larger white population.

Getting What He Can: A Traditional Black Strategy?

One influential African American commentator, Ishmael Reed, has suggested that much of Obama's conformity in regard to these tough political realities is generally necessary given that he is a black man operating in a fully white-controlled society. Reed has criticized white and other progressives who have periodically asserted that "He's weak, he's spineless, he's got no balls, primary him in 2012."[67] Certainly, many white progressives have criticized President Obama for what they call his "weak" attempts at compromising with—and often bending well in the direction of—the very conservative Republican members of Congress. For example, the prominent white progressive analyst, Glenn Greenwald, has regularly criticized Obama for being too compromising in dealing with Republicans and for his weaknesses in pressing for progressive legislation: Obama "doesn't try, doesn't use the weapons at his disposal: the ones he wields when he actually cares about something (such as the ones he uses to ensure ongoing war funding . . . [This] leads to the rational conclusion that he is not actually committed to (or, worse, outright opposes) many of the outcomes which progressive pundits assume he desires."[68]

Indeed, Obama's policy actions, especially on economic matters, have often suggested to many progressives that he is only a political moderate and not the liberal they expected. For example, during the debt crisis of summer 2011, Obama spent much time trying to compromise with an arch-conservative Republican position that insisted on coupling the usually routine increase in the federal debt ceiling with major budget cuts, and he eventually gave in to many conservative demands. In this process, Obama signaled that he was a political centrist trying to create compromise with Republicans unwilling to compromise. Reviewing such Obama negotiations with Republicans, numerous progressive commentators have argued that his adoption of conservative language about the national debt and deficits might or might not have been useful in negotiations, but was weak in that it had a negative effect in further shifting what the Democratic Party publicly stands for in a conservative direction.[69] Still, while many have viewed Obama as politically weak and too conciliatory, yet other political analysts have argued that Obama's operative method actually reflects his community organizing days, during which he operated from the progressive perspective of legendary organizer, Saul Alinsky. Thus, Jonathan Chait has described Obama's conciliatory rhetoric as actually a "ruthless strategy." Quoting *American Prospect* editor, Mark Schmitt, the provocative Chait argues that Obama's savvy method is one of treating bad-faith political antagonists "as if they were operating in good faith" and then drawing "them into a conversation about how they actually would solve the problem." If they do not cooperate in this process, they will presumably pay a significant political price.[70]

Interestingly, too, while opinion polls showed that many voters were upset with the 2011 budget and deficit negotiations and decisions of the president and Congress, a majority still did not view Obama as weak or spineless. In a national survey after those negotiations, substantial majorities felt Obama was still a person who is "trustworthy," "a good communicator," "stands up for what he believes," and "who cares about people like me." There was no sign then that a majority agreed with the harsh general analyses of Obama's political or negotiating style coming from many commentators on both the right and the left.[71]

Looking at these difficult political decisions, moreover, Ishmael Reed has also emphasized that the white progressive critics typically miss certain key racial and other structural realities surrounding President Obama. These white progressives "have been urging the president to 'man up' in the face of the Republicans . . . What the progressives forget is that black intellectuals have been called 'paranoid,' 'bitter,' 'rowdy,' 'angry,' 'bullies,' and accused of tirades and diatribes for more than 100 years."[72] Thus, if President Obama ever appeared too aggressive, he would be strongly dismissed by most whites as another "angry black man," which is a very negative part of traditional white framing. Such widespread dismissals would make any policy goals very difficult to achieve. Instead, President Obama's rather "cool" approach to political action, as Adia Wingfield and I have argued, has involved being at all times and places calm and in control, never really being angry or threatening. The continuing white-racist contexts that prevail inside and outside U.S. politics make this a necessary strategy, as likely seen from Obama's perspective. Recently, Tom Schade, a liberal minister, has suggested that Obama's calm and careful political strategies remind him of those of 1960s civil rights leaders like Dr. Martin Luther King, Jr.—and, thus, not of those of a white Democratic politician such as Bill Clinton. Given that Obama is especially conscious of social and racial inequalities in power, Schade argues, certain of his political strategies might have been expected: "Number one: maintain your dignity. Number two: call your adversaries to the highest principles they hold. Number three: seize the moral high ground. And Number four: win by winning over your adversaries, by revealing the contradiction between their own ideals and their actions."[73]

In addition to suggesting that Obama has been very aware of the way he is racially framed by whites, and thus cautious in his actions, Ishmael Reed has argued that many white progressives do not comprehend what Obama's still supportive black (and as of now Latino) base has understood well: "Unlike white progressives, blacks and Latinos are not used to getting it all. They know how it feels to be unemployed and unable to buy your children Christmas presents. They know when not to shout."[74] Reed and numerous other analysts of color have pointed out that this is still a highly racist society, with a "Jim Crow media" that mostly gives a white perspective on major political issues. In such a difficult societal situation, the first *black* president—and that is the way he and much of his black base have often thought about his pathbreaking situation—must dodge many racial-political land mines and thus operate out of a "cool" racial realism that attempts to get what he can but recognizes significant limits on what a black man can ever do as president.

Nonetheless, by summer 2011 yet more of the ordinary voters in Obama's base were beginning to speak up to their representatives about the depression-like economic crisis in black communities. A member of the CBC, Representative Maxine Waters (D-CA), signaled this sentiment of leaders and voters of color at a 2011 Detroit forum: "We're supportive of the president but we're getting tired . . . We want to give the president every opportunity to show what he can do and what he's prepared to lead on. We want to give him every opportunity . . . but our people are hurting." She asked her substantially black audience if the CBC should put more pressure on the president to act, and many there indicated that the CBC should do so. Still, like Ishmael Reed, politically savvy Representative Waters made it clear that African Americans were overall very supportive of the president and understood well that some political attacks on him were also attacks on the black community. Indeed, she signaled that was a reason why there had not been more public criticism of Obama from the black leaders and communities in his political base.[75]

In an important fall 2011 speech to the CBC, of which Representative Waters was part, President Obama seemed to be responding in part to these calls from his base. He spoke strongly about the need for new jobs programs, with some stern criticism for his Republican opponents and a pitch for fairer taxation of the wealthy. Again he made his presentation with much language and narrative from a strong opportunity framing, urging these black members of Congress to work with him on "giving everybody opportunity" and emphasizing of the United States that "this is the land of opportunity." He praised the "exceptional" American "idea that it does not matter where you come from . . . if you're willing to put in an effort, you should get a shot . . . at the American Dream." His narrative was heavily focused on the need for "widening the circle of opportunity, standing up for everybody's opportunities, increasing each other's prosperity." Underscoring that socioeconomic change often comes slowly and with backtracking, he recounted his successes in expanding unemployment benefits and educational programs and called for congressional support for other proposed employment programs. However, again, Obama did not make direct reference to the specific racial problems of African Americans or other Americans of color, nor did he use any language such as "discrimination," "civil rights enforcement," or "racial justice." At the very end of his speech, he did slip in a vague reference to equality in the midst of a final emphasis on jobs and the need for greater political effort: "With patient and firm determination, I am going to press on for jobs. I'm going to press on for equality. I'm going to press on for the sake of our children."[76]

Obama's Policy Achievements to Date

In addition to distinctive racial barriers, President Obama came into office facing some of the worst economic and political circumstances ever encountered by a U.S. president, most of them inherited from the previous Bush era. These included a near-depression, many major banks and corporations in or near bankruptcy, huge monthly job losses, two trillion-dollar wars, and a generally hostile Republican Party. Even though caught within the vortex of these and other huge societal challenges, Obama was able to achieve in the first years of his presidency some moderately progressive goals that significantly benefitted ordinary Americans, including many Americans of color.

So far, in spite of some political images of him as "weak," Obama has taken significant actions on social issues that are more progressive, and often much more progressive, than what would likely have been taken by any recent Republican president or presidential candidate. For example, President Obama quietly got several agencies like the Department of Justice, under his only major black cabinet member Attorney General Eric Holder, to focus significantly more on enforcing existing civil rights laws than his Republican predecessor. For example, the Department of Justice hired more than 100 lawyers experienced in civil rights litigation on behalf of women, people of color, and gay/lesbian Americans. Additionally, the Obama administration submitted a human rights report under the United Nations Human Rights Council's Universal Periodic Review process and participated in the UN Human Rights Council. Both actions had been rejected by the Bush administration, and major conservative groups protested even this modest human rights action.[77] Researcher Robert Watson listed numerous other progressive achievements of the Obama administration in just his first year or so, among them the following:

1. enforced the law on equal pay for women;
2. stopped the media blackout on war casualties;
3. removed a stem-cell research ban;
4. liberalized travel to Cuba policies;
5. provided new funding for child health care;
6. expanded student and small business loans; and
7. nominated the first Latina Supreme Court justice.[78]

Obama accomplished other progressive political goals, including ending the military's "Don't Ask, Don't Tell" policy (on gay/lesbian issues) and stopping the federal defense of the discriminatory Defense of Marriage Act. The Obama administration also took action to improve funding for black colleges, passed hate-crimes legislation, increased access to medical care, provided more protection from exploitation by credit card firms, increased other consumer protection efforts, expanded support for alternative energy sources, and passed modest new regulations for the financial industry.[79]

What shines through the complexities of Obama's successes and failures in regard to these and other policy goals is the reality of his operating and contending as the first person of color ever to intrude into what is politically the highest inner sanctum of the white male elite. Obama is a classical "outsider within." Sociologist Patricia Hill Collins has developed the idea of the outsider within in examining the coming together of racial and gender characteristics in the situations of African American women, especially in historically white institutions.[80] Not only African American women but also African American men come into historically white institutions as outsiders without certain racial and gender privileges or power of otherwise similar white men, the classical "insiders." Even given the stated legal powers of the presidency, President Obama settled into historically white U.S. political institutions with many outsider disadvantages.

As we have seen, in the midst of recent national economic crises, numerous liberal analysts have called on him to be like previous white presidents who took aggressive positions on policies to deal with major economic problems, such as the New Deal programs forcefully proposed by Franklin Roosevelt during the Great Depression of the 1930s. Yet Franklin Roosevelt was a white male insider with myriad connections to various segments of the dominant elite. His extraordinary connections, and socialization fully within very elite settings, gave Roosevelt an eminent insider status and great power to take aggressive action in difficult times without facing the great headwind of systemic racism. This is definitely *not* the case for President Obama, who did not spend early and long decades being constantly groomed, socialized, and well connected into many of the white elite's networks, exclusive social clubs, and other exclusive private organizations. He has often depended for his advances in the political system on the sometimes vacillating support or sponsorship of some white men in the more moderate and liberal segments of the elite, but by no means has he had the amount of economic, political, and social capital to operate and take action aggressively that a full-fledged member of the dominant white elite would likely have had.

Nonetheless, when segments of the dominant elite have been substantially divided against each other, as on numerous social issues, President Obama has been effective and able to get enough elite backing to secure moderately progressive policy goals. Indeed, periodically, his "cool" and conciliatory approach to certain contested policy issues, drawn at least in part from the black experiential tradition, has provided him with a modest advantage in situations where calmly pressing a progressive case and taking the high moral ground has effected a positive result. Nonetheless, when it comes to a relatively cohesive elite's most sought-after political and economic goals, such as the federal bailout of Wall Street financial companies, Obama has had to more or less conform to their corporate goals and desires, no matter what his personal desires might have been. Moreover, the large-scale bailouts of these and other major capitalist firms actually began under President George W. Bush, but were aggressively continued by the elite and upper-middle-class officials in the new Obama administration.[81]

Conclusion: Obama's Political Future

The recurring racist realities of Obama's 2008 presidential election and of his presidency make the common post-racial narrative's assertions of over-whelming white commitment today to racial equality and justice seem very problematical, if not a bit absurd. So did the racial realities of the 2010 mid-term elections two years into Obama's presidency. The results of those congressional elections suggested a significant decline in public support for President Obama and his policies in various states across the country.

This could be seen most dramatically for white voters. In the mid-term elections the percentage of white voters who opted for Republican congressional candidates set a record for U.S. House races at 60 percent, which included about two-thirds of white blue-collar voters who some years back voted overwhelmingly Democratic. Just 37 percent of white voters chose Democratic candidates, and only 24 percent in the South.[82] Particularly poor political results for Democratic candidates in the South led some political analysts to suggest that, for the time being, the Democratic Party should give up on the South because white voters there were too culturally and politically conservative.[83] More generally, white voters' answers to 2010 exit poll questions revealed much discontent over what they perceived as Obama's great expansion of the federal government and over continuing unemployment problems.[84]

National opinion surveys since the 2010 elections further accent the racial divisions in party identification. In summer 2011, a Pew Research Center analysis found that in 2008 some 46 percent of whites identified as Republicans or leaning to Republicans, with 44 percent identifying as Democrats or leaning to Democrats. By 2011, these percentages had shifted significantly in favor of Republicans, to 52 percent and 39 percent respectively. This significant shift to Republicans was found for most white subgroups, but was especially striking for those under 30 years of age. In 2008, Democrats had a 49 to 42 percent lead in that age group over Republicans; but by 2011 this had reversed to a 52 to 41 percent lead for Republicans. The analysis also revealed, in contrast, that there was no significant shift in party identification or leanings from 2008 to 2011 for black voters (86 percent Democratic) or Latino voters (64 percent Democratic).[85]

The various 2008–2011 exit polls and national surveys suggested that many white voters have come to view the Democratic Party as becoming even more oriented to voters of color and their interests. Indeed, in the 2010 elections Democratic candidates did continue to win substantial proportions of the black and Latino vote (except in Florida among Cuban

Americans) and that vote helped them win congressional seats in important states like California and Nevada. The 2010 exit polls revealed that voters of color were much more likely than whites to view President Obama's policies as helping the country and were less likely to support a reduction in government intervention to improve the economy.[86] Here again was evidence suggesting that many voters of color understood the straightjacket around a president of color that limited how much he could act on certain more progressive political policies.

One thing seems clear from the Democratic and Republican election results in the various 2006–2010 elections. There are two different electorates demographically—one that is very diverse with lots of voters of color who turn out best for presidential elections and that tends to vote for the Democratic Party candidates, and another electorate made up of mostly white and older voters with better turnout rates for non-presidential elections and that tends to vote for Republican candidates.

A few months after the 2010 elections, as they prepared for the 2012 re-election campaign, Obama and his mostly white campaign staff appeared very aware of the social and racial implications of these 2010 results, as well as of society's key demographic changes. The opinion polls in late summer 2011 showed that President Obama still polled well among Latinos in trial heats with likely Republican opponents. Showing significant political savvy, thus, the Obama team brought in Katherine Archuleta, a talented political veteran, to be the new director for the Obama 2012 re-election campaign—the first ever Latina heading up a major presidential campaign. Clearly, the Obama re-election campaign was very aware that their major victory in 2008 had been created by first-rate political organizing and by constructing the first strong multiracial presidential campaign in U.S. history.

However, as they had acted since 2007, Obama's advisers again seemed fearful of alienating too many white voters by seriously discussing any aspects of the country's continuing white-racist realities. Major political advisers like David Axelrod yet again downplayed the reality of racial discrimination and other racism. This was obvious in comments Axelrod made in one important interview that touched on the obsession of the Tea Party activists and other conservatives with Obama's birthplace and birth certificate. Asked on a May 2011 *Meet the Press* program if racism was involved in these "birther" attacks on President Obama, a very hesitant David Axelrod said this:

> I don't think that's a worthy question because, in that sense . . . I don't think it's, I don't think it's, I don't think—but I don't think, I don't think we . . . I think a lot of Americans were offended by it. Of all stripes. Listen, we're a country, and the mayor can speak to this . . .

So—but the point is, we've got big challenges in this country, we've got big problems.

Axelrod's distinctive evasion of the straightforward question about white racism, and his uncharacteristic backtracking and revealing hesitations, indicated his studied unwillingness to deal publicly with the contemporary issues of continuing racism. He also suggested his view of the United States as colorblind by his reference to Americans "of all stripes" being offended.[87]

What the 2012 election might hold for President Obama was unclear at this point in time, but it was clear that he and his mostly white political advisers were still concerned about dealing frontally with the major societal issues of racism—lest they alienate the white voters they viewed, accurately, as necessary for his re-election in the very difficult economic times of this era. Moreover, sensitive to the views of their business and other elite backers, some White House officials and campaign advisers urged President Obama to continue with a pragmatic and moderate political orientation that apparently appealed to many white independents and moderate Democrats. As of this time, thus, they decided not to press for major new stimulus programs to create jobs for ordinary Americans, especially for the millions of Americans of color who still faced depression-level rates of unemployment and home foreclosure.[88]

9

Demographic Change and Political Futures

Recent Census Bureau data reveal a startling level of economic inequality between major racial groups. This racial inequality has significantly increased over the last few decades. One 2011 research analysis of these data revealed that the wealth differential between white Americans and Americans of color was getting ever larger. For whites, the median net "household" worth (assets less debts) was $113,149, some *18 times* that of Latino households ($6,325) and *20 times* that of black households ($5,677). These wealth ratios are the worst that the Census Bureau has found over several decades, and they had become much worse over the depression-like years of the mid- to late-2000s.[1] In addition, we should note the especially significant increases in the income and wealth of the upper 5 percent of U.S. households over recent decades.

Recall David Easton's concept of politics as the process of "authoritative allocation of values for society." This authoritative allocation involves the distribution by government authorities of important tangible and intangible resources and other things that many people value. In addition, clearly, the capitalistic economic system has much impact on this authoritative allocation of valuable resources. Examination of our economic and political history shows that over the centuries a small, most often white and male, elite has had the greatest legitimate economic and political authority not only to shape the allocation of important societal resources but also to construct and control the major economic and political institutions that control resource allocation. By controlling the economy and political system, this oligarchical elite and its immediate subordinates have long made the definitive choices about the allocation of most important societal resources.[2]

Strikingly, this authoritative allocation of resources has *always* been overwhelmingly inegalitarian, tremendously skewed toward elite group interests, and thoroughly legitimated by dominant racial and political frames. Over the centuries, this elite has been extraordinarily effective in crafting and maintaining the political, economic, religious, educational, and other institutions that support and reproduce their interests, as well as the interests of their societal constituency.

194

"We the People" of this United States have never been fairly allocated the rights and valued resources associated with a fully developed political democracy. We did not have such a thoroughgoing democracy in the 18th, 19th, and 20th centuries, and we do not have one now. Moreover, we are not such a political democracy to a substantial degree because of the foundational and systemic reality of racial oppression in our past and present. Recall how this country's early racialized oppression of the "other" took the form of anti-Indian genocide and land theft and African enslavement to work lands of European Americans. White colonizers and founders rationalized land theft and labor oppression with a developed racial frame that often concealed or misrepresented the extraordinarily oppressive realities of the new society, a frame still much in evidence today. Numerous founders viewed themselves as grand patriarchs of their landed domains, an authoritative perspective that closely coupled their racial framing with related patriarchal and class framing aimed at enforcing yet other societal oppressions.

Such extensive oppression eventually reached into many societal areas and generated such a racial hierarchy, such resource inequality, such need for authoritarian control over the oppressed, and such an encompassing racial framing that it not surprisingly shaped the new U.S. political system created by the white male founders in fundamental and foundational ways. Given these extensive realities of oppression, the elite founders could not, and most did not wish to, establish a truly democratic political system for the new United States.

The Rhetorical Liberty and Justice Frame

In the late 18th century the oligarchical elite intentionally buttressed the extreme economic oppression they and their white constituents had created with a substantially undemocratic political system. Yet the undemocratic political system the framers created was often described in terms of an ideological framing of "freedom," "justice," "equality," and "democracy." For centuries now, this powerful and seductive political framing has been routinely intertwined with the dominant racial frame, and both have long remained central to this society.

One of the noteworthy ironies of this society is that over the centuries a mostly white elite, working with its white majority constituency, has routinely claimed to be highly virtuous and the greatest implementer of democracy, liberty, and justice among the world's many countries. This substantially mythical liberty and justice framing has often been operated to cover up the reality of a society built from its earliest century on stolen Native American lands and African American labor. Over the centuries, the white elite, assisted by its white constituency, has continued with yet more such rationalized oppression of other groups of color, including Mexican Americans and Asian Americans beginning in the mid-19th century. The elite has also greatly exploited white working-class Americans and regularly used a racial framing accenting white superiority and privilege to persuade many ordinary whites into becoming a constituency that has mostly supported much of the U.S. racial and class systems of oppression. The ability of the white elite and much of its white constituency to hold a strong liberty and justice framing of this society that is greatly contradicted by actual historical and contemporary oppression and inequalities is remarkable, both in the past and in the present.[3]

Over the centuries this liberty and justice framing has, in the case of most white Americans, generally been a rhetorical framing to be taken seriously only when it is in the interest of whites to do so. This important idealistic framing is centrally about moral issues of right and wrong, yet those with the most significant socio-political power—that is, elite and affluent whites—usually get to decide when and where such grand ideals are actually applied, especially on a large scale. As we have seen throughout this book, over the centuries the white elite, and sometimes whites more generally, have chosen when, where, and to whom the liberty and justice frame effectively gets applied in society.

Nonetheless, today as in the past, the U.S. is regularly confronted by internal contradictions involving the liberty and justice framing. We see this regularly when groups of Americans of color, and other groups, organize to change societal patterns of oppression, for they often use the language of this liberty and justice frame. There are yet other examples of internal contradictions as well. For example, business consultant Paul Hawken carried out an interesting workshop with white managers in a big corporation that makes herbicides and other chemicals. Early in the workshop, these corporate managers strongly *rejected* the idea that creating social justice and resource equity for all people in the United States is essential to the long-term success of the economy and the country. These managers were then given an exercise asking them, in subgroups, to design a spaceship for people like themselves that would go out on a very long trip from the planet and come back within a century with inhabitants who were active and healthy. The managers voted on which group's spaceship design was best, and the winning group had decided that "weeds were important in a healthy ecosystem and banned herbicides" and their food thus had to be organic. These white managers decided too that they would get bored with recorded entertainment and that their spaceship required much diversity of people— many "singers, dancers, artists, and storytellers . . . and engineers alone did not a village make." Moreover, they were asked the question if it would be "OK if 20 percent of the people on the spaceship controlled 80 percent of the resources on board. They immediately and vociferously rejected that notion as unworkable, unjust, and unfair."[4] Strikingly, these corporate managers vigorously rejected typical U.S.-type inequality and injustice on board their own hypothetical spaceship. Not surprisingly, thus, they wanted the liberty and justice frame to be implemented, but only for themselves.

Over recent decades, a majority of white Americans have revealed at best a limited commitment to the common political frame's liberty, justice, and equality ideals in their orientations to Americans of color and, indeed, to poor Americans as a group. Most in the elite and the general white population do not appear to want these liberty and justice ideals actively incorporated into a thoroughly egalitarian and democratic U.S. society, apparently even on a gradual and long-term basis.[5]

Historical Pressures for Democratic Change

Recall the definition of substantial political democracy as a structure and process of governing a country in which "each person affected by the actions" of a political or economic entity actually has a "continuous and equal opportunity to influence actions of that entity."[6] The U.S. political system has never come close to such substantial participatory democracy. Indeed, historically, very few white American leaders have envisaged the United States as a truly just and egalitarian democracy grounded in a solidly democratic constitution. As we have seen, in the late 18th century the founders did not conceive of such, even in the long run. Nor did later celebrated political leaders such as presidents Abraham Lincoln, Woodrow Wilson, Franklin Roosevelt, and Dwight Eisenhower envision a far more egalitarian and fully democratic U.S. future. Nor have most presidents, most other leading politicians, and most business leaders since that time, including in our contemporary era.

Nonetheless, many ordinary Americans have pressed very seriously for societal change, and this society has regularly had protests against the undemocratic political and economic system. An array of people's movements have tried to move the "authoritative allocation" of societal rights and resources much more in an egalitarian and democratic direction. Indeed, periodically over the course of U.S. history we have observed the country move, if often in a halting and backtracking manner, in a more democratic and egalitarian direction. In the first half of the 19th century, for example, organized pressures from ordinary white farmers expanded the country's legal voters from mostly propertied white men to most white men, with the latter having the opportunity to engage in important political activities.

Later on, under great pressure from large-scale societal crises and major people's movements, such as the millions who were part of abolitionist, labor, and civil rights movements, the white male elite has occasionally allowed some more societal changes in a more democratic and egalitarian direction, yet mostly when there has been convergence between the interests of some part of the elite and the interests of the people's movements. For example, recall that during and after the Civil War in the mid-19th century, major attempts were made by some liberal Republicans to respond to the country's crisis of southern white secession—and to pressures coming from abolitionists and freed black Americans (hundreds of thousands of whom fought or worked for Union armies)—by providing a significant reallocation of rights and unjustly held white resources to black Americans. The implementation of the 13th, 14th, and 15th amendments by these liberal Republicans marked a critical effort that, for a short time, moved the United States in a more democratic direction. These pathbreaking amendments and associated antidiscrimination laws and reparative agencies could have, if fully implemented over some decades, permanently reconstituted the United States as a much more desegregated, egalitarian, and democratic country. Unfortunately, as noted in Chapter 3, a substantial majority of the elite soon abandoned these liberty and justice efforts. Effectively using undemocratic features of the political system, including the Supreme Court and electoral college, the elite majority killed off much of this significant democratizing and equalizing effort, and whites as a group thereby retained the very significant privileges and material enrichment they had long unjustly enjoyed.

Some decades later, pressures from labor unions, civil rights groups, and other popular movements during the cataclysmic 1930s Great Depression helped greatly to increase federal labor, civil rights, and social welfare programs benefitting many ordinary white, black, and other Americans. However, by the late 1940s and 1950s the conservative segment of the elite was successful in rolling back some of these major reforms, such as by means of new anti-labor laws significantly weakening unionization. Moreover, the progressive 1960s brought impressive, partially successful attempts to reallocate rights and socioeconomic resources. The significant if partial successes of the black civil rights movement in the 1960s, when the elite was in intense competition with the Soviet Union for global dominance, provide a good example of a temporarily successful people's movement that required such elite interest convergence. Black Americans thereby moved the country in the direction of more participatory democracy, including securing voting and other important civil rights for many Americans of color. Fortunately for democratic progress in the United States, African Americans have periodically developed important protest movements, large and small, over their four centuries of oppression. Note too that the 1960s black rights movements paralleled, and often helped to stimulate, yet other 1960s protest movements, all of which for a time greatly pressed the country's elite in the direction of a more egalitarian allocation of valued civil rights and socioeconomic resources.

White Reactions to Racial Change since the 1960s

Once the pressures of interest convergence that had accelerated in the 1960s had been reduced, especially with the decline of the Soviet Union in the

1980s, the U.S. elite evidently felt much less international pressure in regard to improving civil rights and related resource allocation in this country. Together with other declining pressures on the elite, including a reduction in organized civil rights protests, various conservative presidential administrations since the 1970s have reduced or blocked civil rights enforcement or expansion of civil rights laws. Moreover, in recent decades important segments of the elite have unquestionably become very disturbed over the reallocation of political rights and the redistribution of some socio-political resources to historically oppressed groups that had occurred since the 1960s; as a result significant segments of that elite have periodically, and often successfully, sought to recover their socio-political losses or protect themselves from further such losses.

As I have documented in previous chapters, since the 1960s people's movements the oligarchical elite and its affluent acolytes have made frequent political and other organizational efforts to stop moves toward greater democratization and egalitarianism. One result of this is the sharp racial and political polarization of the major political parties over recent decades. The Republican Party has become ever more centrally the "white party" in composition, orientation, and electoral strategies. In contrast, over the same period the Democratic Party has become much more diverse in composition and orientation, and frequently but not always more diverse in its political strategies.

Today people of color are sought by both parties as rank-and-file voters. However, in the Republican Party people of color very rarely play a significant role in the national leadership, and if they do hold a leadership position briefly, they are expected to emulate the conservative political framing espoused by important white party leaders and funders. In the Democratic Party, there are numerous political leaders of color, mostly at middle and lower levels of party power, yet it too has remained a party within which white men have very disproportionate decision-making power. This shift in the Democratic Party leadership is a significant change from the past history of U.S. political parties, and for the first time in U.S. history significant numbers of people of color are making political decisions at the national, regional, and local levels of a major political party. To some degree, the white male oligarchical control of a party has given way to more diverse decision making. One result is a few more decisions in the direction of protecting civil rights for people of color and other oppressed Americans. This can be seen, for example, in some Democratic Party efforts to more aggressively protect the voting rights of people of color and poor Americans. Yet the modest reductions in white oligarchical control over the Democratic Party have not brought major changes in other areas, for the impact of corporate funding and lobbying can still be observed in the strong support of the Democratic Party leaders for the goals and interests of the corporate elite, such as was observed in the 2009 bailout of troubled Wall Street corporations and the weak attempts by Democratic leaders to re-regulate the finance industry. Even a president of color has made little difference in the impact of this corporate influence. As of now, the powerful and mostly white male corporate and other business leaders who have played the key role in funding U.S. political parties for two centuries continue to have a dominating influence over the most important policy directions, especially on recurring major economic matters, taken by the two leading political parties.

Moreover, much evidence we have examined shows that over recent decades the Republican Party has become a much more right-wing party politically than the Democratic Party, and this is closely associated with the country's significant rightward political shift since the late 1960s. Many scholars and experts have pondered this relatively unprecedented and growing political polarization of the Republican Party and the Democratic Party, yet very rarely have they dealt in any depth with the accompanying racial polarization that has often underlain and interacted with this often dramatic political polarization. Significant aspects of this rightward shift have reflected whites' specific or general reactions to many of the political and other social changes brought by black, Latino, and other civil rights movements since the 1960s, including the multifaceted impacts of these movements and other rights organizations on the discriminatory mechanisms and structures still common across this society. There has been much white resistance to government action at all levels on civil rights enforcement, school and residential desegregation, full employment integration, affirmative action in education, and an array of other remedial programs for ongoing racial discrimination and inequalities. In addition, there has been accompanying white resistance to much 1960s and subsequent liberal legislation and societal change that is not directly linked to the civil rights movement or desegregation except often in the minds of many whites. Influenced greatly over several decades by the conservative elite's manipulation efforts, including those of powerful right-wing media commentators, many whites (and some others) have come to view much Great Society legislation of the 1960s and its later implementation—such as social welfare expansion, various health and employment programs, and educational programs—as undesirable "big government" intervention too heavily benefitting "minorities," even as whites have frequently been the major beneficiaries of many such government programs. Thus, we get an accelerated conservative accent on privatization programs as the answer for this society's ills.

Changing Demographics: White Reactions and Political Futures

In addition to changes in certain government policies that have periodically improved the rights and socioeconomic situations of many Americans of color since the 1960s, large-scale changes in population distribution and growth since that decade have had major and continuing impacts on U.S. society—changes that many white Americans in particular have often found rather troubling. In the 2008 election an American of color, Senator Barack Obama, was elected U.S. president substantially because he got the overwhelming majority of votes of Americans of color. In contrast, a substantial majority of white voters opted for his white Republican opponent, Senator John McCain. Among other things, Barack Obama's election was a conspicuous signal of major changes in the society's demographic character. This election made evident the reality that voters of color had substantially increased as a percentage of U.S. voters in recent years.

Today, Americans of European descent are a decreasing proportion of the U.S. population. They are a statistical minority in California, Texas, New Mexico, and Hawaii, and soon will be in several other states. If future birth and immigration rates remain roughly similar to today's, about half the population will be Americans of color no later than the 2040s. Moreover, by about 2050 a majority of an estimated U.S. population of about 429 million will be Americans of color.[7] Over recent decades, Latino and Asian American populations have grown dramatically and spread to more geographical areas, yet remain substantially geographically concentrated, with around half of both groups living in just 10 metropolitan areas. The African American population has continued to grow as well. In contrast, over recent decades the white population has had relatively low fertility and immigration rates, and has grown more slowly, percentage-wise, than the Latino, Asian, and African American populations.[8]

One significant question these interesting demographic changes raise is just how most whites, especially those in the powerful elite, will react to a very significant and continuing increase in racial diversity over coming decades. Nationally, many whites seem to look at the population changes from within some version of the old white racial frame and thus apparently cannot visualize a United States that is highly diverse in racial terms, is minority white, and perhaps is more democratic and egalitarian in the operation of its political, economic, and other significant institutions.

In a provocative 1990s book, *The Coming White Minority*, journalist Dale Maharidge assessed white Californians' reactions to demographic change and argued that what he saw as the realistic fears of whites were even then being underestimated: "Whites dread the unknown and not-so-distant tomorrow when a statistical turning point will be reached that could have very bad consequences for them . . . They fear losing not only their jobs but also their culture."[9] Many whites, elite leaders, and ordinary citizens view these population changes as very threatening. Today, numerous white media conservatives like Patrick Buchanan, former Republican presidential candidate and prominent media commentator, and Samuel Huntington, influential Harvard professor, have written and spoken from a fearful framing of demographic change, a perspective accenting the declining white percentage as very negative for the future of the Anglo-American culture and "Western civilization." They are not alone, for a major interview study of 100 elite white men found several powerful respondents there expressing concern over the growth of Americans of color, with some likewise viewing Western civilization as under threat.[10]

Consider some aggressive white reactions, actual and potential, to such population change. Over several decades since the 1960s many whites have moved from large cities with growing populations of color to whiter suburbs, exurban and rural areas, or gated communities within these large cities. While the motivations for these moves varied, racial concerns and closely linked economic issues were high on the list of motivations for many whites. Within a great many counties, towns, and cities, this country remains substantially segregated, with most whites and most people of color living largely separate lives outside workplaces and shopping malls.[11] Researching whites who moved to heavily white exurban and other towns, Rich Benjamin has quoted some on why they moved—with a general theme being, as one person put it, that "So many of the people that are here have come from areas where they have seen diversity done badly." Benjamin has described the pull of the heavily white towns: "Americans associate a homogeneous white neighborhood with higher property values, friendliness, orderliness, cleanliness, safety, and comfort" and thus that "Race is often used as a proxy for those neighborhood traits."[12] Actually, however, some of the local comfort noted here for "Americans" is actually for white Americans, for overwhelmingly white towns and neighborhoods can be decidedly unfriendly to many Americans of color. Note too the political implications of this residential segregation of whites; for example, a significant majority of the counties fitting the "exurban" description are strongly Republican in voting orientation.

Many whites have also engaged in organized efforts to restrict immigrants of color, especially those coming from Latin America. Some have joined armed "militia" groups policing parts of the southern U.S. border. In addition, legislative and political attacks on immigrants and their children have periodically been organized by conservative political organizations, including several important Republican groups. Thus, in late 2010, a large group of Republican state legislators laid out model legislation which they viewed as overturning the long-accepted interpretation of the 14th amendment as giving citizenship to anyone born in the United States, including children of undocumented immigrants. Moreover, a recent ThinkProgress study found that about 59 percent of Republican members of Congress had at some time proposed congressional efforts, including some 28 congressional bills, to review or alter this birthright citizenship.[13] And some arch-conservative political groups like American Cause have contended that Republicans are losing elections because the Republican Party does not take strong enough stands against what they have assertively stereotyped as the "Third World Invasion and Conquest of America."[14]

Recall too from Chapter 6 the increased attempts by some Republican leaders and operatives to reduce voting by people of color. Usually with no convincing evidence of significant voting problems, Republican Party operatives and activists have increased so-called ballot security programs involving such tactics as the use of poll watchers to slow down voters' lines and scare off voters with dubious or illegal polling-place strategies.[15] Recently, numerous state laws have been proposed or passed by Republican-controlled legislatures that intentionally make it difficult for some people of color to vote, including mandating identification materials that can be difficult to secure. In addition, one consequence of the racially discriminatory operation of the criminal justice system in recent years has been that many blacks and Latinos with felony convictions (often involving minor drug use that similar white drug users are rarely arrested for) have lost their right to vote, as well as certain other political rights, thereby significantly decreasing these Americans' political impact on U.S. society.[16]

Additionally, some social scientists have argued that one very important 2010 Supreme Court decision represents at least an indirect political response to white fears of major population change. The 2010 Supreme Court decision, *Citizens United* v. *Federal Election Commission*, knocked down federal and state legislative attempts to limit expenditures of corporations, unions, and other groups for political advertising and electioneering communications on behalf of political candidates.[17] As sociologist Glenn Bracey has pointed out, the timing of this rather radical decision by the Supreme Court came just after an African American was elected president and at a time when voters of color were becoming more influential in pivotal elections. Since often-huge corporate expenditures on behalf of political candidates have increasingly favored conservatives and arch-conservatives, this court decision will in coming decades likely help most the more corporate-centered Republican Party and its largely white constituency to maintain great influence over the U.S. government and its policies, even as whites will likely be losing their former demographic dominance. As Bracey notes, the "combination of black and brown leadership, increased black and brown voting activity, decreased white voting potential, and sufficient non-corporate funding pools for campaigns was a new threat to which whites were compelled to respond immediately."[18] Most whites, he notes, assume that they will lose their political and racial dominance as they become a statistical minority. Clearly, since the Richard Nixon era the intentional packing of the Supreme Court by Republican presidents with very conservative judges, who provided the important votes for the key sections of this pathbreaking decision, has been effective in securing major conservative political goals.

Throughout these examples of white resistance we observe significant contemporary racial and class struggles, which are indeed often interrelated. Note again the importance of the mostly white elite. The conservative segment of the elite periodically presses certain groups and organizations in the population, typically white groups and organizations, to assist in countering or blocking various attempts at progressive societal change in the direction of democracy and social justice. Numerous reactionary people's groups line the columns of our history books. Most recently, some Tea Party groups discussed in the last chapter are frequently called "populist," yet are substantially "astro-turf" groups with important support ties to the conservative segment of the elite. That segment has provided substantial funding and other significant support for some Tea Party groups, and the latter have periodically been at the forefront of conservative efforts against antidiscrimination laws and programs such as affirmative action, against efforts to improve the lives of immigrants of color, against efforts to increase voting by Americans of color, or against numerous policy goals of an African American president, Barack Obama, who has often appeared to be taken as representative of the ongoing demographic changes that many of these whites fear.

Given this tremendous power of the organized right, with its many activist and think-tank organizations, huge amounts of money, political influence in Congress, and influence in much of the mainstream media, the civil rights and other progressive groups seeking change in a more democratic and social justice direction have faced major political barriers. In addition, the powerful, usually corporate-backed political pressures from conservative political and economic groups, including major Republican Party groups, help to explain why even Democratic politicians of color like President Obama must, if they are to succeed even in part, operate out of a more moderate political frame and a equal opportunity version of the white racial frame—frames acceptable to at least some moderate segments of the dominant white elite and of the white voting population.

Growing Pressures for Major Political and Economic Reform

The ongoing demographic trends and associated societal changes have clearly helped to spur these white political reactions, yet these demographic trends also often highlight our undemocratic social institutions and increase organized protests by Americans of color against societal inequalities. These protests may eventually bring some democratic and other progressive transformations, including possible increases in human rights, possible reductions in racial discrimination, and better allocations of valued societal resources. Over the next few decades, the dramatic demographic shift toward a population majority of Americans of color will very likely bring much more pressure for important political and economic change. Consider, for example, that today one-third of our large metropolitan areas have populations under 15 years of age that are more than half children of color. In the near future they and their parents will doubtless strive for greater input into the staffing, operation, and curriculum of currently white-dominated school systems. Moreover, by the late 2030s, more than half the working-age population will probably be workers of color. This will give them a greater ability to protest against discrimination and related inequalities in the workplace successfully. This, in turn, may well accelerate organized protests against other forms of racial discrimination, such as in housing and politics.[19]

Over coming decades, moreover, the composition of the voting population will change noticeably. During the 2008 election nearly a quarter of voters were people of color whose votes were essential to some political changes of that year. By the late 2020s, a majority of young adults, and probably of young adult voters in numerous areas, will reportedly be people of color. Even now, the Latino population has played a central role in current growth, and this will figure into congressional reapportionments. Southwestern states with ever larger Latino populations will get new congressional seats because of 2010 census results, and some seats will be in areas now increasingly composed of Latinos. Given that numerous conservative Republican leaders have recently alienated many Latinos with anti-immigrant and other nativistic rhetoric, these areas may well become more Democratic politically.[20] As more Latinos become older and become voters, they are soon going to play a considerably more central political role in southwestern states and probably in other states across the country.

Since the 1990s, moreover, the anti-immigration rhetoric and other anti-civil-rights efforts of many white conservatives have already backfired in some geographical areas, as growing numbers of Latinos have come out to vote substantially for that reason. Even as conservative Republicans made major gains in Congress in the 2010 elections, Latino voters with other voters of color helped to account for some victories by Democratic Party candidates in Nevada, Colorado, and California. In these and other states Latino voters turned out in higher-than-expected numbers in part because of the anti-immigrant rhetoric of some Republican candidates.[21] Rejecting the concerns of Latino voters has already cost the Republican Party certain important elections and may well do so in the future. Clearly, too, there are major implications of these events for the future of an increasingly diverse Democratic Party.

As U.S. voting majorities gradually change from majority white, there will likely be more significant changes in election results, as well as (over time) in jury composition, the operation of the criminal justice system, and legislatures' composition and priorities. Additionally, we will in all likelihood have fewer winning white candidates opposing antidiscrimination laws and pressing for laws further restricting Latin American and Asian immigration, as well as more winning candidates of color.[22]

Over the coming decades these striking demographic changes are likely to generate yet more organizational efforts to bring change in the allocation of valued socioeconomic resources and various other socially valued items. Over the course of U.S. history, progressive developments in civil rights, human rights, and equitable resource allocation have usually involved significant large-scale organization, movements, and protests. As we have observed in several chapters, African Americans have long been at the center of the system of racial oppression, and their protest movements over centuries have regularly challenged this country's enduring racist system. Inspired by African American efforts, and organizing for social justice on their own, many other groups of color have reacted strongly to the racial discrimination and related oppression that targets them. Today, as in the past, we live in a country with many progressive organizations working to change this systemic racism, including many important civil rights groups. Among these are the NAACP, the Mexican American Legal Defense and Education Fund, the Puerto Rican Legal Defense and Educational Fund, the American Indian Movement, the Japanese American Citizens League, the Asian American Legal Defense Fund, and the Organization of Chinese Americans. In addition, these important groups are often joined in specific efforts by numerous other organizations pressing for social justice, including women's rights organizations and gay and lesbian rights organizations.

Important coalitions of such social justice and human rights groups continue to be crucial in putting pressure on the ruling elite. The largest and oldest, the Leadership Conference on Civil and Human Rights, was founded in 1950 by black and Jewish civil rights leaders and now encompasses more than 200 groups. It seeks "to promote and protect the civil and human rights of all persons in the United States. Through advocacy and outreach to targeted constituencies, the Leadership Conference works toward the goal of a more open and just society—an America as good as its ideals."[23] Over the decades this coalition and its member organizations have worked aggressively, and sometimes successfully, in getting much significant civil rights legislation and other social support legislation through the U.S. Congress. Numerous such coalitions on issues of rights and resources are likely to arise over coming decades as the United States becomes yet more socially and politically diverse.

Conclusion

Quite clearly, these are both very exciting and very troubling times for serious advocates of expanded political democracy and the old ideals of liberty and justice. Today, the global political and economic scene is dramatically changing, albeit in an often erratic fashion. International contradictions and conflicts continue to emerge out of a global racial order originally created to implement and legitimate the colonial exploitation and imperialistic expansion of European and North American countries. For centuries now, white Eurocentric economic, cultural, and political institutions have been remarkably globalizing, dominant, and resistant to change. Yet, as we observe in the contemporary United States, many people across the globe have in recent times protested both local and international racial and class exploitation, neocolonialism, and neoliberalism. A great many people of color, and some whites who question such neocolonial exploitation and neoliberal oppression, are regularly organizing for political and other societal changes. In coming decades, as the United States and the world change demographically and in terms of countries' national and international social and political powers, once-dominant whites in many areas may well face ever greater pressures to create and participate in new or reinvigorated socio-political systems that are much less racist and racially exploitative, and perhaps much more just, democratic, and egalitarian in operation.

Many Americans, and especially Americans of color, view the often backward political movement on social inequality and racial discrimination in the United States over recent decades as setting important tasks to build new or renewed political coalitions for progressive societal reform and change. People of all racial and ethnic backgrounds who are committed to a truly implemented liberty and justice framing and structuring of society recognize that repeated organizing for social justice and other progressive goals is necessary when a society's foundations are structurally inegalitarian and oppressive. People in such organized efforts cannot prove that there will be progressive societal change, but they can and do act on the important assumption that it will be much more likely. Human agency is usually possible in spite of oppressive social structures, but such agency must be regularly supported and regenerated, and usually very organized.

The great abolitionist, Frederick Douglass, who was born in slavery and became one of the greatest of all American leaders, underscored the central importance of these continuing struggles for political and social justice in a famous speech in Canandaigua, New York, in August 1857:

> The whole history of the progress of human liberty shows that all concessions yet made to her august claims, have been born of earnest struggle . . . If there is no struggle there is no progress. Those who profess to favor freedom and yet depreciate agitation, are men who want crops without plowing up the ground, they want rain without thunder and lightening. They want the ocean without the awful roar

of its many waters . . . Power concedes nothing without a demand. It never did and it never will. Find out just what any people will quietly submit to and you have found out the exact measure of injustice and wrong which will be imposed upon them, and these will continue till they are resisted with either words or blows, or with both. The limits of tyrants are prescribed by the endurance of those whom they oppress.[24]

Notes

Preface

1   Quoted in Ron Claiborne, "White Party, Black Party: Racial Division in American Politics," ABC News, August 17, 2008, http://abcnews.go.com/Politics/Vote2008/story?id=5598010& amp;page=1 (accessed July 4, 2011).

2   Joseph Lowndes, Julie Novkov, and Dorian T. Warren, "Race and American Political Development," in *Race and American Political Development*, eds. Joseph Lowndes, Julie Novkov, and Dorian Warren (New York: Routledge, 2008), p. 13.

3   See, for example, the important work of Paul Frymer, *Uneasy Alliances: Race and Party Competition in America* (Princeton: Princeton University Press, 1999), p. 27. Frymer deals with racial matters but does not discuss conceptually or empirically institutionalized racism. See also Ernest J. Wilson III, "Why Political Scientists Don't Study Black Politics, But Historians and Sociologists Do," *PS* 18 (Summer, 1985): 600–607. On the historical relationship of political science to U.S. imperialism and white supremacy, see Robert Vitalis, "The Noble American Science of Imperial Relations and Its Laws of Race Development," *Comparative Studies in Society and History* 52 (2010): 909–938; and Errol Henderson, "Navigating the Muddy Waters of the Mainstream: Tracing the Mystification of Racism in International Relations," in *The State of the Political Science Discipline: An African-American Perspective*, ed. Wilbur Rich (Philadelphia: Temple University Press, 2007), pp. 325–363.

4   For more details, see Joe R. Feagin, *Racist America: Roots, Current Realities, and Future Reparations* (Second edition; New York: Routledge, 2010).

5   See Milan Zafirovski, "The Most Cherished Myth: Puritanism and Liberty Reconsidered and Revised," *American Sociologist* 38 (2007): 53–59; and Ronald T. Takaki, *Iron Cages: Race and Culture in 19th Century America* (New York: Oxford University Press, 1990).

6   See Alexis de Tocqueville, *Democracy in America*, trans. Henry Reeve (London: Saunders and Otley, 1835, 1840).

7   For example, Takaki, *Iron Cages*; Feagin, *Racist America*; and Richard Drinnon, *Facing West: The Metaphysics of Indian-Hating and Empire-Building* (Norman, Oklahoma; University of Oklahoma Press, 1997 [1980]).

8   Philip H. Burch, *Elites in American History: The Federalist Years to the Civil War* (New York: Holmes and Meier, 1981); and G. William Domhoff, *Who Rules America? Challenges to Corporate and Class Dominance* (Sixth edition; New York: McGraw-Hill, 2009).

9   Jeffrey A. Winters and Benjamin I. Page, "Oligarchy in the United States?," *Perspectives on Politics* 7 (December 2009): 731.

10 For example, Domhoff, *Who Rules America?* and recent work by Philip Burch.

11 David Easton, *The Political System: An Inquiry into the State of Political Science* (Second edition; New York: Alfred A. Knopf, 1971), p. 134; and David Easton, *A Framework for Political Analysis* (Englewood Cliffs, New Jersey: Prentice-Hall, Inc., 1965). I am indebted here to discussions with Maria Chávez on these political science issues.

1 Framing a Racist America: Puritan Inheritances and Political Framing

1   Alexis de Tocqueville, *Democracy in America*, trans. Henry Reeve (London: Saunders and Otley 1835, 1840), Vol. 2, Kindle DX location 702.

2   Richard Howland Maxwell, "Pilgrim and Puritan: A Delicate Distinction," Pilgrim Society Note, Series Two, March 2003, www.pilgrimhall.org (accessed November 18, 2010). I draw here on data summarized by Maxwell and in Williston Walker, *A History of the Christian Church* (Revised edition; New York: Scribner's, 1959), pp. 403–467; and David Hackett Fischer, *Albion's Seed: Four British Folkways in America* (New York: Oxford, 1989), p. 200.

3   Bob Altemeyer, *The Authoritarians* (Winnipeg, Manitoba: Department of Psychology, University of Manitoba, 2006), p. 2.

4   Milan Zafirovski, "The Most Cherished Myth: Puritanism and Liberty Reconsidered and Revised," *American Sociologist* 38 (2007): 53–59; Maxwell, "Pilgrim and Puritan: A Delicate Distinction."

5   Thomas Jefferson, *Notes on the State of Virginia* (London: John Stockdale, 1787), Query 17, p. 261.

6   David D. Hall, "Peace, Love and Puritanism," *The New York Times* online, http://www.nytimes.com/2010/11/24/opinion/24hall.html?_r=2&hp (accessed November 26, 2010).

7   Robert C. Winthrop, *Life and Letters of John Winthrop* (Second edition; Boston, Massachusetts: Little, Brown, 1869), Vol. 2, p. 430; and Maxwell, "Pilgrim and Puritan: A Delicate Distinction."

8   John Winthrop, "A Modell of Christian Charity (1630)," *Collections of the Massachusetts Historical Society (Boston, 1838),* 3rd series 7: 31–48, http://history.hanover.edu/texts/winthmod.html (accessed November 30, 2010). I have modernized the spelling.

9   See "American Exceptionalism," *New World Encyclopedia*, http://www.newworldencyclopedia.org (accessed July 4, 2011).

10 Winthrop, "A Modell of Christian Charity (1630)." I have modernized the spelling.

11 Deborah Madsen, *American Exceptionalism* (Jackson, Mississippi: The University Press of Mississippi, 1998), pp. 8–9.

12 Karl Marx, *Capital*, Vol. I, chapter 31, http://www.marxists.org/archive/marx/works/1867-c1/ch31.htm (accessed July 4, 2011); see also W. E. B. Du Bois, *The World and Africa* (New York: International Publishers, 1965 [1946]), pp. 56–57.

13 David Harvey, *A Companion to Marx's Capital* (London: Verso, 2010), Kindle DX location 6477.

14 "Interview with James O. Horton," edited transcript, PBS, http://www.pbs.org/race/000_About/002_04-background-02-04.htm (accessed December 19, 2003).

15 Ibid.

16 W. E. B. Du Bois, *The Suppression of the African Slave-Trade to the United States of America 1638–1870* (London, UK: Longman's, Green and Country, 1904), pp. 197–198.

17 Carole E. Scott, "America's Colonial Period," http://freepages.history.rootsweb.com/~cescott/colonial.html (accessed December 19, 2003).

18 Some scholars distinguish between the slavery systems before and after the rise of industrial capitalism. See Dale Tomich in *Through the Prism of Slavery: Labor, Capital, and World Economy* (Lanham, Maryland: Rowman & Littlefield, 2003); and Walter Johnson, "The Pedestal and the Veil: Rethinking the Capitalism/Slavery Question," *Journal of the Early Republic* 24 (2004): 299–308.

19 For details see Joe R. Feagin, *The White Racial Frame: Centuries of Racial Framing and Counter-Framing* (New York: Routledge, 2010).

20 Quoted in Anthony S. Parent, Jr., *Foul Means: The Formation of a Slave Society in Virginia, 1660–1740* (Chapel Hill, North Carolina: University of North Carolina Press, 2003), p. 201.

21 Fritz Hirschfeld, *George Washington and Slavery: A Documentary Portrayal* (Columbia: University of Missouri Press, 1997), p. 58.

22 See Lenny Flank, *Hegemony and Counter-Hegemony: Marxism, Capitalism, and Their Relation to Sexism, Racism, Nationalism, and Authoritarianism* (St. Petersburg, Florida: Red and Black Publishers, 2009).

23 Joan Acker, *Class Questions: Feminist Answers* (Lanham, Maryland: Rowman & Littlefield, 2005), p. 9.

24 Karen Brodkin, "1998 AES Keynote Address: Global Capitalism: What's Race Got to Do with It?," *American Ethnologist* 27 (May 2000): 243.

25 Brodkin, "1998 AES Keynote Address," pp. 243–245.

26 Arthur O. Lovejoy, *The Great Chain of Being: A Study of the History of an Idea* (Cambridge, Massachusetts: Harvard University Press, 1973 [1936]), p. 59. See also Feagin, *The White Racial Frame*, pp. 39–42. I am also influenced generally by George Lakoff and Mark Johnson, *Philosophy in the Flesh: The Embodied Mind and Its Challenge to Western Thought* (New York: Basic Books, 1999), pp. 292–310.

27 See Robert Bucholz and Newton Key, *Early Modern England 1485–1714: A Narrative History* (Oxford: Blackwell Publishing, 2004); and Gordon J. Schochet, *The Authoritarian Family and Political Attitudes in 17th Century England* (New Brunswick, New Jersey: Transaction Books, 1998), pp. xiii–xiv, 5–90.

28 Here and occasionally in the rest of this chapter I extend arguments made in Feagin, *The White Racial Frame*.

29 De Tocqueville, *Democracy in America*, Vol. 2, Kindle DX location 706. Italics added. See Max Weber, *The Protestant Ethic and the Spirit of Capitalism*, trans. T. Parsons (New York: Scribner, 1958).

30 Ronald T. Takaki, *Iron Cages: Race and Culture in 19th Century America* (New York: Oxford University Press, 1990), pp. 12–14.

31 F. Nwabueze Okoye, "Chattel Slavery as the Nightmare of the American Revolutionaries," *William and Mary Quarterly* 37 (January 1980): 13.

32 Peter A. Dorsey, *Common Bondage: Slavery as Metaphor in Revolutionary America* (Nashville: University of Tennessee Press, 2009), p. 7.

33 See Weber, *The Protestant Ethic and the Spirit of Capitalism*.

34 Richard Drinnon, *Facing West: The Metaphysics of Indian-Hating and Empire-Building* (Norman, Oklahoma: University of Oklahoma Press, 1997 [1980]), pp. 506, see also pp. 51–53; and Takaki, *Iron Cages*, pp. 12–15; and Joel Kovel, *White Racism: A Psychohistory* (Revised edition; New York: Columbia University Press, 1984), pp. xli–xlvii.

35 W. E. B. Du Bois, *The World and Africa* (New York: International Publishers, 1965 [1946]), p. 37.

36 George Rawick, as quoted in David R. Roediger, *The Wages of Whiteness: Race and the Making of the American Working Class* (London, UK: Verso, 1991), p. 95.

37 Roediger, *The Wages of Whiteness*, p. 95. Italics added.

38 A. Leon Higginbotham, Jr., *Shades of Freedom: Racial Politics and the Presumptions of the American Legal Process* (New York: Oxford University Press, 1996), pp. 30–38. See also James Walvin, *Questioning Slavery* (New York: Routledge, 1996).

39 John Saffin, "A Brief, Candid Answer to a Late Printed Sheet, Entitled, 'The Selling of Joseph,'" in *A House Divided: The Antebellum Slavery Debates in America, 1776–1865*, ed. Mason I. Lowance, Jr. (Princeton: Princeton University Press, 2003), as reproduced at http://press.princeton.edu/chapters/s7553.html (accessed May 11, 2008); and Samuel Sewall, *The Selling of Joseph, A Memorial* (Boston, Massachusetts: Bartholomew Green and John, 1700), as reproduced at http://www.pbs.org/wgbh/aia/part1/1h301t.html (accessed May 11, 2008). See also Albert J. Von Frank, "John Saffin: Slavery and Racism in Colonial Massachusetts," *Early American Literature* 29 (1994): 254–260.

40 Cotton Mather, *The Negro Christianized An Essay to Excite and Assist the Good Work, The Instruction of Negro-Servants in Christianity* (Boston, Massachusetts: B. Green, 1706), pp. 15, 5. See also Anthony S. Parent, Jr., *Foul Means: The Formation of a Slave Society in Virginia, 1660–1740* (Chapel Hill, North Carolina: University of North Carolina Press, 2003), p. 200. For a much longer analysis of these early white male leaders' views see Feagin, *The White Racial Frame*, pp. 52–57.

41 Toni Morrison, *Playing in the Dark: Whiteness and the Literary Imagination* (New York: Vintage Books, 1992), p. 65.

42 Letter from James Madison to Thomas L. McKenney, February 1826, http://rotunda.upress.virginia.edu/founders/default.xqy?keys=FOEA-print-02-02-02-0623 (accessed November 28, 2010).

43 For much more detail, see Feagin, *The White Racial Frame*, pp. 49–58; Drinnon, *Facing West*, p. 51 and passim; and Audrey Smedley, *Race in North America* (Boulder, Colorado: Westview Press, 1993), pp. 38–57.

44 "Banneker's letter to Jefferson, 1791," PBS Resource Bank, http://www.pbs.org/wgbh/aia/part2/2h71.html (accessed November 28, 2010).

45 Ibid.

46 Seymour Martin Lipset, "The Sources of the 'Radical Right,'" in *The New American Right*, ed. Daniel Bell (New York: Criterion Books, 1955), p. 317.

47 Zafirovski, "The Most Cherished Myth," pp. 53–59.

2 Faking Democracy: Race, Class, and Our Undemocratic Political System

1 For example, the important textbook by Marjorie R. Hershey, *Party Politics in America* (New York: Longman, 2011), does not have an entry for "democracy" in the index.

2 Jim Dator, "Will America Ever Become a Democracy?," in *Democracy and Futures*, eds. Mika Mannermaa, Jim Dator, and Paula Tiihonen (Helsinki: Parliament of Finland, 2006), p. 64.

3 Ibid., p. 65.

4 See, for example, this political blog commentary: "Myth: The U.S. is Not a Democracy," http://www.huppi.com/kangaroo/L-democracy.htm (accessed August 4, 2010).

5 John Hibbing and Elizabeth Theiss-Morse, S*tealth Democracy: Americans' Beliefs about How Government Should Work* (Cambridge, UK: Cambridge University Press, 2002), pp. 1–3. The last quote is from p. 2.

6 Herbert Aptheker, *Early Years of the Republic: From the End of the Revolution to the First Administration of Washington (1783–1793)* (New York: International Publishers, 1976), pp. 55–95.

7 J. Allen Smith, *The Spirit of American Government: A Study of the Constitution, Its Origin, Influence, and Relation to Democracy* (Chautauqua, New York: Chautauqua/Macmillan, 1907), DX Kindle locations 325–331.

8 See the founders quoted in John F. Manley, "Class and Pluralism in America: The Constitution Reconsidered," in *The Case against the Constitution*, eds. J. F. Manley and K. M. Dolbeare (Armonk, New York: M. E. Sharpe, 1987), pp. 108–116; see also Kenneth F. Dolbeare and Linda Medcalf, "The Dark Side of the Constitution," in *The Case against the Constitution*, eds. J. F. Manley and K. M. Dolbeare (Armonk, New York: M. E. Sharpe, 1987), pp. 122–126; and Aptheker, *Early Years of the Republic*, pp. 74–95.

9 See Charles A. Beard, *An Economic Interpretation of the Constitution of the United States* (New York: Free Press, 1986 [1913]). The introduction to this edition by Forrest McDonald critically assesses Beard's main thesis.

10 James Madison, *Federalist 10*, 1787, http://www.constitution.org/fed/federa00.htm (accessed August 5, 2010).

11 The Madison quotes are from Smith, *The Spirit of American Government*, Kindle DX locations 421–427; others are quoted in Dolbeare and Medcalf, "The Dark Side of the Constitution," pp. 122–126.

12 Smith, *The Spirit of American Government*, Kindle DX locations 331–338, 390–396; Aptheker, *Early Years of the Republic*, passim.

13 I draw on summaries of the convention and critical analysis in Smith, *The Spirit of American Government*, Kindle DX locations 421–427.

14 Alexander Hamilton, James Madison, and John Jay, *The Federalist Papers*, http://www. gutenberg.org/ebooks/22788 (accessed July 5, 2011). I searched this edition on my Kindle DX to get these figures.

15 Madison, *Federalist 10*, 1787, http://www.gutenberg.org/ebooks/22788 (accessed July 5, 2011).

16 See National Archives and Records Administration, *Framers of the Constitution* (Washington, D.C.: National Archives Trust Fund Board, 1986).

17 As quoted from Madison's notes by Aptheker, *Early Years of the Republic*, pp. 74–95. The quote is on p. 93.

18 Max Farrand, ed., *The Records of the Federal Convention of 1787* (New Haven: Yale University Press, 1911), Vol. 1, pp. 486–487.

19 Donald E. Lively, *The Constitution and Race* (New York: Praeger, 1992), pp. 4–5. For a more extensive discussion see Joe R. Feagin, *The White Racial Frame: Centuries of Racial Framing and Counter-Framing* (New York: Routledge, 2010), pp. 27–32.

20 David Waldstreicher, *Slavery's Constitution: From Revolution to Ratification* (New York: Hill and Wang, 2009), p. 17.

21 Lawrence Goldstone, *Slavery, Profits, and the Struggle for the Constitution* (New York: Walker and Company, 2005), pp. 115–117.

22 Gautham Rao, "The Federal Posse Comitatus Doctrine: Slavery, Compulsion, and Statecraft in Mid-Nineteenth Century America," *Law and History Review* 26 (Spring 2008), http:// www.historycooperative.org/journals/lhr/26.1/rao.html (accessed February 1, 2008); and Paul Finkelman, *Slavery and the Founders: Race and Liberty in the Age of Jefferson* (Armonk, New York: M. E. Sharpe, 1996).

23 Garry Wills, "*Negro President*": *Jefferson and the Slave Power* (Boston, Massachusetts: Houghton Mifflin, 2003), pp. 5–9; and Irene Diggs, "The Biological and Cultural Impact of Blacks on the United States," *Phylon* 41 (1980): 160.

24 Hamilton, Madison, and Jay, *The Federalist Papers*, http://www.gutenberg.org/ebooks/22788 (accessed July 5, 2011). I searched this edition on my Kindle DX to get these figures. See especially Kindle DX location 4764.

25 Peter A. Dorsey, *Common Bondage: Slavery as Metaphor in Revolutionary America* (Knoxville, Tennessee: University of Tennessee Press, 2009) pp. 2–49.

26 Note too that the lives of most ordinary white women—who did have some white skin privilege over people of color—were determined by a socio-political system that was in numerous ways a type of "male totalitarianism."

27 Jackson Turner Main, *The Antifederalists: Critics of the Constitution* (Chapel Hill, North Carolina: University of North Carolina Press, 1961), pp. 280–281.

28 Smith, *The Spirit of American Government*, Kindle DX locations 434–441, 481–488; and Main, *The Antifederalists*, passim.

29 Waldstreicher, *Slavery's Constitution*, pp. 154–155.

30 Dator, "Will America Ever Become a Democracy?," p. 62.

31 See "Voting Rights Act Timeline," ACLU, http://www.aclu.org/voting-rights/voting-rights-act-timeline (accessed July 28, 2011); and Melanie S. Gustafson, Kristie Miller, and Elisabeth Israels Perr, *We Have Come to Stay: American Women and Political Parties, 1880–1960* (Albuquerque: University of New Mexico Press, 1999).

32 Robert Caro, *The Years of Lyndon Johnson: Master of the Senate* (New York: Knopf, 2002), p. 9.

33 Robert A. Dahl, *How Democratic Is the American Constitution?* (New Haven: Yale University Press, 2001), pp. 47, 52–53. I draw in this section on Joe R. Feagin, "Heeding Black Voices: The Court, Brown, and Challenges in Building a Multiracial Democracy," *University of Pittsburgh Law Review* 66 (Fall 2004): 57–81.

34 Dahl, *How Democratic Is the American Constitution?*, p. 53. See also Robert Caro, *The Years of Lyndon Johnson*, pp. 9–11, 90–94.

35 Dahl, *How Democratic Is the American Constitution?*, pp. 54–55. See *Marbury* v. *Madison*, 5 U.S. 137 (1803). In this section I am indebted to discussions with Roy Brooks.

36 Richard Kluger, *Simple Justice: The History of Brown v. Board of Education and Black America's Struggle for Equality* (New York: Knopf, 1975), Vol. 1, p. 65. I am generally influenced here by Smith, *The Spirit of American Government*, Kindle DX locations 966–973.

37 *Dred Scott* v. *John F. A. Sandford*, 60 U.S. 393, 408 (1857).

38 I draw here on the legal history and analysis of Nathan Newman and J. J. Gass, "A New Birth of Freedom: The Forgotten History of the 13th, 14th, and 15th Amendments," *Judicial Independence Series*, Brennan Center for Justice, New York University Law School, 2004, pp. 1–3.

39 Ibid., pp. 1–4.

40 *United States* v. *Morrison*, 529 U.S. 598 (2000).

41 For details, see Newman and Gass, "A New Birth of Freedom."

42 Robin Einhorn, *American Taxation, American Slavery* (Chicago: University of Chicago Press, 2006), pp. 7–8, 250; Feagin, *The White Racial Frame*, pp. 31–32, 88.

43 "Presidency of the United States of America," *Encyclopedia Britannica Online*, 2010 (accessed December 22, 2010).

44 Aziz Rana, *The Two Faces of American Freedom* (Cambridge, Massachusetts: Harvard University Press, 2010), pp. 326–327.

45 Kevin Phillips, *Wealth and Democracy: A Political History of the American Rich* (New York: Broadway Books, 2002), p. 214.

46 See James O'Connor, *The Fiscal Crisis of the State* (New York: St. Martin's Press, 1973); John Scott, *Corporate Business and Capitalist Classes* (Third edition; New York: Oxford University Press, 1997).

47 Deborah Madsen, *American Exceptionalism* (Jackson, Mississippi: The University Press of Mississippi, 1998), p. 39.

48 Jeffrey A. Winters and Benjamin I. Page, "Oligarchy in the United States?," *Perspectives on Politics* 7 (December 2009): 731. See also 732–739. See also Alyssa Battistoni, "The Public Overwhelmingly Wants It: Why Is Taxing the Rich So Hard?" *AlterNet*, April 23, 2011, http://www.alternet.org/story/150715/the_public_overwhelmingly_wants_it%3A_why_is_taxing_the_rich_so_hard/ (accessed April 24, 2011).

3 Race, Class, and Early U.S. Politics—to the 1930s

1 Marjorie R. Hershey, *Party Politics in America* (Fourteenth edition; New York: Longman, 2011), p. 2.

2 E. E. Schattschneider, *Party Government* (Westport, Connecticut: Greenwood Press, 1942), p. 1.

3 John J. Coleman, Kenneth M. Goldstein, and William G. Howell, *Understanding American Politics and Government* (Revised edition; New York: Longman, 2010), pp. 363–377; and Hershey, *Party Politics in America*, p. 2.

4   "Political Fires Still Raging in Gore Vidal at 81," *Infowars*, October 11, 2006, http://www.
     infowars.com/articles/us/vidal_gore_political_fires_still_raging_at_81.htm (accessed April 21,
     2011).
5   See Joe R. Feagin and Clairece B. Feagin, *Racial and Ethnic Relations* (Ninth edition; Upper
     Saddle River, New Jersey: Prentice Hall, 2011), chapter 3.
6   Hershey, *Party Politics in America*, pp. 12–19; and Coleman, Goldstein, and Howell,
     Understanding American Politics and Government, pp. 382–383.
7   Seymour Martin Lipset, "The Sources of the 'Radical Right,'" *The New American Right*, ed.
     Daniel Bell (New York: Criterion Books, 1955), p. 175.
8   Tali Mendelberg, *The Race Card: Campaign Strategy, Implicit Messages, and the Norm of Equality*
     (Princeton: Princeton University Press, 2001), p. 32.
9   Hershey, *Party Politics in America*, pp. 15–18; Thomas Ferguson, *Golden Rule: The Investment
     Theory of Party Competition and the Logic of Money-Driven Political Systems* (Chicago:
     University of Chicago Press, 1995), pp. 56–57; and Philip H. Burch, *Elites in American History:
     The Federalist Years to the Civil War* (New York: Holmes and Meier, 1981), pp. 129–136.
10   Seymour Martin Lipset, "Introduction," for Harriet Martineau's *Society in America* (Edited
     edition; Garden City, New York: Doubleday Anchor Books, 1962), pp. 21ff.; Burch, *Elites in
     American History*, pp. 129–136.
11   James Richardson, ed., *A Compilation of the Messages and Papers of the Presidents, 1789–1897*
     (New York: Bureau of National Literature, 1969), Vol. 4, pp. 1517–1527.
12   Herbert Aptheker, *The Unfolding Drama: Studies in U.S. History*, ed. Bettina Aptheker (New
     York: International Publishers, 1978), pp. 84ff.
13   Paul Frymer, *Uneasy Alliances: Race and Party Competition in America* (Princeton: Princeton
     University Press, 1999), pp. 7–40.
14   John Louis O'Sullivan, as quoted in *Bartlett's Familiar Quotations*, ed. Emily M. Beck (Fifteenth
     edition; Boston, Massachusetts: Little, Brown, 1980), p. 552. See Joe R. Feagin, "White
     Supremacy and Mexican Americans: Rethinking the 'Black-White Paradigm,'" *Rutgers Law
     Review* 54 (Summer 2002): 959–987.
15   Feagin and Feagin, *Racial and Ethnic Relations*, pp. 140–141.
16   David W. Hall, *The Legacy of John Calvin: His Influence on the Modern World* (Phillipsburg, New
     Jersey: P&R Publishers, 2008); Williston Walker, *A History of the Christian Church* (Revised
     edition: New York: Scribner's, 1959), pp. 403–467.
17   Robert D. Rossel, "The Great Awakening: An Historical Analysis," *American Journal of Sociology*
     75 (May 1970): 907–925; Walker, *A History of the Christian Church*, pp. 466–518; Milan
     Zafirovski, "Protestantism and Authoritarianism: Weber's Secondary Problem," *Journal for the
     Theory of Social Behaviour* 40 (2010): 163–177; and "Manifest Destiny," *U.S. History*,
     http://www.ushistory.org/us/29.asp (accessed December 10, 2010).
18   Reginald Horsman, *Race and Manifest Destiny: The Origins of American Racial Anglo-Saxonism*
     (Cambridge, Massachusetts: Harvard University Press, 1986), p. 209.
19   See John M. Faragher, Mari Jo Buhle, Daniel Czitrom, and Susan H. Armitage, *Out of Many:
     A History of the American People* (Upper Saddle River, New Jersey: Prentice Hall, 2000),
     pp. 401–408; and Horsman, *Race and Manifest Destiny*, pp. 6–7, 208–211.
20   Horsman, *Race and Manifest Destiny*, pp. 212–216. See also Anders Stephanson, *Manifest
     Destiny* (New York: Hill and Wang, 1995), p. 33.
21   Quoted in James L. Huston, *Calculating the Value of the Union: Slavery, Property Rights, and the
     Economic Origins of the Civil War* (Chapel Hill, North Carolina: University of North Carolina
     Press, 2003), pp. 1–2.
22   Ibid., pp. 1–4.
23   Robin Archer, "Secularism and Sectarianism in India and the West: What are the Real Lessons
     of American History?," *Economy and Society* 30 (August 2001): 273–287. See also Robin Archer,
     Why Is There No Labor Party in the United States? (Princeton: Princeton University Press, 2007).
24   Paul E. Johnson, *A Shopkeeper's Millennium: Society and Revivals in Rochester, New York,
     1815–1837* (Second edition; New York: Hill and Wang, 2004).
25   Archer, "Secularism and Sectarianism in India and the West," pp. 281–282.
26   Ibid. See also Archer, *Why Is There No Labor Party in the United States?*
27   Quoted in David Waldstreicher, *Slavery's Constitution: From Revolution to Ratification* (New
     York: Hill and Wang, 2009), p. 157.
28   See Aptheker, *The Unfolding Drama*, p. 83.
29   Merton L. Dillon, *Slavery Attacked: Southern Slaves and Their Allies, 1619–1865* (Baton Rouge:
     Louisiana State University Press, 1990), p. 269.

30   Mendelberg, *The Race Card*, pp. 35–37; and Elise Lemire, *"Miscegenation": Making Race in America* (Philadelphia: University of Pennsylvania Press, 2002), passim.

31   Lemire, *"Miscegenation,"* p. 47 and passim.

32   Abraham Lincoln, "The Sixth Joint Debate at Quincy, October 13, 1858," in *The Lincoln-Douglas Debates: The First Complete, Unexpurgated Text*, ed. Harold Holzer (New York: HarperCollins, 1993), p. 283.

33   Lerone Bennett, *Forced into Glory: Abraham Lincoln's White Dream* (Chicago: Johnson Publishing Co., 1999), pp. 90–150, 610–615; Philip A. Klinkner and Rogers M. Smith, *The Unsteady March: The Rise and Decline of Racial Equality in America* (Chicago: University of Chicago Press, 1999), pp. 70ff.

34   Rhonda V. Magee, "The Master's Tools, from the Bottom Up: Responses to African-American Reparations Theory in Mainstream and Outsider Remedies Discourse," *Virginia Law Review* 79 (May 1993): 886–888. Sumner is quoted on p. 887.

35   Mendelberg, *The Race Card*, pp. 39–51.

36   "Hayes v. Tilden: The Electoral College Controversy of 1876–1877," *Harper's Weekly* website, http://elections.harpweek.com/09Ver2Controversy/Overview-1.htm (accessed July 6, 2011); and Clarence Lusane, *Colin Powell and Condoleezza Rice: Foreign Policy, Race, and the New American Century* (Westport, Connecticut: Praeger, 2006), pp. 40–42.

37   Joe R. Feagin, *Racist America: Roots, Current Realities, and Future Reparations* (Second edition; New York: Routledge, 2010), pp. 17, 49–57; Ruth Thompson-Miller and Joe R. Feagin, "The Reality and Impact of Legal Segregation in the United States," in *Handbook of the Sociology of Racial and Ethnic Relations*, eds. Hernán Vera and Joe R. Feagin (New York: Springer Science, 2007), pp. 455–464; and John W. Cell, *The Highest State of White Supremacy: The Origins of Segregation in South Africa and the American South* (Cambridge, UK: Cambridge University Press, 1982), pp. 168–170. See also David Hackett Fischer, *Albion's Seed: Four British Folkways in America* (New York: Oxford University Press, 1989), pp. 863ff.

38   W. E. B. Du Bois, *Black Reconstruction in America 1860–1880* (New York: Atheneum, 1992 [1935]), pp. 700–701.

39   Michelle Alexander, *The New Jim Crow: Mass Incarceration in the Age of Colorblindness* (New York: New Press, 2010), p. 186.

40   Du Bois, *Black Reconstruction in America 1860–1880*, pp. 703–706.

41   Ferguson, *Golden Rule*, pp. 70–71; Mendelberg, *The Race Card*, pp. 39–51; and Charles Postel, *The Populist Vision* (New York: Oxford University Press, 2007), passim.

42   Frymer, *Uneasy Alliances*, p. 50.

43   Aziz Rana, *The Two Faces of American Freedom* (Cambridge, Massachusetts: Harvard University Press, 2010), pp. 210–211; Ferguson, *Golden Rule*, pp. 77–78.

44   Walter Nugent, *Progressivism: A Very Short Introduction* (New York: Oxford University Press, 2009), pp. 124–126.

45   Archer, *Why Is There No Labor Party in the United States?* Kindle DX locations 3269–3274 and passim.

46   Archer, "Secularism and Sectarianism in India and the West," p. 284.

47   Du Bois, *Black Reconstruction in America 1860–1880*, pp. 182–183.

48   For more detailed discussion, see Joe R. Feagin, *The White Racial Frame: Centuries of Racial Framing and Counter-Framing* (New York: Routledge, 2010), pp. 155–191.

49   Frederick Jackson Turner, *The Frontier in American History* (New York: Henry Holt and Company, 1935). See also Richard Drinnon, *Facing West: The Metaphysics of Indian-Hating and Empire-Building* (Norman, Oklahoma: University of Oklahoma Press, 1997 [1980]), pp. 355–356.

50   Stephanson, *Manifest Destiny*, p. 75.

51   Quoted in ibid., p. 89.

52   Quoted in Robert N. Bellah, *The Broken Covenant* (Second edition; Chicago: University of Chicago Press, 1992), p. 38.

53   Quoted in Stephanson, *Manifest Destiny*, p. 98.

54   Eduardo H. Galeano, *Open Veins of Latin America: Five Centuries of the Pillage of a Continent* (New York: Monthly Review Press, 1997), p. 107.

55   Feagin and Feagin, *Racial and Ethnic Relations*, pp. 71–73; Feagin, *Racist America*, pp. 74–77; John Higham, *Strangers in the Land*, (New York: Atheneum, 1963), pp. 96–152; and Nugent, *Progressivism*, pp. 53–55, 124–126.

56   Doug Blair, "The 1920 Anti-Japanese Crusade and Congressional Hearings," Seattle Civil Rights and Labor History Project, University of Washington, http://depts.washington.edu/

civilr/Japanese_restriction.htm#_edn46 (accessed January 13, 2011); and John Higham, *Send These to Me: Immigrants in Urban America* (Baltimore: Johns Hopkins University Press, 1984), pp. 50–52. See also Feagin and Feagin, *Racial and Ethnic Relations*, passim.

57 Roger Daniels, *Guarding the Golden Door* (New York: Hill and Wang, 2004), p. 55; Blair, "The 1920 Anti-Japanese Crusade and Congressional Hearings"; Higham, *Strangers in the Land*, pp. 148–157.

58 Elizabeth Esch and David Roediger, "One Symptom of Originality: Race and the Management of Labour in the History of the United States," *Historical Materialism* 17 (2009): 1. I also draw in this paragraph on pp. 19, 31, 38–39.

59 Ibid., p. 17.

60 William H. Tucker, *The Science and Politics of Racial Research* (Urbana: University of Illinois Press, 1994), p. 93. For a more extended discussion, see Feagin, *Racist America*, pp. 72–78.

61 Theodore Cross, *Black Power Imperative: Racial Inequality and the Politics of Nonviolence* (New York: Faulkner, 1984), p. 157.

62 Harding and Coolidge are quoted in Tucker, *The Science and Politics of Racial Research*, p. 93. See also Ivan Hannaford, *Race: The History of an Idea in the West* (Baltimore: Johns Hopkins University Press, 1996).

63 Feagin and Feagin, *Racial and Ethnic Relations*, pp. 71–73, 98–99.

64 Allan J. Lichtman, *White Protestant Nation: The Rise of the American Conservative Movement* (New York: Atlantic Monthly Press, 2008), pp. 2–4. See also Lipset, "The Sources of the 'Radical Right,'" pp. 175ff.

65 See Ferguson, *Golden Rule*, pp. 27ff; Burch, *Elites in American History*, pp. 18–20 and passim.

66 Alexis de Tocqueville, *Democracy in America*, trans. Henry Reeve (London: Saunders and Otley 1835, 1840).

67 Kevin Phillips, *Wealth and Democracy: A Political History of the American Rich* (New York: Broadway Books, 2002), pp. 31, 47.

68 See Burch, *Elites in American History*, pp. 85–159.

69 See examples in Ferguson, *Golden Rule*, pp. 28–30, 36, 47–49; and Burch, *Elites in American History*, pp. 85–159.

70 Joe R. Feagin, Clairece B. Feagin, and David V. Baker, *Social Problems: A Critical Power-Conflict Perspective* (Sixth edition; Upper Saddle River, New Jersey: Prentice Hall, 2005), pp. 459–460; and Andrew Mullen, "The Propaganda Model after 20 Years: Interview with Edward S. Herman and Noam Chomsky," *Westminster Papers in Communication and Culture* (2009): 12–22.

71 Mullen, "The Propaganda Model after 20 Years"; and Jacob S. Hacker and Paul Pierson, *Winner-Take-All Politics: How Washington Made the Rich Richer—And Turned Its Back on the Middle Class* (New York: Simon and Schuster, 2010).

72 See documented discussions in Feagin, Feagin, and Baker, *Social Problems*, pp. 462–480; Howard Zinn, *A People's History of the United States* (New York: Harper, 2010), passim; and Robert J. Goldstein, *Political Repression in America: From 1870 to the Present* (New York: Schenkman, 1978), especially pp. 1–131.

4 Race, Class, and U.S. Politics: 1930s–1970s

1 Joe R. Feagin, Clairece B. Feagin, and David V. Baker, *Social Problems: A Critical Power-Conflict Perspective* (Sixth edition; Upper Saddle River, New Jersey: Prentice-Hall, 2005), pp. 388–390; Joe R. Feagin, *Racist America: Roots, Current Realities, and Future Reparations* (Second edition; New York: Routledge, 2010), pp. 55–57.

2 Quoted in C. Vann Woodward, "Home-Grown Radicals," review of David De Leon, *The American as Anarchist: Reflections on Indigenous Radicalism* (Baltimore: Johns Hopkins University Press, 1979), *New York Review of Books* (April 5, 1979): 5.

3 Thomas Ferguson, *Golden Rule: The Investment Theory of Party Competition and the Logic of Money-Driven Political Systems* (Chicago: University of Chicago Press, 1995), pp. 79–81, 150–157.

4 Harvard Sitkoff, *A New Deal for Blacks: The Emergence of Civil Rights as a National Issue* (New York: Oxford University Press, 1978), pp. 37–38; C. G. Wye, "The New Deal and the Negro Community," *Journal of American History* 59 (December 1972): 630–640; Nancy J. Weiss, *Farewell to the Party of Lincoln: Black Politics in the Age of FDR* (Princeton: Princeton University Press, 1983), p. 119. I also draw here on Feagin, *Racist America*, chapter 2.

5 Richard Kluger, *Simple Justice: The History of Brown v. Board Of Education and Black America's Struggle for Equality* (New York: Knopf, 1975), Vol. 2, p. 945.

6 Franklin Roosevelt, "State of the Union," http://www.presidency.ucsb.edu/ws/index.php?pid =16518 (accessed February 28, 2005).

7 Cushing Strout, "Introduction," in *The Spirit of American Government* (Cambridge, Massachusetts: Harvard University Press, 1965), pp. liv–lv.

8 See Jason Morgan Ward, *Defending White Democracy: The Making of a Segregationist Movement and the Remaking of Racial Politics, 1936–1965* (Chapel Hill, North Carolina: University of North Carolina Press, 2011).

9 Kim Phillips-Fein, *Invisible Hands: The Businessmen's Crusade against the New Deal* (New York: W. W. Norton, 2009), Kindle DX locations 130–150, 250–270. See also Morgan Ward, *Defending White Democracy*, passim.

10 Phillips-Fein, *Invisible Hands*, Kindle DX locations 296–314.

11 Bruce Bartlett, "Whitewash: The Racist History the Democratic Party Wants You to Forget," *Wall Street Journal* online, http://opinionjournal.com/extra/?id=110011033 (accessed December 29, 2007).

12 Robert Caro, *The Years of Lyndon Johnson: Master of the Senate* (New York: Knopf, 2002), pp. 97, 100; President's Committee on Civil Rights, *To Secure These Rights* (U.S. Government Printing Office, 1947); "Agency History," Truman Presidential Library, http://www.truman library.org/hstpaper/pccr.htm (accessed July 6, 2011). In the next few paragraphs, I condense and update analysis from Joe R. Feagin, "Heeding Black Voices: The Court, Brown, and Challenges in Building a Multiracial Democracy," *University of Pittsburgh Law Review* 66 (Fall 2004): 57–81.

13 Caro, *The Years of Lyndon Johnson*, pp. 101–103.

14 Joseph E. Lowndes, *From the New Deal to the New Right* (New Haven: Yale University Press, 2008), chapter 1.

15 Caro, *The Years of Lyndon Johnson*, pp. 104, 775.

16 W. E. B. Du Bois, "What is the Meaning of 'All Deliberate Speed?'," in *W. E. B. Du Bois: A Reader*, ed. David L. Lewis (New York: Holt Paperbacks, 1995), p. 422. The article was originally published in 1957.

17 Philip A. Klinkner and Rogers M. Smith, *The Unsteady March: The Rise and Decline of Racial Equality in America* (Chicago: University of Chicago Press, 2002), pp. 3–4.

18 *Brown v. Board of Education of Topeka, 347* U.S. 483 (1954).

19 Derrick Bell, "*Brown v. Board of Education* and the Interest Convergence Dilemma," *Harvard Law Review* 93 (1980): 518. See also *Brown v. Board of Education of Topeka*. The legal brief is quoted in Klinkner and Smith, *The Unsteady March*, p. 235.

20 Nancy MacLean, *Freedom Is Not Enough: The Opening of the American Workplace* (New York: Russell Sage Foundation and Harvard University Press, 2006), pp. 20–21, 31.

21 Caro, *The Years of Lyndon Johnson*, p. 104; and Joe R. Feagin, *The White Racial Frame: Centuries of Racial Framing and Counter-Framing* (New York: Routledge, 2010), pp. 88–89.

22 *Congressional Record*, 84th Congress Second Session, Vol. 102, part 4 (March 12, 1956) (Washington, D.C.: Governmental Printing Office, 1956), pp. 4459–4460.

23 "History of Little Rock Public Schools Desegregation," http://www.centralhigh57.org/1957-58.htm (accessed January 31, 2011).

24 Rick Perlstein, *Before the Storm: Barry Goldwater and the Unmaking of the American Consensus* (Reprint edition; New York: Nation Books, 2009), Kindle DX locations 435–444.

25 Lowndes, *From the New Deal to the New Right*, pp. 142–144, 158–162.

26 Caro, *The Years of Lyndon Johnson*, pp. 97–105; and Edward G. Carmines and James A. Stimson, *Issue Evolution: Race and the Transformation of American Politics* (Princeton: Princeton University Press, 1989), pp. 37–40.

27 Joseph A. Aistrup, *The Southern Strategy Revisited* (Lexington, Kentucky: University Press of Kentucky, 1996), p. 9.

28 Carmines and Stimson, *Issue Evolution*, p. 45.

29 Allan J. Lichtman, *White Protestant Nation: The Rise of the American Conservative Movement* (New York: Atlantic Monthly Press, 2008), p. 259.

30 Chandler Davison and Bernard Grofman, eds., *The Quiet Revolution in the South: The Impact of the Voting Rights Act 1965–1990* (Princeton: Princeton University Press, 1994); Chandler Davidson, Tanya Dunlap, Gale Kenny, and Benjamin Wise, *Republican Ballot Security Programs: Vote Protection or Minority Vote Suppression—Or Both?* (Washington, D.C.: Center for Voting Rights & Protection, 2004).

31 Carmines and Stimson, *Issue Evolution*, p. 57; see also Kevin Phillips, *The Emerging Republican Majority* (New Rochelle, New York: Arlington House, 1969).

32 Feagin, Feagin, and Baker, *Social Problems*, pp. 469–473; Joe R. Feagin and Harlan Hahn, *Ghetto Revolts* (New York: Macmillan, 1973), pp. 92–94; Lerone Bennett, Jr., *Confrontation: Black and White* (Baltimore: Penguin Books, 1966), pp. 164–169.

33 Klinkner and Smith, *The Unsteady March*, pp. 3–4. See also G. William Domhoff, "Bridging the Gap Between Liberals and Leftists: Where Douglas S. Massey's New Liberal Vision Falls Short," January 2006, http://sociology.ucsc.edu/whorulesamerica/change/massey.html (accessed November 12, 2010).

34 Paul Frymer, *Uneasy Alliances: Race and Party Competition in America* (Princeton: Princeton University Press, 1999), pp. 4–26. See also Thomas Ferguson and Joel Rodgers, *Right Turn: The Decline of the Democrats and the Future of American Politics* (New York: Hill and Wang, 1986), pp. 53–57.

35 Carmines and Stimson, *Issue Evolution*, pp. 42–44.

36 Ibid., p. 51.

37 The platform quote is from Carmines and Stimson, *Issue Evolution*, p. 51.

38 Tali Mendelberg, *The Race Card: Campaign Strategy, Implicit Messages, and the Norm of Equality* (Princeton: Princeton University Press, 2001), p. 13.

39 *Report of the National Advisory Commission on Civil Disorders* (Washington, D.C.: U.S. Government Printing Office, 1968), pp. 1, 5.

40 Rick Perlstein, *Nixonland: The Rise of a President and the Fracturing of America* (Reprint edition; New York: Scribner, 2009), Kindle DX locations 460–480, chapter 1. See also Feagin and Hahn, *Ghetto Revolts*.

41 Naomi Murakawa, "The Origins of the Carceral Crisis: Racial Order as 'Law and Order' in Postwar American Politics," in *Race and American Political Development*, eds. Joseph Lowndes, Julie Novkov, and Dorian Warren (New York: Routledge, 2008), p. 234.

42 Ibid., p. 251; and Feagin and Hahn, *Ghetto Revolts*, pp. 1–90 and passim.

43 Murakawa, "The Origins of the Carceral Crisis," pp. 236–244.

44 See surveys in Kevin Phillips, *Wealth and Democracy: A Political History of the American Rich* (New York: Broadway Books, 2002), p. 380.

45 Randolph Hohle, "The Color of Neoliberalism: The 'Modern Southern Businessman' and Post-War Alabama's Challenge to Racial Desegregation," *Sociological Forum* 27 (2012): 142 (Abstract).

46 Ibid.; and Kevin M. Kruse, *White Flight: Atlanta and the Making of Modern Conservatism* (Princeton: Princeton University Press, 2005), p. 8.

47 Ibid., pp. 9–11.

48 Ibid., pp. 10–11, 263.

49 Hohle, "The Color of Neoliberalism," p. 142.

50 Kevin Phillips, *The Emerging Republican Majority*.

51 Lowndes, *From the New Deal to the New Right*, pp. 105, 142–144, 158–162; Hohle, "The Color of Neoliberalism," pp. 142–162.

52 Frymer, *Uneasy Alliances*, p. 104.

53 Judith Stein, "Affirmative Action and the Conservative Agenda: President Richard M. Nixon's Philadelphia Plan of 1969," in *Labor in the Modern South*, ed. G. T. Eskew (Athens, Georgia: University of Georgia Press, 2001), pp. 195–200.

54 Ibid., pp. 103–105; Aistrup, *The Southern Strategy Revisited*, p. 9; and Joseph A. Aistrup, "The Middle Americans," *Time*, January 5, 1970, http://www.time.com/time/subscriber/personof theyear/archive/stories/1969.html (accessed February 4, 2011).

55 Earl Ofari Hutchinson, "The Nixon Tapes, Racism and the Republicans," *AlterNet*, December 18, 2003, http://www.alternet.org/story/17422 (accessed July 7, 2011).

56 Ted Kopell, *Nightline*, ABC News, May 16, 1994.

57 Kenneth O'Reilly, *Nixon's Piano: Presidents and Racial Politics from Washington to Clinton* (New York: Free Press, 1995), pp. 6–7. See also Bruce Oudes, ed., *From: The President: President Nixon's Secret Files* (New York: Harper and Row, 1989), pp. 451ff.

58 Tim Cox, "Rights Groups Cautious about 'Odd Couple' Appearances," United Press International, November 22, 1988.

59 Hutchinson, "The Nixon Tapes, Racism and the Republicans"; O'Reilly, *Nixon's Piano*, pp. 292–330; Kenneth O'Reilly, *Racial Matters: The FBI's Secret File on Black America, 1960–1972* (New York: Simon and Schuster, 1991); and Mendelberg, *The Race Card*, pp. 102–103.

60 Jacob S. Hacker and Paul Pierson, *Winner-Take-All Politics: How Washington Made the Rich Richer—And Turned Its Back on the Middle Class* (New York: Simon and Schuster, 2010), Kindle DX locations 1615–1625.

61 Lowndes, *From the New Deal to the New Right*, Kindle DX Locations 56–57; and Jane H. Hill, *The Everyday Language of White Racism* (New York: Wiley-Blackwell, 2008), pp. 134–157 and passim.

62 Ernest Fergurson, *Hard Right* (New York: Norton, 1986), p. 219; Hill, *The Everyday Language of White Racism*, pp. 134–157.

63 Quoted in Allan J. Lichtman, *White Protestant Nation*, p. 226.

64 Ibid., pp. 153–159 and passim.

65 Seymour Martin Lipset, "The Sources of the 'Radical Right,'" in *The New American Right*, ed. Daniel Bell (New York: Criterion Books, 1955), p. 183.

66 See Todd Gitlin, *The Sixties: Years of Hope, Days of Rage* (Revised edition; New York: Bantam Books, 1993); and Thomas B. Edsall and Mary D. Edsall, *Chain Reaction: The Impact of Race, Rights, and Taxes on American Politics* (New York: W. W. Norton & Company, 1992).

67 Domhoff, "Bridging the Gap Between Liberals and Leftists: Where Douglas S. Massey's New Liberal Vision Falls Short."

5 Race, Class, and U.S. Politics: 1970s–1990s

1 Thomas Ferguson and Joel Rogers, *Right Turn: The Decline of the Democrats and the Future of American Politics* (New York: Hill and Wang, 1986), pp. 78ff.

2 Jacob S. Hacker and Paul Pierson, *Winner-Take-All Politics: How Washington Made the Rich Richer—And Turned Its Back on the Middle Class* (New York: Simon and Schuster, 2010), Kindle DX locations 1978–1982, 2000–2004, 2029–2031.

3 Sidney Blumenthal, *The Rise of the Counter-Establishment* (New York: Times Books, 1986), pp. 4–11, 133–170; Peter Steinfels, *The Neoconservatives: The Men Who are Changing America's Politics* (New York: Touchstone, 1979), pp. 214–277.

4 Ferguson and Rogers, *Right Turn*, p. 79.

5 David T. Courtwright, *No Right Turn: Conservative Politics in a Liberal America* (Cambridge, Massachusetts: Harvard University Press, 2010), passim; and James Davison Hunter, *Culture Wars: The Struggle to Control the Family, Art, Education, Law, and Politics in America* (New York: Basic Books, 1992), passim.

6 Kevin Phillips, *American Theocracy: The Peril and Politics of Radical Religion, Oil, and Borrowed Money in the 21st Century* (New York: Viking, 2006), preface, p. 1.

7 Courtwright, *No Right Turn*, passim.

8 See Allan J. Lichtman, *White Protestant Nation: The Rise of the American Conservative Movement* (New York: Atlantic Monthly Press, 2008), p. 4.

9 Marc J. Hetherington and Jonathan D. Weiler, *Authoritarianism and Polarization in American Politics* (Cambridge, UK: Cambridge University Press, 2009), pp. 1–45.

10 Bob Altemeyer, *The Authoritarians* (Winnipeg, Manitoba: Department of Psychology, University of Manitoba, 2006), p. 37.

11 Todd Gitlin, *The Whole World Is Watching: Mass Media in the Making and Unmaking of the New Left* (Berkeley: University of California Press, 1980), p. 6. I am influenced on framing by the work of George Lakoff, http://www.rockridgeinstitute.org/projects/strategic/nationasfamily/npworldview (accessed November 1, 2004).

12 See, for example, Hetherington and Weiler, *Authoritarianism and Polarization in American Politics*, Kindle DX locations 2–150.

13 Mark A. Noll, *The Scandal of the Evangelical Mind* (Grand Rapids, Michigan: William Eerdmans, 1994), Kindle DX locations 96–103. See also Mark A. Noll, "Introduction," in *Religion and American Politics*, eds. Mark A. Noll and Luke E. Harlow (New York: Oxford University Press, 2007). Noll has shown how over centuries the Protestant tradition has moved from the views of early Protestant Christian thinkers like Jonathan Edwards, who accented the importance of reason in Christian theology, to 19th-century Great Awakening movements that accented religious emotions and biblicism that rejected scientific views such as evolution.

14 Email communication with Bob Altemeyer, February 2011. See the summary of Fromm in C. George Boeree, "Personality Theories," 2006, http://webspace.ship.edu/cgboer/fromm.html (accessed July 21, 2010).

15 Altemeyer, *The Authoritarians*, pp. 11–12.

16 Theodore W. Adorno, Else Frenkel-Brunswik, Daniel J. Levinson, and R. Nevitt Sanford, *The Authoritarian Personality* (New York: Harper, 1950), especially pp. 248–279; C. George Boeree, "Personality Theories," 2006, http://webspace.ship.edu/cgboer/freud.html (accessed July 21, 2010); and John Duckitt, "Differential Effects of Right Wing Authoritarianism and Social Dominance Orientation on Outgroup Attitudes and Their Mediation by Threat from and Competitiveness to Outgroups," *Personality and Social Psychology Bulletin* 32 (2006): 684.

17 Thomas F. Pettigrew, "Commentary: The Indestructible Theory," in *Perspectives on Authoritarianism*, eds. F. Funke, T. Petzel, C. Cohrs, and J. Duckitt (Wiesbaden, Germany: Verlag fuer Sozialwissenschaften, forthcoming).

18 Hetherington and Weiler, *Authoritarianism and Polarization in American Politics*, Kindle DX locations 572–576.

19 Altemeyer, *The Authoritarians*, pp. 200–204.

20 Quoted in Max Blumenthal, "Age of Intolerance," *Nation*, May 28, 2007, http://www.the nation.com/doc/20070528/blumenthal (accessed February 14, 2011).

21 Quoted in James M. Washington, *A Testament of Hope: The Essential Writings of Martin Luther King* (San Francisco: Harper Collins, 1991), pp. xiv–xv.

22 Ibid.

23 Bob Moser, "Holy War," Southern Poverty Law Center, *Intelligence Report* 17 (Spring 2005).

24 Max Blumenthal, *Republican Gomorrah: Inside the Movement that Shattered the Party* (New York: Nation Books, 2010), Kindle DX locations 335ff; Kevin Phillips, *American Theocracy*, pp. 188–189; Kim Phillips-Fein, "Right from the Start: The Roots of the Conservative Grievance Industry," Book Forum, January 2011, http://www.bookforum.com/inprint/017_04/6672 (accessed February 15, 2011).

25 Phillips-Fein, "Right from the Start."

26 Blumenthal, *Republican Gomorrah*, Kindle DX location 335.

27 On collective memory, see Kristen M. Lavelle, "'Our Generation Had Nothing to Do with Discrimination': White Southern Memory of Jim Crow and Civil Rights," PhD dissertation, Texas A&M University, 2011.

28 Ronald Reagan, "City upon a Hill," Conservative Political Action Conference, January 25, 1974.

29 See Anders Stephanson, *Manifest Destiny* (New York: Hill and Wang, 1995), p. 127.

30 Kyle Longley, Jeremy D. Mayer, Michael Schaller, and John W. Sloan, *Deconstructing Reagan: Conservative Mythology and America's Fortieth President* (Armonk, New York: M. E. Sharpe, 2006), p. 78.

31 Quoted in ibid., p. 76.

32 Quoted in Longley, Mayer, Schaller, and Sloan, p. 77.

33 Quoted in Bob Herbert, "The Ugly Side of the G.O.P.," *The New York Times*, September 25, 2007, http://www.nytimes.com/2007/09/25/opinion/25herbert.html (accessed June 19, 2011).

34 Longley, Mayer, Schaller, and Sloan, *Deconstructing Reagan*, pp. 79–81.

35 Ibid., pp. 80–81.

36 Paul Krugman, *The Conscience of a Liberal* (New York: Norton, 2007), p. 181.

37 Thomas Byrne Edsall and Mary D. Edsall, *Chain Reaction: The Impact of Race, Rights, and Taxes on American Politics* (New York: W. W. Norton, 1992), p. 138.

38 Terrel Bell, *The Thirteenth Man* (New York: Free Press, 1988), p. 103.

39 Theodore Reuter, "The New Black Conservatives," in *The Politics of Race*, ed. T. Reuter (Armonk, New York: M. E. Sharpe, 1995), pp. 97–99.

40 Molefi K. Asante and Ronald E. Hall, *Rooming in the Master's House: Power and Privilege in the Rise of Black Conservatism* (Boulder, Colorado: Paradigm Books, 2011), p. 139.

41 Bob Herbert, "Righting Reagan's Wrongs?," *The New York Times*, November 13, 2007, http://www.nytimes.com/2007/11/13/opinion/13herbert.html?_r=2 (accessed March 10, 2011); Kathanne W. Greene, *Affirmative Action and Principles of Justice* (Westport, Connecticut: Greenwood Press, 1989), pp. 5ff; and Joe Davidson, "Reagan: A Contrary View," MSNBC.com, June 7, 2004, http://www.msnbc.msn.com/id/5158315/ns/us_news-life/ (accessed March 10, 2011).

42 Steven Neal, "D-e-a-v-e-r Spells Insensitivity," *Chicago Tribune*, May 9, 1985, Zone C, p. 19.

43 Bell, *The Thirteenth Man*, pp. 104–105; on Watt, see "Big Business," *Financial Times*, January 3, 1991, p. 12.

44 James Gerstenzang, "Bush Vows to Pursue King Dream: 'We Must Not Fail,' He Says on Holiday for Rights Leader," *Los Angeles Times*, January 17, 1989, http://articles.latimes.com/1989-01-17/news/mn-502_1_rights-leader (accessed June 28, 2011).

45 Quoted in Joe Davidson, "Reagan: A Contrary View."
46 *City of Richmond, Virginia* v. *J. A. Croson Co.,* 488 U.S. 469 (1989); see also *Adarand Constructors, Inc.* v. *Pena,* 515 U.S. 200 (1995).
47 Barbara J. Flagg, "Was Blind but Now I See: White Race Consciousness and the Requirement of Discriminatory Intent," *Michigan Law Review* 91 (1993): 953; Wendy Moore, *Reproducing Racism* (Lanham, Maryland: Rowman & Littlefield, 2008). For a more extensive discussion of these issues, see Joe R. Feagin, *Racist America: Roots, Current Realities, and Future Reparations* (Second edition; New York: Routledge, 2010), pp. 145–151.
48 Ferguson and Rogers, *Right Turn,* pp. 134–135.
49 Kevin M. Kruse, *White Flight: Atlanta and the Making of Modern Conservatism* (Princeton: Princeton University Press, 2005), p. 266.
50 Clarence Y. H. Lo, *Small Property versus Big Government: Social Origins of the Property Tax Revolt* (Berkeley: University of California Press, 1990), p. 58.
51 Ibid., pp. 58–59. See also pp. 121–122.
52 Randolph Hohle, "The Color of Neoliberalism: The 'Modern Southern Businessman' and Post-War Alabama's Challenge to Racial Desegregation," *Sociological Forum* 27 (2012): 142–162 (Abstract).
53 Email communication with Randolph Hohle, January 25, 2011.
54 George Lipsitz, *How Racism Takes Place* (Philadelphia: Temple University Press, 2011), p. 35.
55 Ibid.
56 Michelle Alexander, *The New Jim Crow: Mass Incarceration in the Age of Colorblindness* (New York: New Press, 2010), p. 49; and Naomi Murakawa, "The Origins of the Carceral Crisis: Racial Order as 'Law and Order' in Postwar American Politics," in *Race and American Political Development,* eds. Joseph Lowndes, Julie Novkov, and Dorian Warren (New York: Routledge, 2008), pp. 236–248.
57 Alexander, *The New Jim Crow,* pp. 49, 186.
58 Ibid., pp. 53, 186; and Verna M. Weaver, "Frontlash: Race and the Development of Punitive Crime Policy," *Studies in American Political Development* 21 (Fall 2007): 242–243.
59 Murakawa, "The Origins of the Carceral Crisis," p. 251. I also draw on pp. 236–248.
60 Quoted in Winthrop D. Jordan, *White over Black: American Attitudes toward the Negro, 1550–1812* (Chapel Hill, North Carolina: University of North Carolina Press, 1968), p. 110.
61 Joe R. Feagin, *The White Racial Frame* (New York: Routledge, 2010), pp. 52–53, 67, 108 and passim.
62 Amnesty International, *United States of America: Rights for All* (London, UK: Amnesty International Publications, 1998), pp. 3, 109–110. See also *U.S.* v. *Brignoni-Ponce,* 422 U.S. 873 (1975).
63 Manning Marable, "Incarceration vs. Education: Reproducing Racism and Poverty in America," Urban Habitat, Fall 2008, http://www.urbanhabitat.org/node/2808 (accessed June 29, 2009); Bruce Western, *Punishment and Inequality in America* (New York: Russell Sage Foundation, 2006); and Alexander, *The New Jim Crow,* p. 59.
64 Alexander, *The New Jim Crow,* pp. 110–111. On racial bias in sentencing, see Glenn L. Pierce and Michael L. Radelet, "The Impact of Legally Inappropriate Factors on Death Sentencing for California Homicides, 1990–1999," *Santa Clara Law Review* 46 (2005): 1–49.
65 Sheila D. Collins, *The Rainbow Challenge* (New York: Monthly Review Press, 1986), pp. 128–143; Michael Oreskes, "Voters and Jackson," *The New York Times,* August 13, 1988, p. 1.
66 "Origins of the CBC," A Voice Online, 2006, http://www.avoiceonline.org/cbc/timeline.html (accessed March 16, 2011).
67 Tali Mendelberg, *The Race Card: Campaign Strategy, Implicit Messages, and the Norm of Equality* (Princeton: Princeton University Press, 2001), pp. 7–9, 106.
68 Joe R. Feagin, Hernán Vera, and Pinar Batur, *White Racism: The Basics* (Second edition; New York: Routledge, 2000), pp. 152–180; and Sidney Blumenthal, *Pledging Allegiance: The Last Campaign of the Cold War* (New York: Harper Collins, 1990), pp. 224, 264–296.
69 Priscilla Painton, "Quota Quagmire," *Time,* May 27, 1991, p. 20; Rosa Delauro, "The 1990 Elections State by State," *The New York Times,* November 8, 1990, p. B8.
70 Robert C. Newberry, "Bush Joins the Band of Naysayers against Diversity," *Houston Post,* May 8, 1991, p. A23.
71 Jane Mayer and Jill Abramson, *Strange Justice: The Selling of Clarence Thomas* (Boston, Massachusetts: Houghton Mifflin, 1994), p. 64.

72 Ken Foskett, *Judging Thomas: The Life and Times of Clarence Thomas* (New York: Harper Collins, 2004), pp. 173–176. The Thomas quotes are on these pages. I also draw here on "Clarence Thomas: A Silent Justice Speaks Out," abcnews.com, http://abcnews.go.com/The Law/Story?id=3665221&page=4 (accessed March 8, 2011).

73 Mayer and Abramson, *Strange Justice*, pp. 74–75.

74 Quoted in Bob Woodward, *The Agenda: Inside the Clinton White House* (New York: Simon and Schuster, 2005), p. 161.

75 Philip A. Klinkner, Joe Cammarano, Charles O. Jones, Gary Jacobson, and Benjamin D. Ling, *Midterm: The Elections of 1994 in Context* (Boulder, Colorado: Westview Press, 1996), passim.

76 Hacker and Pierson, *Winner-Take-All Politics*, Kindle DX locations 3341–3345; and Klinkner, Cammarano, Jones, Jacobson, and Ling, *Midterm*, passim.

77 Kruse, *White Flight*, p. 263.

78 Paul Krugman, "The Gramm Connection," *The New York Times*, March 29, 2008, http://krugman.blogs.nytimes.com/2008/03/29/the-gramm-connection (accessed June 26, 2011); and Hacker and Pierson, *Winner-Take-All Politics*, Kindle DX locations 3318–3338.

79 Bob Dole's comments were made on "Meet the Press," NBC Television, February 5, 1995.

80 Patrick Buchanan, as quoted in Clarence Page, "U.S. Media Should Stop Abetting Intolerance," *Toronto Star*, December 27, 1991, p. A27.

81 Patrick Buchanan, as quoted in John Dillin, "Immigration Joins List of '92 Issues," *Christian Science Monitor*, December 17, 1991: 6.

82 Pat Buchanan, "1992 Republican National Convention Speech," http://web.archive.org/web/20071018035401/http://www.buchanan.org/pa-92-0817-rnc.html (accessed September 16, 2011).

83 Samuel P. Huntington, "The Erosion of American National Interests," *Foreign Affairs* (September 1997/October 1997): 33.

84 Ibid., p. 38.

85 Samuel P. Huntington, "The Clash of Civilizations?," *Foreign Affairs* 72 (1993): 22–33.

86 Quoted in Kevin Sack, "South's Embrace of G.O.P. Is Near a Turning Point," *The New York Times*, March 16, 1998, p. A1.

87 Daniel M. HoSang, *Racial Propositions: Ballot Initiatives and the Making of Postwar California* (Berkeley: University of California Press, 2010), Kindle DX locations 5851–5859, 5866–5874. I also draw on Kindle DX locations 5769–5776 and 362–365.

88 See Feagin, *The White Racial Frame*, pp. 56–129.

89 Feagin, Vera, and Batur, *White Racism*, pp. 182–185; and David Garrow, "Lani Guinier," *The Progressive*, September 1993, p. 28.

90 Quoted in "Rap's Sister Souljah Raps Clinton's Rebuke," United Press International, press release, June 16, 1992.

91 "Sister Souljah: In the Eye of the Storm," *Larry King Live*, CNN, June 19, 1992.

92 "Sister Souljah," *Crier & Company*, CNN, July 2, 1992.

93 She was quoted in Michael Posner, "Jesse Jackson Hints He Might Not Back Clinton," *Reuters Library Report*, June 17, 1992.

94 Carter was quoted in "Inside Politics," *Washington Times*, June 21, 1992, p. A4.

95 Quoted in Ron Howell and Timothy Clifford, "Jackson: It's Clinton Scheme," *Newsday*, June 21, 1992, p. 6.

96 Paul Frymer, *Uneasy Alliances: Race and Party Competition in America* (Princeton: Princeton University Press, 1999), pp. 4–6, 43, 89–99, 137; and Feagin, Vera, and Batur, *White Racism*, pp. 182ff.

97 Jeffrey M. Berry and Clyde Wilcox, *The Interest Group Society* (Fifth edition; New York: Longman, 2009), passim.

98 Lichtman, *White Protestant Nation*, p. 436. See also p. 443.

6 The George W. Bush Era: Racial and Class Dimensions

1 Marc J. Hetherington and Jonathan D. Weiler, *Authoritarianism and Polarization in American Politics* (Cambridge, UK: Cambridge University Press, 2009), chapter 1, Kindle DX locations 90–94.

2 Ibid., chapter 1, Kindle DX locations 90–111.

3 For example, on U.S. parties as non-ideological and the disappearing center issue, see Marjorie Randon Hershey, *Party Politics in America* (Fourteenth edition; New York: Longman, 2011), pp. 2, 6, 289.

4 Matthew Levendusky, *The Partisan Sort: How Liberals Became Democrats and Conservatives Became Republicans* (Chicago: University of Chicago Press, 2009), chapter 1, Kindle DX locations 100–200; Ronald Brownstein, *The Second Civil War: How Extreme Partisanship Has Paralyzed Washington and Polarized America* (New York: Penguin Press, 2007), chapter 1, Kindle DX locations 292–353.
5 Levendusky, *The Partisan Sort*, chapter 1, Kindle DX locations 100–200.
6 Sean Theriault, *Party Polarization in Congress* (Cambridge, UK: Cambridge University Press, 2008), chapter 1, Kindle DX locations 133–143.
7 Brownstein, *The Second Civil War*, chapter 1, Kindle DX locations 272–292.
8 Levendusky, *The Partisan Sort*, chapter 1, Kindle DX locations 100–200.
9 Brownstein, *The Second Civil War*, chapter 1, Kindle DX locations 360–370; Levendusky, *The Partisan Sort*, chapter 1, Kindle DX locations 100–200.
10 Alan I. Abramowitz, *The Disappearing Center: Engaged Citizens, Polarization, and American Democracy* (New Haven: Yale University Press, 2011); and Brownstein, *The Second Civil War*, chapter 1, Kindle DX locations 412–419.
11 On such clustering, see Hetherington and Weiler, *Authoritarianism and Polarization in American Politics*, chapter 1, Kindle DX locations 125–140.
12 Bill Bishop, "No, We Didn't: America Hasn't Changed as Much as Tuesday's Results Would Indicate," *Slate*, November 10, 2008, http://www.slate.com/blogs/blogs/bigsort/default.aspx (accessed December 17, 2008). See also Paul Taylor and Richard Morin, "Americans Claim to Like Diverse Communities but Do They Really?," Pew Research Center, December 2, 2008, http://pewresearch.org/pubs/1045/americans-claim-to-like-diverse-communities-but-do-they-really (accessed December 17, 2008).
13 Steven Greenhouse, *The Big Squeeze: Tough Times for the American Worker* (New York: Alfred A. Knopf, 2008), chapter 1, Kindle DX locations 109–120.
14 Ibid., chapter 1, Kindle DX locations 121–161.
15 Greenhouse, *The Big Squeeze*, chapter 1, Kindle DX locations 162–228.
16 Dave Gilson and Carolyn Perot, "It's the Inequality Stupid," *Mother Jones*, March/April 2011, http://motherjones.com/politics/2011/02/income-inequality-in-america-chart-graph (accessed March 14, 2011).
17 Julian E. Zelizer, "Establishment Conservative: The Presidency of George W. Bush," in *The Presidency of George W. Bush: A First Historical Assessment*, ed. Julian E. Zelizer (Princeton: Princeton University Press, 2010), Kindle DX locations 298–305.
18 Ibid., Kindle DX locations 291–298.
19 Greenhouse, *The Big Squeeze*, Kindle DX locations 302–314.
20 Michael Powell, "Bank Accused of Pushing Mortgage Deals on Blacks," *The New York Times*, June 6, 2009, http://www.nytimes.com/2009/06/07/us/07baltimore.html?_r=1 (accessed March 16, 2011).
21 Andrew Redleaf and Richard Vigilante, *Panic* (New York: Richard Vigilante Books, 2010), Kindle DX locations 320–360.
22 Public Campaign, Fannie Lou Hamer Project, and William C. Velasquez Institute, *Color Of Money: The 2004 Presidential Race* (Washington, D.C.: Public Campaign, 2004), pp. 1–12; and "Wealthy Campaign Donors Stifle Minority Voices," *USA Today*, December 11, 2003, p. 23a.
23 Frank R. Baumgartner, Jeffrey M. Berry, Marie Hojnacki, David C. Kimball, and Beth L. Leech, *Lobbying and Policy Change: Who Wins, Who Loses, and Why* (Chicago: University of Chicago Press, 2009), chapter 1, Kindle DX locations 17–21, 102–179.
24 Ibid..
25 Nicholas D. Kristof, "A Philosophy with Roots in Conservative Texas Soil," *The New York Times*, May 21, 2000, http://partners.nytimes.com/library/politics/camp/052100wh-gop-bush-bio.html (accessed March 16, 2011).
26 I especially draw here on Gary Gerstle, "Minorities, Multiculturalism, and the Presidency of George W. Bush," in *The Presidency of George W. Bush: A First Historical Assessment*, ed. Julian E. Zelizer (Princeton: Princeton University press, 2010), pp. 252ff.
27 Kevin M. Kruse, *White Flight: Atlanta and the Making of Modern Conservatism* (Princeton: Princeton University Press, 2005), p. 266; and Randolph Hohle, "The Color of Neoliberalism: The 'Modern Southern Businessman' and Post-War Alabama's Challenge to Racial Desegregation," *Sociological Forum* 27 (2012): 142–162 (Abstract).
28 Quoted in Max Blumenthal, *Republican Gomorrah: Inside the Movement that Shattered the Party* (New York: Nation Books, 2010), Kindle DX location 2324.
29 Ibid., Kindle DX location 2308; and Clarence Lusane, *Colin Powell and Condoleezza Rice:*

Foreign Policy, Race, and the New American Century (Westport, Connecticut: Praeger, 2006), pp. 1–79.

30 Chandler Davidson, Tanya Dunlap, Gale Kenny, and Benjamin Wise, *Republican Ballot Security Programs: Vote Protection or Minority Vote Suppression—Or Both?* (Washington, D.C.: Center for Voting Rights & Protection, 2004), pp. 96–106 and passim.

31 Allen Raymond and Ian Spiegelman, *How to Rig an Election: Confessions of a Republican Operative* (Reprint edition; New York: Simon & Schuster, 2008 [2002]).

32 Michael O. Emerson and Christian Smith, *Divided by Faith: Evangelical Religion and the Problem of Race in America* (Oxford: Oxford University Press, 2001).

33 Bebe Moore Campbell, "To Be Black, Gifted, and Alone," *Savvy* 5 (December 1984): 69.

34 Quoted in Lou Dubose, Jan Reid, and Carl M. Cannon, *Boy Genius: Karl Rove, the Brains Behind the Remarkable Political Triumph of George W. Bush* (New York: Public Affairs, 2003), p. 162.

35 Lusane, *Colin Powell and Condoleezza Rice*, pp. 43–79, 188–192.

36 Ron Christie, *Black in the White House* (Nashville: Nelson Current, 2006), p. 122.

37 Jordan T. Camp, "'We Know this Place': Neoliberal Racial Regimes and the Katrina Circumstance," *American Quarterly* 61 (September 2009): 693–717.

38 Gerstle, "Minorities, Multiculturalism, and the Presidency of George W. Bush," pp. 252–264.

39 Ibid., p. 265.

40 See Emerson and Smith, *Divided by Faith*.

41 Office of Civil Rights Evaluation, U.S. Commission on Civil Rights. "Redefining Rights in America. The Civil Rights Record of the George W. Bush Administration, 2001–2004," http://www.thememoryhole.org/pol/usccr_redefining_rights.pdf (accessed April 12, 2005).

42 *Parents Involved in Community Schools* v. *Seattle School District No. 1*, 551 U.S. 701, 803 (2007). This case was heard and ruled in connection with another case, *Meredith* v. *Jefferson County Board of Education*.

43 Ibid., p. 835.

44 *Parents Involved in Community Schools* v. *Seattle School District No. 1*, p. 868.

45 Ibid., p. 769.

46 Thomas F. Pettigrew, "Did Brown Fail?," *Du Bois Review* 8 (2011): 511–516.

47 T. F. Pettigrew and L. R. Tropp, "A Meta-Analytic Test of Intergroup Contact Theory," *Journal of Personality and Social Psychology* 90 (2006): 1–33. See also Martha Minow, *In Brown's Wake: Legacies of America's Educational Landmark* (New York: Oxford University Press, 2010); and Amy Stuart Wells, Jennifer Jellison Holme, Tina Tijerina Revilla, and Awo Korantemaa Atanda, *Both Sides Now: The Story of School Desegregation's Graduates* (Berkeley: University of California Press, 2009).

48 Pettigrew, "Did Brown Fail?"

49 David Corn, *The Lies of George W. Bush: Mastering the Politics of Deception* (New York: Crown, 2003), p. 66.

50 Quoted in Jane H. Hill, *The Everyday Language of White Racism* (Chichester: Wiley-Blackwell, 2008), p. 99.

51 Quoted in ibid., p. 103.

52 Hill, *The Everyday Language of White Racism*, pp. 99–103.

53 See Seymour Martin Lipset, "The Sources of the 'Radical Right,'" in *The New American Right*, ed. Daniel Bell (New York: Criterion Books, 1955), pp. 182ff; and Milan Zafirovski, *The Protestant Ethic and the Spirit of Authoritarianism: Puritanism, Democracy, and Society* (New York: Springer, 2007).

54 I am influenced here by Michael Parenti, *Against Empire* (San Francisco: City Lights Books, 1995); and Michael Parenti, *The Face of Imperialism* (Boulder, Colorado: Paradigm Press, 2011).

7 The Barack Obama Presidential Campaign

1 In this period I was checking arch-conservative and racist websites and saw some of the racially slanted story on Dr. Wright there before the mainstream media picked it up.

2 For a more detailed discussion, see Adia Harvey Wingfield and Joe R. Feagin, *Yes We Can? White Racial Framing and the 2008 Campaign* (New York: Routledge, 2010), pp. 122–130; and Joe Feagin, "Dr. Wright is Still Right on Racism: Check the Research Data," Racism Review, April 28, 2008, http://www.racismreview.com/blog/2008/04/28/dr-wright-is-still-right-on-racism-check-the-research-data (accessed April 29, 2011).

3 Rev. John H. Thomas, "What Kind of Prophet?," http://www.ucc.org/news/responding-to-wright.html (accessed April 11, 2011). This is the United Church of Christ website.

4   Ibid.
5   Frank Schaeffer, "Obama's Minister Committed 'Treason' but when My Father Said the Same Thing He was a Republican Hero," Huffington Post, March 16, 2008, http://www.huffington post.com/frank-schaeffer/obamas-minister-committed_b_91774.html (accessed April 25, 2011).
6   Barack Obama, "A More Perfect Union," http://my.barackobama.com/page/content/hisown words (accessed December 4, 2011). See Wingfield and Feagin, Yes We Can?, pp. 131–139, for a more detailed discussion of this speech.
7   Obama, "A More Perfect Union." On persisting discrimination and black views, see Joe R. Feagin, Racist America: Roots, Current Realities, and Future Reparations (Second edition; New York: Routledge, 2010), especially chapters 3–6.
8   Obama, "A More Perfect Union."
9   See Wingfield and Feagin, Yes We Can?, passim.
10 Penn is quoted in Joshua Green, "The Front-Runner's Fall," Atlantic Monthly, September 2008, http://www.theatlantic.com/magazine/archive/2008/09/the-front-runner-8217-s-fall/6944/5/ (accessed July 19, 2011); see also Mike Allen, "Clinton Told to Portray Obama as Foreign," Politico, August 10, 2008, http://www.politico.com/news/stories/0808/12420.html (accessed April 10, 2011).
11 Geraldine A. Ferraro, "Healing the Wounds of Democrats' Sexism," The Boston Globe, May 30, 2008, http://www.boston.com/bostonglobe/editorial_opinion/oped/articles/2008/05/30/healing_the_wounds_of_democrats_sexism (accessed April 26, 2011).
12 Ibid.
13 Amiri Baraka, "Barack and Moving Forward," Black and Progressive Sociologists for Obama, August 19, 2008, http://sociologistsforobama.blogspot.com/2008/08/amiri-baraka-barack-and-moving-forward.html (accessed April 10, 2011).
14 Darryl Fears, "House Issues an Apology for Slavery," Washington Post, July 30, 2008, http://www.washingtonpost.com/wp-dyn/content/article/2008/07/29/AR2008072902279.html (accessed May 1, 2011).
15 George Lakoff, "The Palin Choice: The Reality of the Political Mind," Common Dreams, September 2, 2008, http://www.commondreams.org/view/2008/09/02 (accessed April 26, 2011).
16 Ibid.
17 Lakoff, "The Palin Choice."
18 Mark Schmitt, "Can Identity Politics Save the Right?," The American Prospect, May 27, 2008, http://www.prospect.org/cs/articles?article=can_identity_politics_save_the_right (accessed April 26, 2011).
19 The Frum quote is in ibid.
20 Jacqueline Soteropoulos, "Skeptics Put Cops on Trial: The American Public Isn't Giving Government or Police Officers the Blind Trust It Once Did," Tampa Tribune, April 17, 1995, p. A1. I draw here on Nick Mrozinske, "Derivational Thinking and Racism," unpublished research paper, University of Florida, Fall 1998.
21 Thierry Devos and Mahzarin R. Banaji, "American = White?," Journal of Personality and Social Psychology 88 (2005): 447–466. See also other research papers at http://www.projectimplicit.net/articles.php (accessed April 26, 2011).
22 Quoted in Russ Mitchell, "King Announced Bid for Fourth Term," Spencer Daily Reporter, March 8, 2008, http://www.spencerdailyreporter.com/story/1316727.html (accessed April 26, 2011).
23 "Text of Forwarded E-Mail," Tampa Bay Online, October 30, 2008, http://beta2.tbo.com/news/politics/2008/oct/30/text-forwarded-e-mail-ar-104478/ (accessed April 28, 2011). For a full discussion, see Wingfield and Feagin, Yes We Can?, pp. 1–4.
24 Joseph Abrams, "The Indiana Congressional Candidate the GOP Wishes Would Go Away," FoxNews.com, April 30, 2008, http://www.foxnews.com/story/0,2933,353536,00.html (accessed April 28, 2011).
25 Max Blumenthal, Republican Gomorrah: Inside the Movement that Shattered the Party (New York: Nation Books, 2010), Kindle DX location 2074.
26 James Wright, "Black Republicans Ponder Their Future," Afro Newspapers, November 24, 2008, http://news.newamericamedia.org/news/view_article.html?article_id= (accessed December 18, 2008).
27 Cliff Schecter, "John McCain's White Supremacist Problem," Huffington Post, April 28, 2008, http://www.huffingtonpost.com/cliff-schecter/john-mccains-white-suprem_b_99014.html (accessed April 28, 2011).

28 Blumenthal, *Republican Gomorrah*, Kindle DX locations 4816–4817.
29 Terence Fitzgerald, "Change? Don't Count on It: American Racism is on Full Display," RacismReview, September 15, 2008, http://www.racismreview.com (accessed April 5, 2011); Terence Fitzgerald, "Politically Recycling the Great Divide," RacismReview, October 20, 2008, http://www.racismreview.com/blog/2008/10/20/politically-recycling-the-great-divide/ (accessed April 10, 2011).
30 Jim Brunner, "Snohomish County GOP Pulls '$3 Bills' Smearing Obama from Fair Booth," *Seattle Times*, August 27, 2008, http://seattletimes.nwsource.com/html/localnews/2008140846_fair27m0.html (accessed April 26, 2011).
31 Michelle Dearmond, "GOP Mailing Depicts Obama on Food Stamp," *The Press-Enterprise*, October 16, 2008, http://www.pe.com/localnews/inland/stories/PE_News_Local_S_webbuck1.e7982b.html (accessed April 26, 2011).
32 Quoted in Amy Goodman, "Former McCain Supporter: McCain is 'Unleashing the Monster of American Prejudice,'" *Democracy Now*, October 13, 2008, http://www.alternet.org/rights/102837/former_mccain_supporter%3A_mccain_is_%22unleashing_the_monster_of_american_prejudice%22/?page=2 (accessed April 25, 2011).
33 Frank Schaeffer, "Open Letter to the Republican Traitors (from a Former Republican)," Huffington Post, March 8, 2009, http://www.huffingtonpost.com/frank-schaeffer/open-letter-to-the-republ_b_172822.html (accessed April 25, 2011).
34 Adam Nossiter, "For Some, Uncertainty Starts at Racial Identity," *The New York Times*, October 14, 2008, http://www.nytimes.com/2008/10/15/us/politics/15biracial.html (accessed December 12, 2008). For a more detailed discussion, see Wingfield and Feagin, *Yes We Can?*, pp. 180–184.
35 Jennifer Steinhauer, "Volunteers for Obama Face a Complex Issue," *The New York Times*, October 14, 2008, http://www.nytimes.com/2008/10/15/us/politics/15nevada.html (accessed December 12, 2008).
36 The white volunteer responded with this comment to a summary post on our sociological research blog, www.racismreview.com.
37 Roger Simon, "A Measure of Racism: 15 Percent?," politico.com, April 21, 2008, http://www.politico.com/news/stories/0408/9761.html (accessed April 25, 2011).
38 Ibid.
39 "Exit Polls," cnn.com (undated), http://www.cnn.com/ELECTION/2008/results/polls/#USP00p1 (accessed March 11, 2011).
40 Ibid. The Native American data were compiled by Shari Valentine.
41 See Ana-Maria Arumi, as cited in Tom Curry, "Young Voters Not Essential to Obama Triumph," MSNBC.com, November 7, 2008, http://www.msnbc.msn.com/id/27582147 (accessed April 5, 2011).
42 Marjorie R. Hershey, *Party Politics in America* (New York: Longman, 2011), pp. 131–132.
43 Ibid.
44 Paul Jenkins, "The GOP's White Supremacy," Huffington Post, December 28, 2008, http://www.huffingtonpost.com/paul-jenkins/the-gops-white-supremacy_b_153823.html (accessed December 29, 2008); and James Wright, "Black Republicans Ponder Their Future," *Afro Newspapers*, November 24, 2008, http://news.newamericamedia.org/news/view_article.html?article_id= (accessed December 18, 2008).
45 David A. Bositis, "Blacks and the 2004 Republican National Convention," Joint Center for Political and Economic Studies, Washington, D.C., 2004, pp. 1–10; David A. Bositis, "Blacks and the 2008 Democratic National Convention," Joint Center for Political and Economic Studies, Washington, D.C., 2008. I am indebted here to research tabulations by Louwanda Evans.
46 Matt Bai, "Is Obama the End of Black Politics?," *The New York Times Magazine*, August 6, 2008, http://www.nytimes.com/2008/08/10/magazine/10politics-t.html?_r=1 (accessed April 10, 2011).
47 Baraka, "Barack and Moving Forward."
48 Maulana Karenga, "Post-Black and Continuous White: Misreading the Meaning of Obama," Black and Progressive Sociologists for Obama, August 19, 2008, http://sociologistsforobama.blogspot.com/2008/08/karenga-on-post-black.html (accessed April 10, 2011).
49 "President-Elect Obama: The Voters Rebuke Republicans for Economic Failure," *Wall Street Journal*, November 5, 2008, http://online.wsj.com/article/SB122586244657800863.html (accessed December 28, 2008). For a detailed discussion, see Wingfield and Feagin, *Yes We Can?*, pp. 220–221.

8 Barack Obama's Presidency: Racial and Class Dimensions

1 "Inaugural Poem," *The New York Times*, January 20, 2009, http://www.nytimes.com/2009/01/20/us/politics/20text-poem.html?ref=books (accessed May 8, 2011). See also Jessie Daniels, "Obama's Inauguration & a New Era of Learning about Racism," http://www.racismreview.com/blog/2009/01/21/obama-inauguration-racism/ (accessed April 12, 2011).

2 David Ehrenstein, "Obama the 'Magic Negro,'" *Los Angeles Times*, March 19, 2007, http://www.latimes.com/news/opinion/la-oe-ehrenstein19mar19,0,5335087.story?coll=la-opinion-center (accessed May 9, 2011).

3 Nicholas Graham, "RNC Candidate Distributes 'Barack The Magic Negro' Song," Huffington Post, December 26, 2008, http://www.huffingtonpost.com/2008/12/26/rnc-candidate-distributes_n_153585.html (accessed May 9, 2011).

4 "Limbaugh: 'I Do Believe . . . Obama is an 'Angry Black Guy'," MediaMatters, July 27, 2009, http://mediamatters.org/mmtv/200907270023 (accessed May 4, 2011).

5 Quoted in Laura Bassett, "Rush Limbaugh: Obama Created Recession as 'Payback' for Racism," Huffington Post, July 7, 2010, http://www.huffingtonpost.com/2010/07/07/rush-limbaugh-obama-creat_n_637716.html (accessed May 4, 2011).

6 "Mayor to Quit over Obama Watermelon E-mail," MSNBC.com, February 27, 2009, http://www.msnbc.msn.com/id/29423045/ (accessed May 5, 2011).

7 "Racist and Ridiculous," Newscoma, June 15, 2009, http://newscoma.com/2009/06/15/racist-and-ridiculous/ (accessed April 12, 2011).

8 Randy Krehbiel, "Coburn Sour on the Economy," *Tulsa World*, August 18, 2011, http://www.tulsaworld.com/news/article.aspx?subjectid=336&articleid=20110818_16_A14_CUTLIN497125 (accessed August 19, 2011).

9 Mark Kantrowitz, "The Distribution of Grants and Scholarships by Race," http://www.finaid.org, September 2, 2011 (accessed October 24, 2011).

10 Wire Services, "Orange County GOP Official Refuses to Resign over Racist Email," *Los Angeles Wave*, April 16, 2011, http://www.wavenewspapers.com/news/orange-county-racist-ape-chimp-email-gop-republican-obama-davenport-119993794.html (accessed May 5, 2011).

11 Liz Garrigan, "Nothing Funny about this Monkey Mail," Nashville Scene, March 5, 2010, http://www.nashvillescene.com/pitw/archives/2010/03/05/nothing-funny-about-this-monkey-mail (accessed May 9, 2011).

12 See Leslie H. Picca and Joe R. Feagin, *Two-Faced Racism: Whites in the Frontstage and Backstage* (New York: Routledge, 2007).

13 TMZ Staff, "Sharpton Spanks the Monkey Cartoon," TMZ, February 18, 2009, www.tmz.com/2009/02/18/al-sharpton-monkey-cartoon-obama/ (accessed May 5, 2011).

14 See Picca and Feagin, *Two-Faced Racism*, pp. 68–74, 249–251.

15 Matthew Rothschild, "Racist Beehive Buzzing," *The Progressive* (October 2009): 4.

16 Brian Montopoli, "Von Brunn: 'Obama was Created by Jews,'" *CBS News*, June 11, 2009, http://www.cbsnews.com/8301-503544_162-5081368-503544.html (accessed July 21, 2011).

17 Bryan Bender, "Secret Service Strained as Leaders Face More Threats," *Boston Globe*, October 18, 2009, http://www.boston.com/news/nation/washington/articles/2009/10/18/secret_service_under_strain_as_leaders_face_more_threats/?page=2 (accessed May 11, 2011).

18 "Hang Obama by F*ck Haiti Earthquake Facebook Group," Governmentalityblog, January 29, 2010, http://www.governmentalityblog.com/my_weblog/2010/01/hang-obama-from-fck-the-haiti-facebook-group.html (accessed May 5, 2011).

19 The hanging is reported in "Obama Burned in Effigy," *TMJ4 News*, at http://www.youtube.com/watch?v=zaz2nDlQLu4&feature=player_embedded (accessed May 5, 2011); on the sign, see Bossip Staff, "Billboard Depicts President Obama as Terrorist, Mobster, Illegal Immigrant, Gay Man," Bossip.Com, October 14, 2010, http://bossip.com/295723/billboard-depicts-president-obama-as-terrorist-mobster-illegal-immigrant-gay-man12006/ (accessed May 9, 2011).

20 Brian Tashman, "Gheen Floats Military Coup and Arrest to 'Remove' Obama from Office 'As Soon As Possible,'" RightWingWatch, August 24, 2011, http://www.rightwingwatch.org/content/gheen-floats-military-coup-and-arrest-remove-obama-office-soon-possible (accessed August 25, 2011).

21 Joe Sonka, "Rand Paul's Spokesperson is a Satanic Metal God in KKK Gear," Barefoot and Progressive, December 16, 2009, http://barefootandprogressive.blogspot.com/2009/12/rand-pauls-spokesperson-is-satanic.html (accessed May 4, 2011).

22 "Rand Paul on 'Maddow' Defends Criticism of Civil Rights Act, Says He Would Have Worked to Change Bill," Huffington Post, May 20, 2010, http://www.huffingtonpost.com/2010/05/20/rand-paul-tells-maddow-th_n_582872.html (accessed May 4, 2011).

23 Stephanie Condon, "Haley Barbour Criticized for Praising Segregationist Group," CBS News, http://www.cbsnews.com/8301-503544_162-20026232-503544.html (accessed May 4, 2011).

24 See Kristen M. Lavelle, "'Our Generation Had Nothing to Do with Discrimination': White Southern Memory of Jim Crow and Civil Rights," PhD dissertation, Texas A&M University, 2011.

25 Southern Poverty Law Center, "Hate Group Numbers Up by 54% since 2000," February 26, 2009, http://www.splcenter.org/news/item.jsp?aid=366 (accessed June 19, 2009); and Jessie Daniels, "Man Arrested for Threats on White Supremacist Website," February 19, 2010, RacismReview, http://www.racismreview.com/blog/2010/02/19/man-arrested-for-threats-on-white-supremacist-website/ (accessed April 12, 2011).

26 "David Duke Holds Memphis News Conference," WhiteReference, November 2008, http://whitereference.blogspot.com/2008/11/dr-david-duke-holds-memphis-news.html (accessed December 26, 2008).

27 "Tea Party Supporters: Who They Are and What They Believe," CBS News, April 14, 2010, http://www.cbsnews.com/8301-503544_162-20002529-503544.html (accessed April 15, 2011); and Lydia Saad, "Tea Partiers Are Fairly Mainstream in Their Demographics," Gallup, http://www.gallup.com/poll/127181/tea-partiers-fairly-mainstream-demographics.aspx (accessed May 5, 2011).

28 Devin Burghart, Leonard Zeskind, and the Institute for Research & Education on Human Rights, "Tea Party Nationalism," August 2010, http://www.teapartynationalism.com/the-reportbriall-of-tea-party-nationalismi/introduction (accessed April 15, 2011); and Kate Zernike, *Boiling Mad: Inside Tea Party America* (New York: Henry Holt Times Books, 2010), passim.

29 Luke Meredith, "Iowa Tea Party Billboard Compares Obama to Hitler, Lenin," Huffington Post, July 13, 2010, http://www.huffingtonpost.com/2010/07/13/obama-hitler-tea-party-billboard_n_645203.html (accessed April 15, 2011).

30 Richard Greener, "Obama's 'Middle Class Working People' Support: See Any White Folks?," Huffington Post, April 3, 2010, http://www.huffingtonpost.com/richard-greener/obamas-middle-class-worki_b_524265.html (accessed May 6, 2011); and Burghart, Zeskind, and the Institute for Research & Education on Human Rights, "Tea Party Nationalism."

31 G. William Domhoff, *Who Rules America? Challenges to Corporate and Class Dominance* (Sixth edition; New York: McGraw-Hill, 2009); and Jessica Holden Sherwood, *Wealth, Whiteness, and the Matrix of Privilege: The View from the Country Club* (Lanham, Maryland: Lexington Books, 2010).

32 Quoted in Devin Burghart, "Tea Party Nation Warns of White Anglo-Saxon Protestant 'Extinction'," Institute for Research & Education on Human Rights, March 29, 2011, http://www.irehr.org/issue-areas/tea-parties/19-news/76-tea-party-nation-warns-of-white-anglo-saxon-protestant-extinction (accessed April 15, 2011).

33 See "Excerpt from Leonard Zeskind's Presentation to the NAACP National Convention Saturday," Institute for Research & Education on Human Rights, 2010, http://www.irehr.org/index.php?option=com_content&view=article&id=61:excerpt-from-leonard-zeskinds-presentation-to-the-naacp-national-convention&catid=16:blog&Itemid=4 (accessed April 15, 2011).

34 Brian Montopoli, "NAACP Passes Tea Party Racism Resolution," July 2010, http://www.loonwatch.com/2010/07/naacp-tea-party-movement-is-racist/ (accessed April 15, 2011).

35 "Palin: Obama's Disconnect With American People Evident in Arizona, Gulf," Fox News, July 13, 2010, http://www.foxnews.com/story/0,2933,596592,00.html#ixzz1Jbz2dtau (accessed April 15, 2011).

36 Burghart, Zeskind, and the Institute for Research & Education on Human Rights, "Tea Party Nationalism."

37 "In Pictures: Faces of the Super Wealthy," Forbes, September 2010, http://www.forbes.com/wealth/forbes-400?boxes=listschannellists (accessed June 20, 2011). I am indebted to Louwanda Evans for doing tallies from this and related listings.

38 Rebecca Fortner, "Cracking the Plexi-Glass Ceiling," RiseUp, February 9, 2011, http://www.usariseup.com/eyes-enterprise/cracking-plexi-glass-ceiling-2010-fortune-500-ceos-color (accessed May 11, 2011); and Catalyst Inc., "Minorities and Women Lose Ground on Fortune 500 Corporate Boards, Alliance for Board Diversity Census Shows," Equality Magazines, May 2, 2011, http://www.equalitymagazines.com/index.php/news/minority-news/144-minorities-and-women-lose-ground (accessed May 11, 2011).

39 Roll Call, *Guide to the New Congress* (Washington, D.C.: CQ Roll Call, 2010). See also Jennifer E. Manning, "Membership of the 111th Congress: A Profile," Congressional Research Service, October 2010, www.crs.gov (accessed July 22, 2011).

40 Manning, "Membership of the 11th Congress."

41 See Erika Lovley, "237 Millionaires in Congress," Politico, November 6, 2009, www.politico.com/news/stories/1109/29235.html (accessed October 22, 2010); Howard W. Allen and Robert Slagter, "Congress in Crisis: Changes in Personnel and the Legislative Agenda in the U.S. Congress in the 1890s," *Social Science History* 16 (Autumn 1992): 407–409.

42 Anna Palmer and Matthew Murray, "For Black Lobbyists, Progress Is Real but Big Challenges Remain," Roll Call Staff, June 9, 2009, http://www.rollcall.com/issues/54_142/-35651-1.html (accessed May 10, 2011); Erika Lovley, "Hill Lags in Hiring Hispanics," Roll Call, February 4, 2010, http://www.hispaniclobbyists.org/node/102 (accessed May 10, 2011).

43 Marcus Stern and Jennifer LaFleur, "Leadership PACs: Let the Good Times Roll," September 26, 2009, http://www.propublica.org/article/leadership-pacs-let-the-good-times-roll-925 (accessed October 22, 2010).

44 "Banking on Connections," Center for Responsive Politics, June 3, 2010, http://www.opensecrets.org/news/FinancialRevolvingDoors.pdf (accessed October 22, 2010).

45 "Washington Post-ABC News Poll," *The Washington Post,* April 18, 2011, http://www.washingtonpost.com/wp-srv/politics/polls/postpoll_04172011.html (accessed April 24, 2011).

46 Larry M. Bartels, "Economic Inequality and Political Representation," Princeton University, August 2005, http://www.princeton.edu/~bartels/economic.pdf (accessed April 24, 2011).

47 Sherwood, *Wealth, Whiteness, and the Matrix of Privilege.*

48 Jeffrey A. Winters and Benjamin I. Page, "Oligarchy in the United States?," *Perspectives on Politics* 7 (December 2009): 732.

49 Robert W. McChesney, "The New Global Media: It's a Small World of Big Conglomerates," *The Nation,* November 29, 1999, http://www.hartfordwp.com/archives/29/053.html (accessed July 3, 2008); and Anup Shah, "Media Conglomerates, Mergers, Concentration of Ownership," *Global Issues* (February 2, 2009): 159–160, http://www.globalissues.org/article/159/media-conglomerates-mergers-concentration-of-ownership (accessed May 10, 2011).

50 See Franklin D. Gilliam, Jr. and Shanto Iyengar, "Prime Suspects: The Effects of Local News on the Viewing Public," unpublished paper, University of California at Los Angeles, undated; S. Derek Turner and Mark Cooper, "Out of the Picture: Minority and Female TV Station Ownership in the United States," October 2006, FreePress, www.freepress.net (accessed February 26, 2009); S. Derek Turner, "Off the Dial: Female and Minority Radio Station Ownership in the United States: How FCC Policy and Media Consolidation Diminished Diversity on the Public Airwaves," June 2007, FreePress, www.freepress.net (accessed February 26, 2009). See also David K. Shipler, "Blacks in the Newsroom," *Columbia Journalism Review* (May/June 1998): 26–29; and Robert M. Entman et al., *Mass Media and Reconciliation: A Report to the Advisory Board and Staff, the President's Initiative on Race* (Washington, D.C., U.S. Government Printing Office, 1998).

51 Andrew Mullen, "The Propaganda Model after 20 Years: Interview with Edward S. Herman and Noam Chomsky," *Westminster Papers in Communication and Culture* (2009): 12–22.

52 Richard Cohen, "Ignorant, Apathetic and Smug," *The Washington Post,* February 2, 1996, p. A19; Bobbie Harville, "History: Knowledge is Lacking; Americans' Understanding of the Country's History is Thin, a New Survey Reveals," *Dayton Daily News,* July 14, 1996, p. 15A. For more discussion, see Joe R. Feagin, *Racist America: Roots, Current Realities, and Future Reparations* (Second edition; New York: Routledge, 2010), chapter 3.

53 Jacob S. Hacker and Paul Pierson, *Winner-Take-All Politics: How Washington Made the Rich Richer—And Turned Its Back on the Middle Class* (New York: Simon and Schuster, 2010), Kindle DX locations 1815–1845.

54 Dave Gilson and Carolyn Perot, "It's the Inequality Stupid," *Mother Jones,* March/April 2011, http://motherjones.com/politics/2011/02/income-inequality-in-america-chart-graph (accessed March 14, 2011).

55 Blackwaterdog (blogger), "The Arrogance of Being President While Being Black," DailyKos, February 27, 2020, http://www.dailykos.com/story/2010/02/27/841263/-The-arrogance-of-being-president-while-being-black-%28Updated%29 (accessed May 9, 2011).

56 Jessie Daniels, "'Guess I'm a Racist': Anti-Health Care Ad," RacismReview, http://www.racismreview.com/blog/2009/12/09/guess-im-a-racist-anti-health-care-ad/ (accessed April 12, 2011).

57 See, for example, the report on Richard Berman, CBS News, July 17, 2007, http://www.cbs
    news.com/stories/2007/04/05/60minutes/main2653020.shtml (accessed May 4, 2011); and
    Jessie Daniels, *Cyber Racism* (Lanham, Maryland: Rowman and Littlefield, 2009).

58 April Ryan, "Interview with President Barack Obama," December 21, 2009 Ryan Website,
    http://aprildryan.com/2009/12/ (accessed May 8, 2011). See also Carol E. Lee, "Obama
    Concedes 'Grumbling'," Politico, December 21, 2009, http://www.politico.com/politico44/
    perm/1209/obama_concedes_grumbling_d3f4e3ea-9672-407a-8c9c-2898cc184375.html
    (accessed May 8, 2011).

59 Richard Delgado, "Linking Arms: Recent Books on Interracial Coalition as an Avenue of Social
    Reform," *Cornell Law Review* 88 (March 2003): 871.

60 See Picca and Feagin, *Two-Faced Racism*, especially chapters 1–3.

61 James Kirchick, "Squanderer in Chief," *Los Angeles Times*, April 28, 2009, http://www.la
    times.com/news/opinion/la-oe-kirchick28-2009apr28,0,4218519.story (accessed December 15,
    2010).

62 "News Conference," Apri 4, 2009, http://www.whitehouse.gov/the-press-office/news-
    conference-president-obama-4042009 (accessed December 15, 2010).

63 Clyburn's quote is from the Black Caucus website, http://www.crewof42.com (accessed January
    7, 2011).

64 Quoted in Chris Hedges, "The Obama Deception: Why Cornel West Went Ballistic," TruthDig,
    May 16, 2011, http://www.truthdig.com/report/item/the_obama_deception_why_cornel_west_
    went_ballistic_20 (accessed May 18, 2011).

65 Domhoff, *Who Rules America?*, chapters 7–8.

66 Quoted in Hedges, "The Obama Deception."

67 Ishmael Reed, "What Progressives Don't Understand about Obama," *The New York Times*,
    December 11, 2010, http://www.nytimes.com/2010/12/12/opinion/12reed.html?_r=2&nl=
    todaysheadlines&emc=a212 (accessed May 8, 2011).

68 Glenn Greenwald, "Obama v. Bush on Power over Congress," Salon, August 18, 2011,
    http://www.salon.com/news/politics/barack_obama/index.html?story=/opinion/greenwald/20
    11/08/18/obama_v_bush (accessed August 24, 2011).

69 See, for instance, Joshua Holland, "The Obama Wars," *AlterNet*, August 16, 2011, http://www.
    alternet.org/story/152055/ (accessed August 19, 2011).

70 Jonathan Chait, "The Obama Method," *New Republic*, July 1, 2009, http://www.tnr.com/
    article/the-obama-method (accessed August 26, 2011).

71 "Obama Leadership Image Takes a Hit, GOP Ratings Decline," Pew Research Center, August
    25, 2011, http://people-press.org/2011/08/25/obama-leadership-image-takes-a-hit-gop-ratings-
    decline/ (accessed August 26, 2011).

72 Reed, "What Progressives Don't Understand about Obama."

73 Tom Schade, "Progressives Don't See Obama Clearly Because of Our Racial Blind Spots,"
    Schade Website, http://www.tomschade.com/2011/08/progressives-dont-see-obama-clearly.
    html (accessed August 18, 2011).

74 Reed, "What Progressives Don't Understand about Obama."

75 Jeff Johnson, "Rep. Waters to Black Voters: 'Unleash Us' on Obama," http://www.thegrio.
    com/politics/frustration-boils-over-at-black-caucus-detroit-town-hall.php (accessed August
    19, 2011).

76 Trymaine Lee, "Obama's Speech to CBC a Call to Arms, Not a Calling Out: White House
    Spokesman," Huffington Post, September 27, 2011, http://www.huffingtonpost.com/
    2011/ 09/27/white-house-spokesman-oba_n_983864.html?page=2 (accessed September 28,
    2011).

77 See Office of the Spokesman, Department of State, "Media Note," August 24, 2010,
    http://www.state.gov/r/pa/prs/ps/2010/08/146233.htm (accessed May 8, 2011).

78 He lists many more, as presented in Will Moredock, "The Accomplishments of President
    Obama—It's More than You Would Think," *Charleston City Paper*, November 17, 2009,
    http://www.charlestoncitypaper.com/TheGoodFight/archives/2009/11/17/the-
    accomplishiments-of-president-obama-its-more-than-you-would-think (accessed May 16,
    2011).

79 See "A Word on Greenwald's Worldview," Booman Tribune, August 16, 2011, http://www.
    boomantribune.com/story/2011/8/16/223210/466 (accessed August 19, 2011).

80 Patricia Hill Collins, "Learning from the Outsider Within: The Sociological Significance of
    Black Feminist Thought," *Social Problems* 33 (1986): 14–32.

81 See Adia Harvey Wingfield and Joe R. Feagin, *Yes We Can? White Racial Framing and the 2008 Campaign* (New York: Routledge, 2010), chapters 1, 7–8.

82 Ronald Brownstein, "White Flight," *National Journal*, January 7, 2011, http://nationaljournal.com/magazine/in-2012-obama-may-need-a-new-coalition-20110107 (accessed March 13, 2011).

83 Thomas F. Schaller, *Whistling Past Dixie* (New York: Simon & Schuster, 2006).

84 Greg Smith and Scott Clement, "Religion in the 2010 Elections," Pew Research Center, November 3, 2010, http://pewresearch.org/pubs/1791/2010-midterm-elections-exit-poll-religion-vote (accessed April 5, 2011).

85 Pew Research Center, "GOP Makes Big Gains among White Voters," July 22, 2011, http://pewresearch.org/pubs/2067/2012-electorate-partisan-affiliations-gop-gains-white-voters (accessed August 19, 2011).

86 Brownstein, "White Flight," *National Journal*; and Pew Research Center, "The Latino Vote in the 2010 Elections," November 17, 2010, http://pewresearch.org/pubs/1790/2010-midterm-elections-exit-poll-hispanic-vote (accessed May 8, 2011).

87 David Axelrod, "Meet the Press," MSNBC.com, May 1, 2011, http://www.msnbc.msn.com/id/42822623/ns/meet_the_press-transcripts/ (accessed May 2, 2011).

88 See Joshua Holland, "The Obama Wars," *AlterNet*, August 16, 2011, http://www.alternet.org/story/152055/ (accessed August 19, 2011).

9 Demographic Change and Political Futures

1 Rakesh Kochhar, Richard Fry, and Paul Taylor, "Wealth Gaps Rise to Record Highs between Whites, Blacks, Hispanics Twenty-to-One," Pew Research Center, July 2011, http://pewsocialtrends.org/2011/07/26/wealth-gaps-rise-to-record-highs-between-whites-blacks-hispanics/ (accessed August 18, 2011).

2 See David Easton, *The Political System: An Inquiry into the State of Political Science* (Second edition; New York: Alfred A. Knopf, 1971), p. 134. I am indebted here to discussions with Maria Chávez.

3 For detailed evidence, see Joe R. Feagin, *The White Racial Frame: Centuries of Racial Framing and Counter-Framing* (New York: Routledge, 2010), especially chapters 1–3.

4 Interview with Paul Hawken, "Corporate Futures," *Yes! A Journal of Positive Futures*, Summer 1999, at http://www.futurenet.org/10citiesofexuberance/corporatefutures.html (accessed August 8, 2001); and Paul Hawken, *Blessed Unrest: How the Largest Movement in the World Came into Being and Why No One Saw It Coming* (New York: Viking, 2007), pp. 180–181.

5 See, for example, Michael Hughes, "Symbolic Racism, Old-Fashioned Racism, and Whites' Opposition to Affirmative Action," in *Racial Attitudes in the 1990s: Continuity and Change*, eds. Steven A. Tuch and Jack K. Martin (Westport, Connecticut: Praeger, 1997), pp. 73–74; and Joe R. Feagin and Eileen O'Brien, *White Men on Race: Power, Privilege and the Shaping of Cultural Consciousness* (Boston, Massachusetts: Beacon, 2003).

6 Jim Dator, "Will America Ever Become a Democracy?," in *Democracy and Futures*, eds. Mika Mannermaa, Jim Dator, and Paula Tiihonen (Helsinki: Parliament of Finland, 2006), p. 64.

7 Steve H. Murdock, *An America Challenged: Population Change and the Future of the United States* (Boulder, Colorado: Westview Press, 1995), pp. 33–47; and U.S. Census Bureau, "An Older and More Diverse Nation by Midcentury," August 2008, http://www.census.gov/Press-Release/www/releases/archives/population/012496.html (accessed June 12, 2009).

8 William H. Frey, Alan Berube, Audrey Singer, and Jill H. Wilson, "Getting Current: Recent Demographic Trends in Metropolitan America," Brookings Institution, March 2009, http://www.brookings.edu/reports/2009/~/media/Files/rc/reports/2009/03_metro_demographic_trends/03_metro_demographic_trends.pdf (accessed June 12, 2009).

9 Dale Maharidge, *The Coming White Minority: California's Eruptions and America's Future* (New York: Random House, 1996), p. 11.

10 Feagin and O'Brien, *White Men on Race*, passim.

11 William H. Frey, "Domestic and Immigrant Migrants: Where Do They Go?," *Current* (January 22, 1997): n.p.; and William H. Frey, "Metropolitan Magnets for International and Domestic Migrants," Frey Website, http://www.frey-demographer.org/reports/Brook3-2.pdf (accessed June 19, 2009).

12 Rich Benjamin, "Refugees of Diversity," *The American Prospect* 20 (October 2009): 18–19.

13 "130 Republicans in Congress Want to Consider Ending Birthright Citizenship," ThinkProgress, October 26, 2010, http://thinkprogress.org/2010/10/26/gop-birthright-citizenship/ (accessed April 18, 2011).

14 "The Nativists are Restless," *The New York Times*, January 31, 2009, http://www.nytimes.com/2009/02/01/opinion/01sun1.html (accessed August 4, 2011).

15 Chandler Davidson, Tanya Dunlap, Gale Kenny, and Benjamin Wise, *Republican Ballot Security Programs: Vote Protection or Minority Vote Suppression—Or Both?* (Washington, D.C.: Center for Voting Rights & Protection, 2004), pp. 96–106 and passim. See also Allen Raymond and Ian Spiegelman, *How to Rig an Election: Confessions of a Republican Operative* (Reprint edition; New York: Simon & Schuster, 2008 [2002]).

16 Cord Jefferson, "Voting Rights Act at 45: What's to Celebrate?," The Root, August 6, 2010, http://www.theroot.com/views/voting-rights-act-45-whats-celebrate?page=0,1 (accessed August 3, 2011).

17 *Citizens United* v. *Federal Election Commission*, 558 U.S. 08-205 (2010).

18 Glenn Bracey, "A White Supremacist Century: Supreme Court as White Oligarchical Power," RacismReview, January 24, 2010, http://www.racismreview.com/blog/2010/01/24/a-white-supremacist-century-supreme-court-as-white-oligarchical-power/ (accessed April 12, 2011).

19 Joe R. Feagin, "The Future of U.S. Society in an Era of Racism, Group Segregation, and Demographic Revolution," in *Sociology for the 21st Century: Continuities and Cutting Edges,* ed. Janet Abu-Lughod (Chicago: University of Chicago Press, 1999), pp. 199–212; U.S. Census Bureau, "An Older and More Diverse Nation by Midcentury," August 2008, http://www.census.gov/Press-Release/www/releases/archives/population/012496.html (accessed June 12, 2009); and William H. Frey, "Diversity Spreads Out," Brookings Institution, http://www.frey-demographer.org/reports/Brook06.pdf (accessed June 19, 2009).

20 Mark Hugo Lopez and Paul Taylor, "The 2010 Congressional Reapportionment and Latinos," Pew Hispanic Center, January 5, 2011, http://pewhispanic.org/reports/report.php?ReportID=132 (accessed August 3, 2011).

21 Angela Maria Kelley, Marshall Fitz, Gebe Martinez, Vanessa Cárdenas, "Latinos Make Their Mark," Center for American Progress, November 9, 2010, http://www.americanprogress.org/issues/2010/11/latino_vote.html (accessed August 10, 2011); and Daniel M. HoSang, *Racial Propositions: Ballot Initiatives and the Making of Postwar California* (Berkeley: University of California Press, 2010), Kindle DX locations 5954–5962.

22 See Feagin, "The Future of U.S. Society in an Era of Racism, Group Segregation, and Demographic Revolution"; and Frey, "Diversity Spreads Out."

23 "History of the Leadership Conference on Civil and Human Rights & The Leadership Conference Education Fund," http://www.civilrights.org/about/ (accessed August 8, 2011).

24 Frederick Douglass, "The Significance of Emancipation in the West Indies," in *The Frederick Douglass Papers*, ed. John W. Blassingame (New Haven: Yale University Press, 1986), Vol. 3, p. 204.

Index